CREATING HEALTHY ORGANIZATIONS

How Vibrant Workplaces Inspire Employees to
Achieve Sustainable Success

GRAHAM LOWE

Creating Healthy Organizations

How Vibrant Workplaces Inspire
Employees to Achieve
Sustainable Success

UNIVERSITY OF TORONTO PRESS
Toronto Buffalo London

ISBN 978-0-8020-9980-8

Printed on acid-free, 100% post-consumer recycled paper with
vegetable-based inks.

Library and Archives Canada Cataloguing in Publication

Lowe, Graham S.
Creating healthy organizations : how vibrant workplaces inspire
employees to achieve sustainable success / Graham Lowe.

Includes bibliographical references and index.
ISBN 978-0-8020-9980-8

1. Employee motivation.   2. Job satisfaction.   3. Employee health
promotion.   4. Quality of work life.   5. Leadership.   6. Corporate culture.
7. Organizational effectiveness.   8. Organizational change.   I. Title.

HF5549.5.M63L69 2010   658.3'14   C2010-900545-7

University of Toronto Press acknowledges the financial assistance to its
publishing program of the Canada Council for the Arts and the Ontario
Arts Council.

 Canada Council   Conseil des Arts
for the Arts   du Canada    **ONTARIO ARTS COUNCIL**
CONSEIL DES ARTS DE L'ONTARIO

University of Toronto Press acknowledges the financial support for its
publishing activities of the Government of Canada through the Book
Publishing Industry Development Program (BPIDP).

To Ella and Penny

Contents

Figures

Acknowledgments

Producing this book was a collaborative enterprise. Many individuals generously shared with me their ideas and experiences. Others provided me with opportunities to learn first hand about how they were creating healthy organizations.

The framing of quality of work life and organizational performance in health terms goes back to work I did between 1999 and 2001 at Canadian Policy Research Networks, especially projects with Grant Schellenberg and Harry Shannon, with encouragement from Judith Maxwell. My immersion in the research on workplace health promotion deepened when Health Canada contracted me to write two discussion papers, one on healthy workplace strategies and the other on healthy workplaces and productivity. Deborah Connors and organizers of the annual Health, Work and Wellness conference in Canada connected me over the years with a dedicated network of workplace change agents, from whom I learned much. Ongoing discussions and collaborations with Greg Banwell and Craig Thompson at Wilson Banwell Human Solutions also helped to shape my thinking about healthy organizations.

As a consultant, workshop leader, and conference speaker, I have had the privilege of hearing and seeing hundreds of examples of individuals and organizations moving down a healthy trajectory. Several organizations have agreed to share their stories here. In this regard, I would particularly like to thank Mike Martin at Teck Cominco's Trail Operations, Richard Gotfried at Trico Homes, Jeff MacPherson at the City of Edmonton, Leanne Bilodeau at University of British Columbia Okanagan, Jeff Fielding at the City of London, David Minns at the National Research Council's Institute for Fuel Cell Innovation, Marie Sopko at

Nexen, Karen Jackson at Trillium Health Centre, and Seow Ping at the Singapore Health Promotion Board.

Jennifer Dixon provided research assistance with chapter 7. Joanne McKechnie helped to analyse the data from Great Place to Work Institute Canada's 2007 '50 Best Workplaces in Canada' list that I use in various chapters. I gained an inside view of outstanding workplaces during the 2005 to 2008 period, when Joanne and I were co-principals in the Great Place to Work Institute's Canadian affiliate before selling to new owners. Continued access to the institute's data is appreciated. I also draw on survey data from 'Rethinking Work,' a joint venture with Ekos Research, where Susan Galley was a creative source of ideas on workplace issues.

I also want to acknowledge the input I have received from the numerous participants at my workshops and conference presentations. More than anything, these conversations confirmed to me the need for a practical guide to creating healthier organizations.

Jennifer DiDomenico at the University of Toronto Press offered the right balance of encouragement, advice, and patience needed for me to complete this project.

CREATING HEALTHY ORGANIZATIONS

How Vibrant Workplaces Inspire Employees to Achieve Sustainable Success

As the corporate hub of Canada's boom-bust energy economy, Calgary experienced a white-hot real estate market for most of this decade. Home prices in the Alberta city of 1 million people skyrocketed as buyers lined up to outbid each other. Then, in 2008 the global financial crisis and plummeting oil prices knocked the bottom out of Calgary's housing market. Home sales that year dropped about 50 per cent, unsold property piled up, and prices fell. It is now a buyers' market, but fewer people are buying, fearful about an uncertain future. Construction is a cyclical industry, caught in the updrafts and downdrafts of the economy. Yet despite knowing the good times could not last, many companies were caught off guard in 2008. Some closed their doors completely; others cut their workforce by 30 to 40 per cent.

However, at least one company – Calgary-based Trico Homes – likely will emerge from the economic crisis even stronger. The reasons are both simple and complex: Trico Homes is a healthy organization. It has designed, marketed, and built over 4,000 homes in the Calgary area and the interior of British Columbia. The company has won numerous building industry accolades. It has been recognized as one of the '50 Best Managed Companies' and '50 Best Workplaces' in Canada. But these accomplishments are not what make Trico a healthy organization. What is important is *how* it achieved these results. To understand the how, we have to appreciate Trico's operating philosophy – in other words, its corporate character. The company's character is rooted in a culture that blends social responsibility, caring values, and a performance-oriented ethic of teamwork.

The Trico philosophy is expressed in its vision and grounded in its values. The company vision is to enhance its customers' lives while en-

riching the community. Wayne Chiu, founder and CEO of Trico Ho
believes that a company should leave a legacy by contributing to t
communities in which it does business. For Trico, philanthropy in
volves more than writing a cheque – it's about building lasting partnerships that strengthen communities. Trico has earned a reputation as a
community leader through its partnerships and employee volunteering
with the Kids Cancer Care Foundation, Bow Valley College, GlobalFest,
UNICEF Canada, Volunteer Calgary, and Immigrant Services Calgary.
Recently, Trico Homes initiated a $1.5 million partnership with south-
east Calgary's Family Leisure Centre in support of a significant expan-
sion program and the establishment of the Trico Centre for Family
Wellness.

The corporate values are T.R.I.C.O. – trust, respect, integrity, community, and opportunity. Trico cultivates trusting and respectful relationships among employees, trades, suppliers, and community partners.
All feel part of the Trico extended family. Employee surveys found
high positive scores on management integrity and credibility, fairness,
respect, team spirit, and pride. During the boom years, staff turnover
stayed well below the industry average. People's interests and passions
are tapped through training and career development opportunities. At
weekly team meetings, a 'no bad ideas' philosophy encourages creative
input from employees. When Trico's employees speak for themselves,
here is how they described, in an anonymous survey, why it is a great
company to work for:

- Right from the beginning of my employment with Trico I was welcomed
  as 'one of the family'. Even though I am a receptionist, I am taken seriously and the work I do here is appreciated. I am told often how much
  I mean to the company.
- Trico Homes is dedicated to making a difference in the community and
  encourages employee involvement in this process … Trico Home's culture has a strong business ethic which encourages growth and development for the company.
- The people are willing to help you in any situation. Giving back to the
  community has a great deal of importance for management and the
  staff. The staff get recognized for their accomplishments, their extra effort, and good ideas that help the company save time and money.
- Management treats me as a member of this big family, not just as an
  employee. They care about my needs and give flexibility for my own
  family and personal life.

Trico managers believe there are opportunities for well-managed companies to gain market share if they position themselves now for the recovery. As Richard Gotfried, vice-president of Corporate Communications, puts it: 'We can shine if we do things right.' Richard explains that 'right' for Trico means true to its philosophy and culture. By drawing on the strength and resilience of relationships within its extended family of employees and partners, Trico has so far weathered the economic storm.

Actually, Trico saw the storm coming. Trico's managers and employees knew the housing boom was unsustainable and saw signs of this in 2007. Trico's ability to adapt to the economic downturn was embedded all along in its sustainable people practices and business processes. During growth years, the company hired new employees only after ensuring that everything had been done to gain efficiencies by adjusting processes and workloads. Consistent with its values, Trico wanted to honour its commitment to employees over the longer term. Regarding business processes, Trico is always on the lookout for new products and services that will benefit customers. As building activity slowed, it had the time to reassess all aspects of a home, from design and customer appeal to materials and products used, to how it is built. By collaborating, Trico employees and business partners found cost savings through new products and streamlined construction methods.

Trico quickly did three things to survive the declining market. It offered a price assurance program, which adjusts the presale price of a house to the market value at time of occupancy if the market goes down. Customers also have a guarantee program – a preset price for their existing home if it does not sell before they move into their new Trico home. Trico also negotiated attractive financing options with its mortgage partners and committed to becoming a leader in affordable home ownership. The company now targets average-income workers who were frozen out of the overheated Calgary market – such as the three firefighters who were recruited from another city, but had to return because they could not afford to buy a family home in Calgary.

So far, the new strategy is working. But there was a painful price: staff cuts. When the global recession hit full force in the fall of 2008, Trico managers were communicating regularly with employees, explaining changes in the market, how the company was affected, and how it was responding. The CEO made it clear he was prepared to keep as many of the team employed as possible. The key message was that the continued success of the company depends on its dedicated staff and strong culture. Fortunately, Trico had gradually brought staffing levels down through attrition. But after much thinking and planning, the executive team announced in December 2008 that seven positions would be cut. Focusing on the team that will be needed when the market stabilizes, managers used performance-related criteria to identify who would leave. The workforce declined from 106 at its peak to 80 after the job reductions.

When Wayne Chiu explained to employees why the layoffs were being made, he also committed to no further job cuts for the twelve months starting in January 2009 in order to ease employees' insecurity. Because Trico's culture is performance oriented, the criteria for the layoffs were understood by everyone. Remaining team members saw the integrity in this approach. Trico's caring culture ensured that the people who left were treated fairly and with dignity, in accord with the company's values. The executive team wanted the departing staff to be proud of time they spent with the company. If anything, employees were surprised that the layoffs were not deeper. Morale rose after the layoffs because employees now had a greater sense of stability and security.

Trico took two other steps that strengthened it for the future. One step was to approach its six major community partners and confirm the company's commitment to maintaining ongoing financial contributions and volunteer support. After all, these long-term community partnerships had helped to define the character of the company. The other step was to invite any interested employee to join a new home design team competition. Employees and managers formed four teams, each with a professional designer to translate people's ideas into plans. The design parameters were challenging: a compact, environmentally friendly house on a small city lot. The four designs were independently judged, and the company has already built the 26-foot-wide design competition winner – 'The Liberty' – as a model home in a new community. This collaborative approach to design would have been difficult to use during boom times. In addition, it was fun for everyone involved.

Trico's story is about how a successful business with a progressive philosophy is navigating its way through a recession. Like a healthy person, the company is adaptable and resilient when faced with adversity. At a deeper level, the Trico story also is about the evolution of a healthy and sustainable organization. Indeed, the word *healthy* accurately describes companies – or organizations in the public or nonprofit sectors – with qualities similar to those of Trico Homes.

The Healthy Organization Ideal

This book outlines how to create healthier organizations. Being healthy is an ideal that any organization can aspire to achieve. We talk about healthy people using words such as *vigorous, flourishing, robust, thriving, resilient,* and *fit.* The same words also can be used to describe healthy organizations. Healthy persons experience physical and mental well-being because all physical, mental, and emotional systems are in sync. They effectively perform their roles as workers, citizens, partners, and parents while further developing their potential. And they have a positive relationship with the environment in which they live, drawing from it while contributing to it. The same can be said for a healthy organization. Its systems are well integrated, it operates successfully today, develops new capacity to thrive tomorrow, and it has mutually beneficial relationships with customers and communities, and the environment.

My goal is to provide a fresh perspective on how organizations operate and how they can be made more enduring in human terms. A healthy organization is at once healthy, successful, and responsible. I incorporate in a healthy organization model three previously separate streams of management practice and research: workplace health promotion, organizational performance, and social responsibility. These areas recently have started to converge. My contribution is to push this cross-fertilization to a higher level. So, while the ideas I present are not new on their own, what is new is how I bring them together in an integrated, healthy organization framework.

Looking at Your Organization through a Health Lens

What is to be gained by looking at your organization through a health lens? The main advantage is that when you make the connections between people, performance, and community more visible, it will be easier make your organization sustainable into the future. A health lens provides insights about how to improve people practices, performance and community relationships. It encourages holistic and long-term thinking about what drives an organization's success.

My model of a healthy organization, presented in chapter 1, shows how the organization's structures, systems, and culture influence both employee well-being and business performance. What I call the 'healthy organization value chain' expands the idea of an employee-customer value chain by linking future success to how the organization nurtures its employees' capabilities and quality of life over the long term. A health lens also highlights an organization's evolving relationships with its customers or clients, shareholders or citizens, and the communities in which it operates. Ultimately, a healthy organization succeeds by renewing and replenishing its human and social capital. That is what I mean by sustainable success.

Business experts have done surprisingly little to adapt health ideas to corporate performance. I say 'surprisingly,' because the analogies are potentially powerful. Consider two interesting exceptions. When McKinsey consultants wrote about 'healthy organizations,' they had in mind caring for the long-term well-being, resilience, and renewal of the company rather than short-term financial results.[1] Organizational researchers Michael Beer and Russell Eisenstat borrowed the 'silent killer' idea, likening barriers to strategy implementation and organizational learning to cholesterol.[2] Poor vertical communication, they concluded, is one of the biggest silent killers of both strategy and learning.

Workplace health promotion experts operate in a separate sphere, which is part of the problem. Workplace health experts lack convincing ways to talk to managers and executives about the performance impacts of healthy and unhealthy employees and workplaces. As a result, the ample research on healthy workplaces has not been communicated to managers and other practitioners in terms that make sense for business strategy. For instance, *Healthy Work: Stress, Productivity, and the Reconstruction of Working Life* is a pioneering book on job stress written by Robert Karasek and Töres Theorell almost twenty years ago.[3] The book marked a huge advance in the field of workplace health, but went largely unnoticed by managers or organizational researchers. The authors' performance-enhancing solutions to job stress involved reorganizing work to improve 'creativity, skill development, and quality.'[4] In short, a healthy workplace also could be a higher-performing workplace.

Above all, healthy organizations forge an enduring link between employee well-being and performance. This link must become central to the business's philosophy, long-term strategy, and the way it operates day to day. I believe that this people-performance link can be strengthened if we have the right tools for thinking and talking about how organizations can be healthy – tools that I provide throughout this book.

Helping Change Agents

A growing number of managers, human resource (HR) practitioners, health and wellness professionals, and front-line employees are committed to achieving their own versions of the healthy organization ideal. These are the people I call 'change agents,' and this book is written mainly for them, so that they can exert even more positive influence inside their workplace.

Before the recession hit in 2008, these change agents were seeking ways to make workplaces healthier in order to address the growing challenges of recruiting, retaining, developing, and engaging employees. The economic crisis has not deterred these change agents, even if their steps forward now may be smaller and slower. While some companies have been forced by economic conditions into survival mode, others are seizing the opportunity to engage employees in figuring out how to do things better for the longer term. As Trico Homes found, it is important is to tap into your already healthy roots to adapt in creative ways to the market downturn. Because, as the recovery gets traction, that resilience you foster today will be critical for addressing the same employee challenges that beset organizations earlier in this decade.

For any organization adopting this positive mindset, the good news is that our understanding of health and performance has come a long way in recent years. To illustrate the progress that has been made, here are three examples:

- Back then, workplace health practitioners talked a lot about making the 'business case' for investing in employee wellness and healthy work environments. I recall a keynote speaker at a major workplace health conference in 2002 arguing that workplace health and well-being are barely on the HR radar screen, never mind the business radar screen. The message for practitioners back then was 'make yourselves organizationally relevant.' Indeed, many change agents have done just that.
- An occupational physician pointed out to me that, despite data from health benefit providers that showed mental health problems imposing huge costs on employers, there was little interest in addressing root causes. That is because the root causes of stress, burnout, and work-life conflict require changing the work environment – a black box that managers avoided opening. But workplace health professionals persisted, using what this physician called a 'foot in

the door' approach with CEOs and executive teams to make the case that a healthy social and psychological work environment is a bottom-line issue.

- At a conference of senior health benefits managers, one participant summed up how people experience a healthy workplace: 'It is so nice to go to work in a good mood and leave that way.' A good mood is a sure sign of positive mental, physical, and emotional health. It also is a sure sign of an employee who enjoys their work and takes pride in their contributions to the organization's goals. The fact that employee engagement has become a top priority for managers underscores the need to create positive employee work experiences – which require a healthy work environment.

I encourage change agents to focus on their organization's existing potential, strengths, and opportunities. You need to look for ways to build on these attributes. Certainly, an accurate diagnosis of problems is a basis for designing solutions. I propose a solutions-oriented mindset, given that we know a lot about the causes and consequences of unhealthy and unproductive workplaces. Viewing organizations through a 'health' lens helps us to imagine what is possible. This approach is gaining momentum through the growing field of positive organizational studies. Researchers in this area apply concepts such as resilience, wellness, innovation, creativity, justice, engagement, and mindfulness as tools for understanding how to develop the human potential in any organization.[5]

Similarly, viewing organizations through a health lens reveals how employees at all levels can be resourceful in doing their jobs and improving their immediate work environments. Often, this involves employees' taking initiative, alone or together, within their limited sphere of influence to create small but tangible improvements. It is at the level of micro-action that progress towards a healthy organization ideal can be best made.

I encourage readers to develop a personal vision of a healthy organization, which describes what your organization has the potential to become. When this personal vision becomes part of a shared vision with co-workers, you will have a powerful catalyst for change. Using your own language, this vision can guide improvements in performance and the quality of work life. Charting that path to a healthy organization cannot be based on a simple formula or a CEO directive. Building a healthier organization is a shared responsibility: everyone, regardless of level or position in the organization, can and should participate. What I offer are examples, ideas, and tools that can help you to mobilize others in pursuit of that shared healthy organization vision.

Leveraging Where You Are Today

In order to move forward, we need to understand where we are today. In this regard, I use the word *creating* in the title of the book to refer to an evolving and continual process. I am not suggesting that you, or your organization, are starting from scratch. I realize that most organizations are already on a healthy organization trajectory, through initiatives such as an occupational health and safety program, a wellness committee, or employee surveys. So, from a change perspective, what is important is to build from where you are, leveraging workplace health promotion and performance improvement initiatives that are already under way.

A particular challenge for organizations that are recognized leaders is sustaining their healthy cultures, high levels of employee dedication, and excellent performance – especially during tough economic times. As the CEO of Wegmans, a U.S. grocery store chain that ranked first on *Fortune* magazine's 2005 list of '100 Best Companies to Work For In America,' commented, 'we'll never be there, we're always on a journey.'

A relatively small number of companies, such as Wegmans or Trico Homes, are award winners, making it onto best workplaces, most admired companies, or corporate social responsibility awards lists. However, companies on these lists are atypical. They belong to a top tier of organizations – probably no more than 10 per cent – that are outstanding by business, workplace, and social responsibility criteria. My experience as a workplace consultant has taught me that many organizations are somewhere in the middle of the pack, maybe a little behind or just ahead of their peers. This book's messages are aimed primarily at this audience – the large group of organizations that are making some progress, but aspire to more.

I believe that many organizations of all sizes in all sectors strive to be better than they are in terms of the quality of their workplaces, performance, and community relationships. And as progress is made on these fronts, the bar is constantly raised. In this sense, becoming a healthier organization refers to an ongoing journey rather than a destination. This book is intended to help change agents make that journey faster and further.

Learning from Your Peers

While there is much to learn from high-profile award winners, we can draw equally valuable lessons from typical organizations that in their own way are trying to be healthier. These organizations are your peers. Perhaps the most important lesson is that there is hidden potential in most organizations to move further down a healthy organization pathway and there are employees and managers who are ready, willing, and able to lead this change.

Three examples illustrate how fairly typical organizations have seized opportunities to become healthier:

- A manager of internal audits in a large professional service organization launched a 'healthy organization' assessment, with a mandate from the executive team to figure out 'how to energize the organization to bring it to the next step.' The impetus for the assessment came not from human resources or occupational health and safety, but from a less likely source of change – an audit team. Over a period of several years of team-building, and after much reflection by managers, the culture shifted and became more supportive of both employee health and performance.
- An organizational development manager at a forest products company led an initiative to foster a collaborative management style. The first question the management team had to answer was 'what do we mean by collaboration?' The answer, in short, was 'it's how we work together' – in other words, healthy relationships. As a start, the management team worked for nine months to get a vision and guiding principles, which were rolled out to all production sites and used to update management training. This process took several years and had unexpected setbacks, owing to a tough market for wood products, but the company did move to a more values-based style of management.
- At a management retreat for a large municipality, a new HR strategy (called the 'people plan') and refreshed values focused attention on healthy workplace issues. One discussion turned to this question: 'what can you do to make time for people issues?' Creative ideas for addressing the workload problem were discussed. Someone pointed out that in her area, 'nobody is beating down doors to be a general manager.' Another manager stood up and admitted: 'I used to be proud of what I do. Now I just struggle to get through the day.' This

retreat accelerated actions already under way in various parts of the organization to create healthier work environments.

These examples involve mid-level and senior managers. Yet in each organization there also were employees taking active roles in healthy change. The managers realized they had to tap the energy of these front-line change agents. Furthermore, the kind of conversations taking place among managers already had occurred in some work units or teams. So there were pockets of innovation within each organization that exemplified the healthy ideal, yet had not been recognized or shared internally. The main point is that in most organizations there are ripe opportunities to harness and mobilize healthy organizational change.

Chapter Overview

The chapters that follow address three core questions:

1. What are the building blocks of a healthy organization?
2. How can you move down your own healthy organization path?
3. How can you measure and sustain progress?

Chapter 1 outlines a healthy organization model. The model combines elements from workplace health promotion, human resources, organizational performance, and corporate social responsibility. Convergent trends will help you to identify new opportunities to improve both the quality of work life and organizational results. Four building blocks support sustainable success. These building blocks are positive cultures, inclusive leadership, vibrant workplaces, and inspired employees. The model provides you with a guide for planning and action by encouraging integrative thinking about the underlying drivers of well-being, performance, and responsible business practices.

Chapter 2 lays out the limits – and promise – of practice and research on workplace health promotion. There is untapped potential to extend the benefits of your current healthy workplace practices beyond reduced employee health risks, health benefit savings, and lower levels of absenteeism. Workplace health promotion can be a springboard for a more holistic, organizational perspective, tightening the links between employee well-being and performance. Providing this springboard requires improvements in the psychological and social aspects of work that define a vibrant workplace. Employee health and wellness then become assets that contribute to a capable and inspired workforce.

Chapter 3 shows how your organization can achieve higher levels of employee wellness and performance by putting in place the ingredients of vibrant workplaces that truly inspire employees in their jobs. A vibrant workplace is grounded on the quality of relationships, jobs, teamwork, and human resource support systems. A vibrant workplace is more than healthy: it supports employees in learning, collaborating, and innovating in the interests of customers and society. By cultivating these conditions, you will do more than just engage your employees. You can inspire them to contribute their best and to feel part of a workplace community with a bigger purpose.

Chapter 4 explores the culture building block of a healthy organization. The chapter suggests steps you can take to nurture a positive culture. Strong, people-centred values are the foundation, shaping day-to-day interactions among co-workers; between managers and employees; and between employees and their customers or clients, suppliers, business partners, and the larger community. There is growing awareness among executives that a company's culture contributes in many ways to its business success. Indeed, your organization's culture can become a strategic advantage.

Chapter 5 outlines the way that leadership in healthy organizations must be widely shared. The chapter describes six elements of inclusive leadership. Employees are actively involved in shaping the organization's healthy trajectory; they do not need permission to do so because such behaviour is collectively valued. Certainly, executive support is a key enabler of healthy change, but an inclusive approach to leadership mobilizes everyone. Healthy organizations, then, are co-created through ongoing and coordinated actions across the entire workplace community, and change agents play a pivotal role.

Chapter 6 looks inside the change process, focusing on the dynamics of how healthy organizations actually evolve. The chapter offers practical insights for navigating change so that the experience for those affected is healthy. Examples are offered from a wide range of organizations that are improving the work environment, involving employees in the process, and achieving performance improvements. Five broad principles for healthy change are outlined: understand the readiness for change in your organization; align structure and culture; link changes to the business strategy; widen the circle of involvement; and learn and innovate along the way.

Chapter 7 discusses what sustainable success could mean for your organization and its implications for your human resources, environmental, and community practices. Practical ways your organization can thrive so that all stakeholders benefit are examined. The focus is on two significant drivers of sustainable success: the quality of relationships with stakeholders and the future workforce capabilities required for the organization to thrive. The chapter's theme is renewal, specifically how you can renew your relationships with customers and your community stakeholders and how you can renew your workforce.

Chapter 8 provides practical advice and resources for measuring progress along your healthy organization trajectory. Having the relevant metrics available contributes to healthy change and a positive culture. The chapter focuses on how to make better use of your own evidence to plan, implement, and monitor organizational improvements. There is no handy one-size-fits-all tool for evaluating whether an organization is becoming more, or less, healthy. Organizations therefore have no choice but to come to grips with why they need healthy organization measures, what measures are needed, and how to make the fullest use of them to learn and improve.

Chapter 9 is an action-oriented summary of the insights, arguments, and evidence provided throughout the book. I distil each chapter into a checklist of points for discussion, planning, and implementation. Readers are encouraged to use this guide to design your own strategies. Your focus can be a team, work unit, department, or your entire organization. Whether you sit at the executive table or are a front-line worker, there is a role you can play in helping your organization to achieve a better quality of work life for employees and improved performance.

1 The Healthy Organization

A subtle but profound shift is under way in workplaces. Human resources and workplace health experts are focusing increasingly on how employees' work environment influences their health and job performance. Managers are searching for ways to fully engage employees and unleash hidden talents. More companies are seeking to follow through on their social responsibility commitments in an era when public expectations for ethical business practices are rising. These trends are converging, opening up new opportunities to improve the quality of work life, organizational performance, and communities – all at the same time. It is not unrealistic to imagine a future in which boundaries have dissolved between employee wellness, performance, and corporate social responsibility and where these goals are central to every manager's job.

While this projection sounds promising, we have some distance yet to go. Even the most comprehensive health promotion initiatives have at best modest impacts on the overall well-being and performance of an organization's workforce. Employee engagement still is viewed as an HR issue, and limited efforts have been made to uncover its underlying 'drivers' in the work environment. While social responsibility codes surely apply to how an organization treats its own employees, these implications are only now being explored.

To help to close these gaps between thinking and practice, this chapter lays out a model of a healthy organization. The healthy organization model is intended to help executives, managers, practitioners in human resources and workplace wellness, and a host of change agents scattered throughout workplaces find better ways to connect work environments, quality of life on and off the job, business results, and community benefits.

Five key points are made:

1. Employee well-being is an organizational performance issue, not simply a matter of personal health.
2. There are good reasons to move beyond employers' current focus on employee engagement and healthy workplaces.
3. The model of a healthy organization helps us to think in holistic, long-term ways about the underlying drivers of well-being and performance.
4. A healthy organization rests on four pillars: vibrant workplaces, inspired employees, positive cultures, and shared leadership.
5. Healthy organizations put in place conditions for sustainable success, renewing their workforce capabilities and relationships with customers and communities.

Integrating Well-Being and Performance

By presenting a healthy organization model, I am challenging you to take a big step beyond what you may now think of as a 'healthy workplace.' My concept of a healthy organization combines ideas about what contributes to employee well-being and organizational performance from different areas of expertise. Economists want to know how firms can achieve more output for the same units of input. Managers and organizational experts are concerned about how organizations achieve higher levels of performance in ethical and socially responsible ways. Health promotion practitioners need to know how to involve managers and employees in creating genuinely health-promoting work environments. And those in the growing field of business ethics want social responsibility to apply to everything a company does.

These sound like separate agendas, but the healthy organization concept unifies them into a change tool that is far more useful than workplace health promotion will ever be on its own. That is because, in the twenty-first century knowledge economy, national prosperity and the performance of individual companies depend more than ever on human skills and abilities. Indeed, decades of research on the determinants of population health show that for people to thrive, they must live in environments that enable them to realize their human potential. In short, wellness and work performance go hand in hand.

Leading thinkers in the fields of occupational health and safety, workplace health promotion, and epidemiology agree that the most successful interventions target underlying workplace and organizational factors. Over the past decade this perception has led to calls for a holistic or systemic view of the determinants of employee health and well-being. Health then becomes a defining feature of the entire organization.

A holistic approach also emphasizes the importance of a healthy change process. This is achieved when workers and managers actively collaborate to identify and design improvements to their own work environments. Having employees at all levels co-create healthy and productive work environments builds on the World Health Organization's definition of health promotion as 'the process of enabling individuals and communities to increase control over the determinants of health and thereby improve their health.'[1] The two key words in this definition are 'control' and 'determinants.' In a healthy organization, employees at all levels are able to influence key aspects of the environments in which they work, including the culture of the organization.

An organizational perspective on employee health slowly has taken hold over the past decade. However, it has yet to get full traction. In the 1990s the U.S. National Institute for Occupational Safety and Health (NIOSH) stated that a healthy work organization is 'one whose culture, climate and practices create an environment that promotes employee health and safety as well as organizational effectiveness.'[2] More specifically, NIOSH identifies the importance of an organizational climate in which employees feel valued and are able to resolve group conflicts. Equally important are management practices that support workers to learn, collaborate, and grow.

In summary, employers and employees stand to reap substantial benefits by integrating work environments with individual health outcomes and organizational performance. Practically speaking, an integrated approach to workplace health requires leadership by senior management, active involvement of employees, and cooperation among diverse stakeholders. They include practitioners in occupational health and safety, human resources, health promotion, line managers, and employees' representatives in professional associations and unions. Individuals and groups in any of these positions can be agents of change – as can front-line employees who take initiative to improve their immediate work environment. Ideally, wellness goals must be embedded in the organization's strategy and employees need to feel a sense of shared responsibility for reaching them. The healthy organization model moves us in this direction.

Healthy Organizations in Action

Leading employers in Europe, North America, and elsewhere have developed their own approaches to health and performance. The European Network for Workplace Health Promotion (ENWHP) has been operating since 1996, providing a forum for employers, policy-makers, and occupational health and safety and health promotion practitioners to develop standardized criteria for workplace health promotion and to disseminate effective practices. I participated in one of the ENWHP meetings and was impressed with network members' integrative thinking about healthy work environments, employee wellness, business success, and social responsibility. This approach came from some global brand-name employers: Shell, Stora Enso, Volkswagen, GSK, Hilti, to name a few. The network's vision is 'healthy employees in healthy organizations.' Achieving this vision is seen as a key to social and economic prosperity.

Exemplifying a healthy organization is Stora Enso, an integrated forest-products company headquartered in Finland. Its major challenge is creating a performance culture among 45,000 employees in forty countries. Developing a highly skilled, motivated, and healthy workforce is a strategic priority. Regular Web-based surveys monitor workplace culture, employee satisfaction and well-being, and management practices to ensure they support these goals. This scrutiny complements rigorous safety practices. Survey results are reported to all work units, and accountability is through action plans, targeted improvements, and a performance-based reward system for managers. Environmental sustainability also is integral to the company's operating philosophy. Dr Paavo Jäppinen, a Stora Enso vice-president, explains: 'For customers and the general public it is becoming increasingly important that economic success is based on social responsibility. At Stora Enso, workplace health management and corporate culture based on partnership are essential elements of our human resource development, helping us to achieve our corporate goals.'[3] This cannot be dismissed as simply a corporate version of Nordic social democracy. Indeed, Stora Enso operates according to this philosophy in dozens of countries around the world.

In the United States, an outstanding example of a healthy organization is the SAS Institute, a leader in business intelligence software. At SAS, innovation and business growth are built on long-term relationships with employees and customers. As SAS president and CEO Jim

Goodnight explains: 'We've worked hard to create a corporate culture that is based on trust between our employees and the company, a culture that rewards innovation, encourages employees to try new things and yet doesn't penalize them for taking chances, and a culture that cares about employees' personal and professional growth.' SAS has been on *Fortune* magazine's 100 Best Companies to Work For In America list for ten consecutive years. SAS also has created a robust accountability framework using metrics and ongoing employee feedback. SAS's caring culture places importance on work/life balance and, by doing so, enables employees not only to have time for personal and family needs, but also to actively participate in their communities.

A Canadian example is Trillium Health Centre. As one of the largest tertiary care hospitals in Canada, Trillium offers advanced cardiac, neurosurgery, stroke, and orthopaedic services. Trillium's two sites provide emergency, inpatient, ambulatory and community-based care to over 1 million people in Mississauga, Ontario, and the surrounding area. With over 4,000 employees and 1,100 volunteers, one of Trillium's strategic directions was to 'engage people fully.'

The concept of an 'organic organization' was used by founding CEO, Ken White, to describe a non-bureaucratic environment that encourages innovation and individual leadership by fully engaging all employees, physicians, and volunteers to make decisions and take ownership for them. For people to be fully engaged, they must be supported by a healthy environment. That is why Trillium has set the explicit goal of creating and maintaining healthy workplaces. Trillium annually surveys staff, physicians, and volunteers to assess health, wellness, and work experiences. Managers are accountable for acting on the survey results and employees also are involved in this process. Healthy workplace changes support other major human resource goals, including recruitment, flexible work options, talent management, and professional development. The current strategic theme, 'outstanding people,' reflects how the present CEO, Janet Davidson, has build on this strong foundation with a dual focus on developing people and creating a working and volunteering environment that attracts outstanding new talent.

While Stora Enso, SAS, and Trillium follow different paths and use different language, each has a deeply rooted culture based on a virtuous connection between how employees are treated and business success. Each supports people in a healthy and productive environment, recognizing this as the best way to excel in meeting the needs of all major stakeholders: managers, employees, employees' families, shareholders or owners, partners and suppliers, and communities. These organizations also have adopted what experts identify as best practices for people management and organizational performance. Leading-edge HR management places a high value on treating employees as core business assets and 'bundles' practices such as teamwork, extensive training, employment security, reduced hierarchy, performance-based pay, employee involvement in decision making, and employee wellness into a comprehensive strategy directly tied to business goals.[4]

A Healthy Organization Model

As a guide for assessing the health of your company, worksite, or department, I offer a basic model of a healthy organization. This model generalizes from the examples just described, drawing widely on research evidence that shows the importance of work environments, employee experiences, culture, and leadership. The model also has been confirmed in practice, through my consulting work with numerous organizations wanting to move in this direction and through conversations with hundreds of managers and employees across Canada and internationally.

I present the model in two steps. First, I identify in figure 1.1 the four building blocks of a healthy organization: a positive culture, an inclusive approach to leadership, and vibrant workplaces that inspire employees. Taking action to make your organization healthier requires a clear understanding of how the main components of the healthy organization model are connected. So my second step, in figure 1.2, is to describe the logic of a healthy organization. I do this by adapting the concept of a value chain, which will be familiar to managers who track the relationship between employee and customer experiences.

A vibrant workplace is really the centrepiece of the model, because this is the environment in which people work day in and day out. Vibrant workplaces do more than engage employees. They actually cultivate a sense of personal inspiration about the work in hand. An engaged employee is satisfied and loyal. An inspired employee is more than this, actively seeking out ways to develop and use skills, knowledge, and abilities to further corporate goals. In today's knowledge-based economy, it is not enough for individuals to be skilled and well educated. In order for employees to apply their capabilities, they need relationships, resources, and systems that enable them to collaborate. When workers collaborate, the sum becomes greater than the parts: teams and organi-

Figure 1.1 Building blocks of a healthy organization

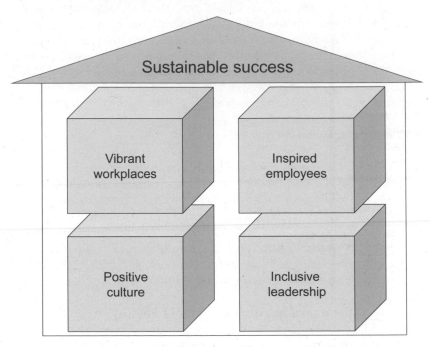

zation develop capabilities for performance, innovation, and creativity that far surpass what each individual member brings to their job – and to the organization, its customers, and society.

Two critical enablers of a vibrant workplace are culture and leadership. A positive culture based on strong people values will resonate with employees and managers, providing guidelines for healthy and productive work behaviours. While leadership from the top for a healthy organization vision and goals is important, this alone will not mobilize the workforce to move down the healthy organization path. What is needed is an inclusive approach to leadership that empowers all members of an organization to take responsibility for healthy changes.

Success is multidimensional. A healthy organization meets or exceeds its business goals in terms of customers' needs and financial results. It also does more than promote personal health and wellness, providing an overall high quality of work life for employees based on their to-

Figure 1.2 The healthy organization value chain

tal experience of their job and work environment. It also provides net benefits for communities by operating in socially responsible ways. In both business and human terms, these are the conditions for sustainable success. In every sector of the economy, we can find employers that have developed in their own way a healthy organization. While these journeys have not been guided by a pre-existing model, the approaches follow the same basic logic.

Here is the underlying logic. The stage is set for high quality of work life *and* high performance by having a strong culture grounded on people values, a commitment from top managers to improve the workplace as a way of achieving business results, and active encouragement for all employees to demonstrate leadership in their roles. These components of a healthy organization are foundational, which is why I devote entire chapters to the topics of culture and leadership. Living the values is a hallmark of a healthy organization. One of its clearest expressions can be found in an organization's people policies, programs, and practices – how it approaches all human resource management issues. As you will see, many of my examples illustrate the healthy organization building blocks by featuring specific people practices. At the core of a healthy organization are vibrant workplaces that inspire employees – goals that are within reach if all people policies, programs, and management actions reinforce and support them.

In the late 1990s Anthony Rucci, Steven Kirn, and Richard Quinn published their path-breaking *Harvard Business Review* article on the employee-customer-profit chain at Sears.[5] While Sears has since faltered, their theory that satisfied employees lead to satisfied customers who drive up profits has entered mainstream management thinking. This idea has strong intuitive appeal to managers, and it certainly has been used by HR professionals to make a case for their contribution to the bottom line. But it also is evident that senior managers have paid more attention to the customer-profit part of the chain, to the neglect of the first and perhaps most crucial link: employees. And when employees have been part of the value chain, managers have focused on the attitudes – usually satisfaction or engagement – that are correlated with customer service, and have paid less attention to their determinants.

Since this *HBR* article, new evidence has confirmed the importance of the employee link in the value chain. When the employee link is applied to a healthy organization, we see that other links also are important, because they put in place the preconditions for a vibrant workplace that will inspire employees. Anchor points in the value chain are culture and leadership, which give shape to effective and supportive people practices. By expanding the seminal work of Rucci and his co-authors, I describe what may be called a healthy organization value chain, where 'value' is defined as what matters most to customers, employees, shareholders, and communities.

The components of a healthy organization are mutually reinforcing, and success produces an upward spiral that further strengthens the culture, validates the importance of shared leadership, maintains vibrant workplace conditions, and continues to inspire employees. The more employees feel they are able to contribute to the organization's success, the more they feel empowered to further expand their capabilities in innovative ways. This process of innovation also encompasses refinements to the work environment, continually adapting jobs, processes, structures, and systems in ways that maximize people's contributions. Again, wellness is not an end goal but a natural result of healthy processes for involving individuals in improving all aspects of the organization's operations.

The rest of this chapter overviews the four building blocks of a healthy organization – vibrant workplaces, inspired employees, positive culture, and inspired leadership – and their interconnections. I illustrate how these building blocks contribute to higher levels of well-being and performance. This leads to sustainable success, which is how organizations can continue to benefit all stakeholders in future.

Vibrant Workplaces

To emphasize, a vibrant workplace is at the core of a healthy organization. Most successful organizations today have policies and programs in place designed to keep their employees safe and healthy. Increasingly, safety and health are viewed from the perspective of total physical, mental, and emotional wellness. This is my starting point for defining a vibrant workplace. The next plateau of wellness is attainable only by addressing the job characteristics, relationship qualities, work environments, and organizational supports known to shape positive employee experiences and develop performance capabilities. At the end of the work day or week, employees' well-being is enriched by their knowing they have made a meaningful contribution to a larger purpose.

Let us look more closely at the specific features of relationships, jobs, work environments, and organizational supports that constitute a vibrant workplace:

- *Jobs*: Employees have the autonomy to direct their own work, which they find both challenging and meaningful. Employees have ample opportunity to learn and to develop and apply their skills and abilities on the job. They know how their role fits in and makes a difference. Compensation and other rewards are fair and at a decent level.
- *Relationships*: Mutual respect characterizes working relationships among co-workers and between employees and managers. People trust each other and are committed to a shared vision and mission. Employees experience a sense of belonging because the workplace is a true community.
- *Environments*: The work environment is open, collaborative, and participatory. There is a premium on two-way communication throughout the organization. Employees have meaningful input into decisions affecting them. All employees' contributions are valued and recognized. Work is team based and cooperative.
- *Supports*: Supervisors support employees to succeed in their jobs,

develop their talents, and have a balanced life. Employees have adequate facilities, equipment, tools, and other resources needed to do their job well. There are appropriate policies and programs in place to promote health, safety, and effective human resource management practices.

Notice that few of these key ingredients specifically refer to health. Thus, a vibrant workplace is more than a healthy or safe workplace. It is all about the drivers of well-being and performance. For example, two major workplace challenges today are work/life imbalance and job stress. These issues are highlighted in media reports of employees not taking their vacations, working unpaid overtime because of job insecurity, younger workers' reluctance to become managers because of burnout fears, and the blurring of boundaries between personal and work time by 'smart' phones such as the BlackBerry.

Job stress and work/life imbalance are catch-all labels for a range of unhealthy and unproductive workplace conditions that undermine quality of work life, performance, and socially responsible business practices. Solutions to stress and imbalance require action aimed at the ingredients of a vibrant workplace – which essentially is the mirror image of an unhealthy, dysfunctional, and unproductive workplace. The most effective solutions to stress and imbalance involve finding the right mix of job autonomy, decision input, support, resources, and flexibility to offset job demands. Thus, by taking actions that address the root causes of stress and work/life imbalance, managers and human resources professionals will not only reduce workplace risks to both employee well-being and performance, but will be creating a more vibrant workplace.

Inspired Employees

Vibrant workplaces are the contexts in which employees in any position or corporate level are able to thrive at work. A vibrant workplace inspires employees to continually develop and apply their capabilities to deliver excellent results. Employees not only achieve their personal health and wellness goals – most of all, being highly satisfied with their jobs and employer – but they also learn and collaborate, two activities essential for an organization to fully tap into its human capabilities.

Workers who feel inspired actively learn, share their knowledge, and apply their skills. They collaborate effectively with co-workers, customers, and partners to ensure the highest quality of services or products. And they are able to adapt to changes in the business environment, customers' needs and preferences, and within the organization. They look forward to coming to work each day because they know they can make a difference, grow personally, and feel the pride of meaningful accomplishments. They do so within a web of supportive relationships, composed of co-workers, their immediate supervisor and the management group to whom they or their team reports, informal networks of colleagues, and their clients or customers. Experiencing work in this way, an employee moves beyond simply being engaged in her or his job.

Beyond Engagement

Engagement now sits alongside strategy as one of the most overused and fuzzy terms in the management vocabulary. Let us consider a definition of engagement that reflects what managers really want employees to experience in their work: 'Engagement is above and beyond simple satisfaction with the employment arrangement or basic loyalty to the employer – characteristics that most companies have measured for many years. Engagement, in contrast, is about passion and commitment – the willingness to invest oneself and expend one's discretionary effort to help the employer succeed.'[6]

What does it mean to invest oneself and give discretionary effort? Today, organizations need more than extra effort. Rather, they need employees who can be creative, innovative, think and act proactively, and find ways to exceed customers' expectations. Inspired employees do more than give extra effort. They channel their passion for their work and their commitment to the organization and its customers into how they work with others, how they acquire skills and knowledge and apply these in new ways for the benefit of the organization and its stakeholders, how they set high standards for themselves and their team, and how they anticipate and respond to internal and external change. This is a virtuous circle. The positive experiences of learning, teamwork, achieving job and career goals, and contributing to organizational success deepen that psychological state of feeling inspired.

The healthy organization model calls for a rethinking of employers' current fixation with workforce engagement. In its *2007 Global Workforce Study*, consulting firm Towers Perrin discovered that a mere 21 per cent of the 88,600 workers it surveyed in eighteen countries were engaged in their jobs. This hampers firm performance, Towers Perrin explains, by creating an 'engagement gap' between what employees are prepared to commit to and invest in their job and their employer's ability to tap into this potential. As Julie Gebauer, a Towers Perrin workforce effectiveness consultant puts it: 'Organizations ... are not getting the discretionary effort they need from their people to drive their performance and growth agendas, and it's hurting both their top and bottom lines.'[7] According to the report, the best way for senior managers to get higher levels of employee engagement is to inspire employees in their work, provide ample opportunities for skill development, build a solid reputation as a responsible corporation, and generally show an interest in their well-being.

But how do managers inspire the entire workforce of an organization? How do employees inspire each other? Answering these questions requires a clearer understanding of *how* employees' work experiences matter for business performance.

There are two reasons why employers do not achieve the engagement goals they seek. First is the confusion between engagement as an outcome and the actions, processes, and conditions that lead to this outcome. Second is the lack of a clear distinction between the behavioural and attitudinal aspects of engagement. Certainly, it is useful to know from surveys to what extent employees feel proud and passionate about their work. However, what really matters for performance is how these feelings are converted into productive workplace behaviours. What is more, these behaviours matter more than attitudes to an employee's well-being. Employee engagement surveys typically measure working conditions that lead employees to contribute to the performance of their work unit. The actual state of being engaged remains opaque. So I encourage HR and workplace wellness professionals to actively employ the concept of 'engagement.' Doing so will focus senior management's attention on healthy processes for involving (i.e., 'engaging') employees in decisions, initiatives, and changes that build more vibrant workplaces – thereby inspiring employees in their work.

The Capabilities of an Inspired Workforce

Inspiration describes how an individual experiences their work. But it exists only because an employee is in a supportive and enabling work setting. Think of the musician who practises on her own for many hours each day. This private activity provides a sense of accomplishment – getting it right, achieving higher personal standards – but what really matters for an inspired performance is the actual or virtual relationship the solo musician has with her audience, either as concert goers or listeners to her CDs or MP3 tracks. And if she performs with an ensemble, then critical to the inspirational process is her chemistry with the conductor and other musicians who together create the performance. Simply put, inspired performances depend on a web of positive relationships.

Inspired employees work collaboratively. By collaborating, individual employees and teams collectively generate and apply new knowledge and skills – leading to innovation. Management guru Peter Drucker observed that knowledge workers teach each other and learn together. Innovation flows from this collaborative teaching and learning, keeping an organization ahead of the competition or able to provide even higher levels of public service at lower costs. Richard Lyons, the chief learning officer at investment bank Goldman Sachs, defines innovation as 'fresh thinking that creates value.'[8] Innovation depends on employees taking practical insights from their knowledge and creatively applying their skills. Useable information is transmitted through interpersonal communication, a basic point that has given new relevance to what social scientists call 'social capital' and 'social networks.'

Two examples show the importance of workplace relationships to innovation. The first example takes us to a pulp and paper mill, where a paper-making machine operator retired after thirty years of service and was generously feted by his co-workers at a dinner. Within weeks of his departure, the paper-making machine malfunctioned. Facing lost production costs of about $400,000 daily, the company brought in engineers from the machine's maker to investigate the causes of the problem. Then someone thought to call the retired worker, whose first question was, 'has anyone been cleaning the paper dust from behind the machine?' This procedure is not in the operating manual, but the operator had figured it out as he mastered the machine's idiosyncrasies. He had come up with a simple innovation for keeping the machine running, but because plant communications traditionally were on a 'need to know' basis, this critical piece of knowledge remained in his head. The retired operator was passionate about keeping 'his' machine running, but a supportive context for making this private information organizational knowledge was lacking.

Another example is a telecommunications company's call centre, where hundreds of customer services representatives scramble to stay on top of a steady stream of new products and services. The company's knowledge management system, which customer service reps access online, was unable to keep up with all these changes. So the workers in this call centre invented informal ways to share their knowledge and to support each other. Recognizing that nobody could know everything about each of the new products and services, employees regularly shared their solutions and helped each other during customer calls (we hope that is happening when we are put on hold). This innovation in teamwork may seem small, but in a business where customer satisfaction drives revenues, every improvement in service counts. For the employees in this call centre, being able to devise and share their own solutions to customer problems boosted morale and instilled pride. What is more, these employees also had less stress and achieved higher call quality ratings than the company's other call centres.

Learning

Vibrant workplaces also encourage individual and group learning. Active learning is therefore a mark of the inspired employee. Leading thinkers on learning organizations agree that people learn in workplaces through a process that extends over time, is collaborative, and is based on continual knowledge acquisition and dissemination. Learning helps workers to avoid repeating mistakes, to reproduce successes, and to discover new work methods, services, or products. Harvard University's David Garvin describes 'learning facilitators' as those features of an organization and its people that support continual, widespread learning. In learning organizations, according to Garvin, employees at all levels and in all positions are able to actively acquire, interpret, and apply new knowledge or ideas. Learning facilitators include what I identify as attributes of vibrant workplaces: openly sharing and debating different perspectives, timely and accurate feedback, time and space for learning, and a 'sense of psychological safety.'[9]

There are parallels here with what often is labelled a 'learning organization.' In a learning organization, individuals and teams generate and share new knowledge, engage in critical thinking that is system focused, and are supported by a culture that values experimentation.[10] Organizational learning generates the capacity to continually improve performance. However, the learning organization concept is concerned with the connection between learning activities and work performance. While it is obviously important for companies to adapt and prosper, learning is only one feature of a healthy organization. Rather than treating learning as a defining characteristic of an organization, I see it as what inspired employees do when they are in vibrant work environments with positive cultures. In this way, learning is part of the internal dynamic of a healthy organization, contributing to employees' well-being and job satisfaction as well as their capacity to perform better.

As Peter Senge argues in *The Fifth Discipline*, his influential book on learning organizations, most organizations learn poorly because they are designed and managed in ways that actually create 'learning disabilities.'[11] These barriers to learning are visible in the failure of many large-scale organizational change initiatives, from the implementation of new IT systems to total quality management or business process reengineering. Projects like these fail to deliver desired productivity improvements because the people involved have neither the time nor the support to apply lessons from earlier systems to the new system. Learning also requires a longer-term perspective on people development, which calls for a marked departure from the short-term focus of most current workplace training programs.

Common people practices associated with learning include a long-term focus on people, supporting and developing employees, and an abiding belief that when these practices are followed, customers and shareholders benefit. For example, Graniterock is a California-based quarrying, concrete supply, and construction company with over 700 employees.[12] The company's quality goals and business plans are based on its customers' needs, efforts that have won it the National Baldridge Award for Quality. The company also places a high priority on employee development, health and welfare, and safety. Graniterock has performance measures on people development, financial performance, supplier performance, and customer needs. Work is team based, involving task forces, functional teams, and quality teams. Team members use individual development plans to track their own skill and knowledge development and to set long-term training and development goals. The company's future human resource needs and its quality objectives are linked with individual employees' aspirations and abilities. To support this approach, all managers are extensively trained in coaching and people skills. Employee development and performance are seen not as 'HR' issues, but as a shared responsibility for everyone in the organization.

Collaboration

Learning and collaboration go hand in hand. The twenty-first-century version of the learning organization can be called the collaborative organization. The twinning of learning and collaboration better reflects the realities of an emerging global economy that places a premium on creatively applying knowledge.

The project teams, business networks, and global supply chains of today's successful corporations require new ways for workers to create solutions. The emerging form of work organization in this century is post-bureaucratic. It is fluid, flexible, and ceaselessly recombining knowledge into business solutions. Some experts refer to the knowledge-based, flexible organization as a collaborative community, grounded in a shared ethic of interdependent contributions.[13] This makes trust in working relationships critical for the level of collaboration that successful businesses require. The twenty-first-century flexible organization takes many forms, such as short-term projects, supply chains, business alliances and partnerships, and outsourcing arrangements. It also can be virtual, such as communities of software developers that come together to expand open-source operating systems, such as Linux, or to create free online resources such as Wikipedia. Indeed, behind what is called Web 2.0 is any internet-based technology that enables higher levels of interaction and collaboration among users.

Being careful not to over-extrapolate from the IT world, there is still no denying the growing importance of collaboration in all businesses. Consider two cases from very different sectors: construction and health care. The industrial construction sector makes airports, pipelines, tunnels, refineries, and large facilities. Stakeholder relationships more often than not have been adversarial and the industry lags behind others in its HR practices. The sector is engineering dominated. Project management has been viewed as a way to limit project costs and marshal resources. But there is growing recognition that more cooperation, communication, and trust are needed as a basis for project success. A construction project is a complex web of short-term relationships involving different members with diverse skills. Project success depends on the strength and quality of these relationships. According to construction project management experts: 'a cooperative approach between construction organizations would bring about trust and commitment-induced efficiency, and better resource allocation and utilization which leads to increased industry performance.'[14] In short, the ability of project stakeholders to collaborate is what leads to projects being completed on time and on budget and to high technical standards.

The Mayo Clinic is an outstanding example of health care teamwork developed to a fine art. Len Berry, a Texas A&M University professor who spent months observing how the Mayo's teams serve patients, calls it simply 'a collaborative organization.'[15] While the clinic enjoys an enviable global brand and can attract leading talent, it is the Mayo's philosophy – pursuing the ideal of service ahead of profits, sincere concern for the welfare of each patient, and continuing interest among staff in each other's professional development – in which collaboration is grounded. At the Mayo, it takes a team to care for a patient. Collaborative patient care is supported through recruitment, leadership development and training, and infrastructure (from IT systems to physical work space). And it infuses the culture. When the Mayo conducted focus groups with patients, their families, staff, and volunteers to document the common elements in their experience, the dominant image that emerged was of people holding hands.

Whether it is online creation of wikis or open-source software, learning organizations like Graniterock, or the team-based health care practised by the Mayo Clinic, such examples point to a common feature in healthy organizations: people are inspired by opportunities to learn, collaborate, and contribute. Through these activities, people in a healthy organization also are resilient in the face of change. Indeed, they will be better able to anticipate and adapt to change. The Mayo Clinic trains for the future by focusing on the needs of tomorrow's patients. This orientation towards the future is also part and parcel of innovation, which demands thinking ahead to anticipate needs.

Culture and Leadership

Two other building blocks of healthy organizations – culture and leadership – are intertwined. A positive culture exudes the high value placed on employees, customers, and society. Inclusive leadership practises these values. It is a mindset that everyone in the organization has a responsibility to improve the workplace as the route to better business results – and a better society.

Culture and Leadership in Action

Baptist Health Care is a good illustration of how a positive culture and shared leadership for making improvements support employees to achieve excellent results. Baptist Health Care employs 5,500 workers in five acute-care hospitals, nursing homes, mental health facilities, and outpatient centres in Pensacola, Florida. Baptist Health Care attributes its current high levels of service excellence to the transformation of its culture and work environment, guided by three principles: employee satisfaction, patient satisfaction, and leadership development. It began this transformation in 1996 with the goal of improving the poor quality of its health services. Patient satisfaction was in the 18th percentile, positive employee morale was at 44 per cent, and turnover was 27 per cent annually. The five directions of transformation were creating and maintaining a great culture, selecting and retaining great employees, committing to service excellence, continually developing great leaders, and hardwiring success through systems of accountability. As a result of succeeding in all these areas, by 2003 Baptist Health Care was in the 99th percentile in patient satisfaction, positive employee morale was 83 per cent, and turnover had dropped to 14 per cent.

Baptist Health Care defines the key characteristics of a healthy culture as open communication, no secrets, a sense of employee ownership, and no excuses.[16] Responsibility for renewing the culture was handed over to employee-led committees. There are teams on culture, communication, customer loyalty, employee loyalty, and physician loyalty. Teams use a variety of measures to create transparency and accountability for key goals. Regular surveys of employees, physicians, and patients inform continual communication and action planning. People practices are consistent with the values, meeting employees' work/life needs.

CEO Al Stubblefield sums up the Baptist Health Care approach, emphasizing the importance of reinventing the organization's culture: 'At Baptist Health Care, we recognize the strong correlation between employee commitment and customer satisfaction. We know that happy, committed employees work more productively and provide better service. By valuing and recognizing our staff, we harness the power of motivation and generate sustained levels of achievement.'[17] Baptist Health Care mapped its own route to a vibrant workplace that inspires its staff to deliver excellent health care services. This, in brief, is the healthy organization value chain in action.

Better Workplaces

Baptist Health Care is on *Fortune* magazine's annual list of 100 Best Companies to Work For In America and has won awards for the quality of its patient care. Some of my other examples also are on the *Fortune* list, namely, Graniterock, Mayo Clinic, and SAS. The list is based on research by Great Place to Work Institute, a global workplace consulting firm that compiles annual 'best workplaces' lists in North and South America, Europe, Australia, and Asia. Because the *Fortune* list has been published annually since 1998 and features some of the most successful and widely admired publicly traded companies in the United States, we can gain useful lessons about what makes these companies inspiring to work for. The main insight from research on the *Fortune* list is that positive workplace cultures drive superior performance.

Great workplaces have high-trust cultures with strong core values, such as respect, fairness, and integrity. Great Place to Work Institute's research shows that employees trust managers who are concerned about their well-being, listen and respond to their input, are open and honest about change, and consistently reflect the organization's values. Trust is a fragile property of all employee-management relationships. The level of trust in workplace makes the difference between mediocre and exceptional performance. Employees who trust the people they work for also have pride in their work and feel a true sense of camaraderie with co-workers. The synergy between trust, pride, and camaraderie inspires employees to be creative and innovative. They are more likely to take the kind of risks expected of entrepreneurial business owners. More than three-quarters of the employees in companies on the *Fortune* list of 100 Best Companies to Work for in America look forward to coming to work every day. Most other organizations are lucky to achieve half that level of enthusiasm.

Evidence for the culture-performance link comes from independent financial analysts and academic researchers who have combed through the financial results for companies on the *Fortune* list.[18] The Russell Investment Group has calculated the annualized returns for the '100 Best' and the stock market (the S&P 500 and the Russell 3000 stock indexes). Between 1998 and 2007 a portfolio that had equal dollar amounts of stock in the companies on the 1998 list would have had 10.65 per cent annual returns if held until 2006, compared with rates of return of about 6 per cent for the two market indices. If the portfolio of '100 Best' companies was reset each year to reflect changes on the *Fortune* list, the annualized rate of return jumped to 14.16 per cent, or 2.3 times the market average.

Academics also have put the *Fortune* list through rigorous tests to see if the positive employee relationships – what financial experts call 'intangible assets' – influence market performance. One study compared the stock returns, return on assets, and ratio of market to book value of equity for fifty companies on the 100 Best list and fifty market peers (based on size, industry, operating revenues) not on the list.[19] On all measures, the 100 Best firms outperformed their peers. This better performance enables firms on the 100 Best list to provide the working conditions and perks that attract and retain talented and inspired workers. Amplifying these findings, research by Alex Edmans at the University of Pennsylvania's Wharton School shows that a portfolio of stocks from the 1998 list of 100 Best earned more than double the market return over an eight-year period.[20] In short, investing in people pays off over the long term.

Sustainable Success

An organization's future will be bleak indeed if it burns out employees, exhausts credit lines, alienates customers, acts unethically, and is irresponsible towards the environment. Quite simply, these practices deplete key resources, from operating capital and people to reputation. Failure is likely. By contrast, organizations that thrive constantly regenerate their resources. This requires long-term and holistic thinking, exactly as we have come to view the challenges facing the natural environment. Organizations, too, are fragile ecosystems. Continued success depends on renewing the fine balance needed between culture, people practices, systems, and structures.

I use the term 'sustainable success' to link financial, people, and ethical goals. This revises the triple bottom-line view of 'people, planet, profits' by highlighting how organizations can renew themselves. In this regard, organizations need to renew the capabilities of their workforce and they need to renew their relationships with customers and communities. At the top of the healthy organization value chain, the links between people and performance also benefit communities. Employees' pride comes from contributing to excellent products or services, as well as from being part of an organization that 'gives back' to the community by supporting public initiatives. I elaborate these points in chapter 7. For now, I encourage you to take a look at how local and national community-based non-profit organizations and charities are forming closer partnerships with businesses. A selling point for such partnerships is that they provide a way to realize corporate commitments to social responsibility and create employee volunteering opportunities. But none of this is possible, of course, without success in basic business terms. That is precisely why the vibrant workplace is at the heart of my healthy organization model. These kinds of workplaces are the generators of both economic and social performance.

Stronger People-Performance Links

There is a plain truth about organizational performance: enabling people to contribute their best work translates into better organizational results. This point is confirmed in studies involving many different organizations. Research shows that a cluster of working conditions and management practices, similar to what I call a vibrant workplace, encourages employees to achieve higher levels of job performance. In short, people-performance links can be made stronger, providing the basis for continued success.

An article in the *Journal of Applied Psychology* used Gallup organization data from 198,514 employees in 7,939 business units in thirty-six companies to test the relationship between employees' overall job satisfaction and their level of engagement in the performance of the business unit.[21] Business performance was measured by customer satisfaction, profitability, revenues, turnover, and safety (lost-time work injuries). Business units performed better when employees were satisfied and had managers and working conditions that engaged them. A book by two Gallup consultants, *12: The Elements of Great Managing*,[22] outlines the twelve key engagement drivers. These include clear job expectations, the resources needed to do the job, recognition, supportive supervisors and co-workers who care, doing what you do best, opportunities to learn and develop, connection to the company's mission, and having decision input.

Similar conclusions were reached by David Sirota, Louis Mischkind, and Michael Irwin Meltzer in their book, *The Enthusiastic Employee*.[23] Sirota and his colleagues view high employee morale as the key to a firm's performance. They extensively surveyed employees' attitudes as a way to help organizations improve their effectiveness. Employees' experiences of equity (being treated justly), achievement (doing challenging and skilled work, being recognized for and taking pride in one's contributions, and being proud to work for the company), and camaraderie (positive and cooperative relationships with co-workers) are strongly associated with both morale and performance. Companies with high morale, measured by overall employee satisfaction, performed about 20 per cent better than their industry peers. Enthusiastic workers also improve quality, reduce defects, and boost customer satisfaction and sales. The management practices that have the biggest positive impact on morale are actions addressing employees' needs for equity, achievement, and camaraderie.

For additional evidence of how vibrant workplaces produce healthy outcomes, we can turn to studies of high-performance workplaces (HPW).[24] These are productive and innovative firms that place human resources at the centre of their business strategy. As Jeffrey Pfeffer, a Stanford University organizational expert, explains: 'The fundamental premise of high performance management systems is that organizations perform at a higher level when they are able to tap the ideas, skill and effort of all their people.'[25] HPWs have flexible work systems that provide workers with considerable support and scope to make decisions and provide input. Thus, another label for a HPW is a high-involvement or high-trust workplace.

Indeed, there are parallels between a vibrant workplace and Gallup's data on employee engagement, Sirota et al.'s emphasis on employee morale, and high-performance workplace studies. But these approaches lack two main ingredients of sustainable success. First, they do not address whether the workplace conditions leading to higher job performance contribute to employees' overall health and wellness. Second, there is no community connection. The advantage of the healthy organization model, and the value chain described earlier, is that performance, wellness, and community benefits are interwoven.

Healthier Employees and Communities

Let us briefly consider these other links in the healthy organization value chain. The dynamics of a healthy organization generate benefits for the communities in which it operates. For example, healthier employees are less likely to use health care services. This has important implications for publicly funded health services and for employer-provided health benefit costs. The supportive work environment of a healthy organization helps employees to enjoy a fulfilling personal and family life. Employees have more time and energy to contribute to raising their children, assisting their aging parents, and volunteering in community activities that matter to them. The philosophy of a healthy organization is, above all, people focused, so there is consistency between treating employees and customers well and being a responsible corporate citizen. In short, a healthy organization's relationships

with its external stakeholders will generate mutually beneficial outcomes.

The people-based values of a healthy organization also are evident
externally in socially and environmentally responsible business practices. These values and ethics require longer-term, holistic thinking that
balances profits (or in the public sector, 'value for money'), with what is
good for community stakeholders. By doing good in this way, corporations can shore up public trust that has been eroded over this decade
by a string of Enron-like corporate scandals up to the 2008 Wall Street-
induced global financial crisis. They also are addressing a long list of
consumer and investor concerns, from human rights and fair trade to a
reduced carbon footprint, which were barely on the radar ten years ago.

As companies sort out how to strengthen their ethical standards
and take actions that make meaningful contributions to good causes,
employees, too, are holding employers to higher standards. While corporate responsibility comes in many forms, what is pivotal to 'walking the talk' is having a strong connection with human resource goals
and practices. Branding a company as a responsible corporate citizen
signals to prospective employees – especially young recruits – that the
company cares, treats others well, and reflects their personal values. It
also sets the bar higher for how employers actually support employees
to personally contribute to the community, on company time and on
their own time. In high-pressure workplaces that demand long hours,
there is an obvious disconnect with corporate ethics of supporting local
charities through volunteering.

Healthy organizations have figured out ways to integrate corporate
social responsibility with their people practices. As critics have noted,
CSR without HR is PR. This is a trap into which I have seen a number of
organizations fall. For example, it is fine for senior executives to make
time in their schedules to be on the board of the local United Way or
other prominent community charities. Yet front-line employees are expected not only to make personal donations, but beyond that, to get
personally involved in fund-raising campaigns, which their workloads
and the emphasis the company places on achieving operational goals,
not on community service, make extremely difficult. The World Bank's
definition of CSR places employees at the centre: 'Corporate social responsibility is the commitment of businesses to contribute to sustainable economic development by working with employees, their families,
the local community and society at large to improve their lives in ways
that are good for business and for development.'[26] New research in-

deed confirms that companies with comprehensive CSR practices do have stronger employee relations.[27]

Clearly we need an expanded value chain for organizational performance, one that includes employees, customers, shareholders, and the community. Essentially, the issue comes down to integrity. If an organization claims to be a good corporate citizen committed to improving the quality of life, then how can it not apply the same principle internally? And if a company emphasizes to its employees the importance of open, respectful communication, how can it not apply this principle to employees' dealings with community stakeholders? Readers may well answer, 'it's not that simple.' But as I show in later chapters, by consistently and thoroughly living their values, healthy organizations expand their value chain to include employees and communities.

Making Well-Being a Priority

To recap, a healthy organization cultivates vibrant workplaces in which employees feel inspired. This process builds capabilities for ongoing success. The criteria for success will vary, or course, depending on the size, sector, and location of the organization. But generally speaking, benefits will flow to employees, customers, and owners and to the larger community in which the business operates. In short, the healthy organization can achieve a triple win.

For employees, benefits can be measured in terms of overall health and wellness, work/life balance, professional development and personal growth, and a generally high quality of work life. For the organization, success would include financial performance, operating efficiency, reduced human capital risks and costs, and future sustainability. There also are community benefits. The people-focused values of a healthy organization are expressed in a range of socially and environmentally responsible actions, from charitable contributions, to support for employee volunteering, to reduction of the organization's carbon footprint. And by contributing to a healthy and skilled workforce, the organization is reducing the burden on publicly funded health care and building capabilities that individual employees can carry into their personal, family, and community activities.

I also have emphasized that the healthy organization model invites us to take an integrative, future-oriented view of workplaces. The model provides an opportunity to connect internal people practices and values with how the organization operates within its communities. The concept of a value chain is a useful tool for thinking about how multiple internal and external stakeholders can be part of and benefit from the activities of the organization. A healthy organization is responsive to the needs of its employees, its social and physical environment, and most important, the needs of its customers or clients. Above all, it strives to improve the well-being of all these stakeholders. As chapter 2 will show, the very idea of a health organization has its roots in workplace health promotion. Indeed, the limits of the workplace health promotion paradigm are what led me to the expanded view of well-being and performance captured in the vision of a healthy organization.

2 Beyond Workplace Health Promotion

Visitors to Singapore are impressed by the city-state's economic dynamism, high living standards, and cosmopolitanism – not to mention its clean sidewalks and efficient public transit system. The Singapore government and business community have done many innovative things to build a knowledge-based commercial, financial, and manufacturing powerhouse. One of the country's success factors is the active promotion of healthy employees in healthy workplaces.

The 2008 biennial Singapore HEALTH awards, which I attended as a speaker and workshop leader, offer a window on the potential of workplace health promotion to take a more organizational focus.[1] The award, which stands for 'Helping Employees Achieve Life-Time Health,' is sponsored by the government's Health Promotion Board. The goal is a healthier workforce and ultimately higher economic productivity and living standards. In 2008 there were 358 public and private sector employers receiving awards in four categories: bronze, silver, gold, and platinum. To start the ball rolling, the Singapore government provides matching grants to employers to fund health promotion programs and it supports internal 'health facilitators' to be change agents. Beyond the government funding, what really seems to motivate employers and employees to participate in the HEALTH awards process is the useful feedback they receive, the public recognition from being an award winner, and recruitment and retention benefits. Also, for those in the gold and platinum levels, there are performance dividends.

Listening to the stories of the companies and public sector organizations at the awards event, I was struck by how many have progressed from basic health promotion towards their own vision of a 'healthy organization.' Bronze award recipients typically are new comers to the idea of health promotion. These companies and government agencies have a mix of programs that encourage healthy eating, physical activity, mental well-being, chronic disease management, prevention of communicable disease, and smoking cessation – the basics in a comprehensive health promotion approach to workplace wellness. But this year's bronze award winners aspire to win a silver, gold, or even platinum award next time. As organizations move to higher levels, the distinction between health and organizational performance dissolves. At the platinum level, one sees organizations with healthy cultures. Business strategies incorporate employee health and well-being, providing a clear competitive advantage. And managers intuitively understand that a healthy and a high-performing workforce are one and the same.

Typical of platinum award winners are Nanyang Polytechnic and NatSteel Holdings. The chair of the workplace health promotion committee at Nanyang Polytechnic talked about the importance of core values and policies that supported a nurturing and caring culture and 'borderless' teamwork – factors that enabled successful workplace health promotion as well as innovation. The vice-president of human resources at NatSteel Holdings, which manufactures steel products for residential, commercial and infrastructure projects, described the sophisticated tools the company uses to assess needs and track and report progress on a wide range of workforce health and well-being issues. The goal is to create a 'happy, motivated and challenged' workforce and to galvanize the company's reputation as 'a great place to work.' These examples show that by challenging employers and employees to step forward and be evaluated and recognized for their workplace health promotion efforts, the Singapore government has put in place enabling conditions for truly healthy organizations. The more significant lesson is that employers and employees have taken up this challenge. As a result, workplace health promotion is a springboard for moving to a higher level of well-being and performance.

This chapter makes the case for a healthy organization by exploring the benefits and limitations of workplace health promotion. As in Singapore, workplace health promotion has taken root in many countries and businesses in the past decade, generating pent-up demand for an organizational approach to employee well-being. Workplace health promotion initiatives are, in my view, a launching pad for achieving better employee well-being and organizational performance. Workplace health promotion can put in place the building blocks for healthy organizations, contributing to more vibrant workplaces that actively involve employees in shaping a positive, supportive, and wellness-oriented corporate culture. As we saw in the Singapore HEALTH Awards, the next step for employers that have implemented wellness programs is to leverage them to uncover the organizational factors influencing success. This chapter offers change agents who are seeking to build on current health promotion approaches in their own workplace the following guideposts:

1. There is a solid business case for comprehensive workplace health promotion and prevention programs.
2. There is good potential to expand workplace health promotion by addressing the underlying causes of presenteeism, stress, and work/life imbalance.
3. Current health promotion initiatives can be a stepping stone to a more holistic organizational perspective that links employee well-being with performance.
4. For companies to move in this direction, employee health and wellness must be viewed as an organizational asset that contributes to a skilled and motivated workforce.
5. Also critical is understanding the root causes of health and performance, especially the psychological and social aspects of work.

The Wellness Paradox

Champions of workplace wellness must resolve a basic paradox in order to make progress: despite rising investments by growing numbers of employers in employee health and wellness, the performance benefits are limited mainly to savings related to lower absenteeism and benefit costs. Other innovations that have transformed workplaces – from information technology and improved knowledge management systems to business process redesign – have more visible performance payoffs, enabling people to create more value by working better. So why can similar performance benefits not flow from investments in healthier workplaces? The answer is that we have run up against the limits of health promotion.

I believe that the wellness paradox can be resolved by thinking in terms of organizational health. This approach helps us to see the value chain I laid out in chapter 1 – and shows us ways to move up that value chain.

Increasingly, managers, workplace wellness practitioners, and researchers recognize the need to examine the underlying workplace determinants of health and productivity. Actions are guided by the World Health Organization's (WHO) definition of health as complete physical, mental, and social well-being, not simply absence of disease or ill health. Job and organizational factors should, ideally, support positive mental and physical health outcomes for employees. It is widely assumed that healthy employees are more productive. It is now common, especially in the United States, to use the term 'health and productivity management' to integrate health promotion into all corporate functions from human resources, benefits, employee assistance programs, occupational health and safety, workers' compensation, organizational development, and business operations.

However, major stumbling blocks remain. Canada is typical of many countries in this regard. According to Buffett & Company Worksite Wellness Inc., the proportion of Canadian employers participating in its National Wellness Surveys that offered at least one wellness initiative to employees rose from 44 per cent in 1997 to 91 per cent by 2009.[2] Echoing international experts, Buffett & Company considers that comprehensive wellness includes multiple wellness initiatives, data analysis, employee follow-up and counselling, continual evaluation, and the calculation of return on investment. Yet relatively few employers make health and wellness a core component of their business strategy.

Employers' search for solutions to rising health and disability benefits costs has generated much rhetoric about the need to create healthier workplaces. However, action has been slower in coming. It is not that the current approach to workplace health is not paying off. Comprehensive workplace health promotion programs can reduce employee health risk factors, reduce employers' health care costs, and improve productivity. Yet most of the productivity gain is realized through reduced absenteeism.

This narrow focus fails to capture the many other sources of productivity affected by healthy or unhealthy work environment. So change agents must embrace a larger vision of a work environment in which employees thrive. Such visions are cast in terms of organizational effectiveness, performance, and social responsibility. Achieving individual well-being is a by-product of work systems, management practices, and organizational cultures that inspire employees to collaborate in the interests of customers or clients, shareholders, and the larger community.

Healthy Workplace Pay-Offs and Potential

I often am asked by managers and employees who are trying to improve their work environment: 'How do we make changes based on evidence?' 'How will we know the value of a healthier workplace?' Answers to both questions can be found in workplace health promotion research. As a brief review of these studies shows, we actually know a great deal about the kinds of changes that best contribute to healthy outcomes for individuals and organizations and the expected returns from healthy workplace investments.

Wellness Returns on Investment

A growing number of worksite health promotion programs have been subjected to rigorous cost-benefit analysis that calculates the employer's return on investment (ROI). Some studies also look at improvements in employees' health status, but it is notable from a healthy organization perspective that workplace health promotion ROI is all about employer costs. ROI is the most clear-cut 'business case' one can make for a workplace health and wellness program. And, as I show below, the business case for health promotion is compelling: reductions in employer health care costs, productivity gains, and better health outcomes for employees. The big result is improved quality of life.

We can identify three evidence-based insights about the strengths, limitations, and potential of workplace health promotion. These insights underscore the momentum that is has been building for a broader organizational focus on health and performance:[3]

1. Focused worksite health promotion programs aimed at modifying an employee's diet, physical activity, and other lifestyle factors have limited results in terms of reducing health risk factors.
2. Comprehensive worksite health promotion and disease management programs generally have positive clinical and cost outcomes, showing the best results for employees who have the highest risk of heart disease and have other chronic conditions.
3. There is a growing consensus among experts that further improvements in employee well-being and organizational performance will require changes in work environments. In other words, an organizational approach is needed.

Much research exists showing the positive impact of worksite health promotion programs. We know that workplace health promotion interventions that are comprehensive, well designed, and successfully implemented will have a net positive ROI. Many studies also show that, in addition to cost savings, programs aimed at high-risk groups – such as smokers and obese individuals – contribute to improved health outcomes. So for employers, the issue is not whether to introduce such programs to reduce health risks and increase productivity, but how to design, implement and evaluate programs to achieve the best outcomes for employees and the organization.

Part of the motivation for employers to promote wellness is the potential to reduce or contain the rising costs of health benefits, thereby avoiding the alternative of cutting back benefits coverage. If anything, the recent recession prompted a line-by-line review of health benefits budgets. Employers taking the long view, as Trico Homes did, were seeking savings without reducing the benefits that are so important to retaining staff, maintaining a performance culture during tough times, and staying competitive for future recruitment.

Healthy Lifestyle Programs

Anyone working in an office, shopping mall, government facility, or large industrial site in the late 1980s and early 1990s in most parts of Canada and the United States witnessed one of the most remarkable single-issue public health initiatives ever. I remember the first winter the Canadian federal government banned smoking in all its offices in the late 1980s. As groups of smokers huddled around doorways in the frigid cold, the dark humour among bureaucrats was that pneumonia was now smokers' greatest health risk.

In fact, worksite smoking cessation policies and programs are the most widespread and successful initiatives by employers and governments to address pre-existing employee health risks. Results have been impressive: a steady decline in smoking rates in countries adopting such measures. Indeed, the elimination of smoking from most North America workplaces marks a significant public health milestone.

There is overwhelming evidence that smoking increases annual health care costs.[4] Medical costs of smoking in the United States range from 6 per cent to 14 per cent of annual personal health care costs. A study of telephone customer service workers estimated that smokers lost an average of 4.1 hours per week due to illness-related absences, short-term disability, and lost productivity (the latter is the largest component, at 3.5 hours). The Canadian Cancer Society suggests that the annual cost savings to employers when an employee quits smoking can be as high as $3,396 when absenteeism, decreased productivity from smoke breaks, and the costs of smoking facilities are included.[5]

Yet it would be a stretch to claim that companies and government departments have become high performing just because they introduced a smoking cessation campaign or set up an on-site gym. In short, beyond the health benefits to those employees who participate in these programs – and their non-smoking colleagues in the case of worksite smoking bans – there is little evidence of sustained performance benefits to organizations. However, the performance payoffs increase when single-focus programs are combined within a wider range of supports and resources that promote employee well-being.

Today, obesity has replaced smoking as the number one public health issue in the advanced industrial countries. According to the WHO, 'obesity has reached epidemic proportions globally.'[6] Some areas of North America, the United Kingdom, and Australia have seen a three-fold increase in obesity rates since 1980. Obesity increases a person's risk of preventable chronic diseases, such as cardiovascular disease, hypertension, type-2 diabetes, arthritis, and some types of cancer. Direct costs of weight-related major chronic diseases to Canada's health system were estimated at nearly $1.6 billion in 2001, rising to $4.3 billion when indirect costs were included.[7] From the perspective of the healthy organization model presented in chapter 1, obesity can be seen as a societal issue that responsible employers can help to address through workplace actions. Success would be measured in terms of healthier employees, improvements in quality of life, and a more sustainable health care system.

Unlike smoking in workplaces, obesity does not impair the health of co-workers or impose fire and safety risks or added cleaning costs on employers. Consequently, employers are more reticent to directly take on what is a personal health issue. Even so, some employers are taking action to support healthy eating and exercise. Yet contributions to a more vibrant workplace will be minimal if actions to reduce obesity are just that – solving the obesity problem by targeting individuals' lifestyles. However, if such initiatives take the shape of employee-led activity challenges – such as using the stairs instead of the elevator, counting daily steps on pedometers, or seeing which group can 'walk around the world' – then we are into a whole other realm of fun, team-building, and generating a healthy culture.

Yet this approach may be expecting a great deal, however, because studies of the benefits of fitness programs find mixed results. Potential net financial benefits for employers who introduce fitness programs include reduced health care costs, absenteeism, injury rates, and turn-over and improved job performance, productivity, and morale.[8] Reviews of the financial impact show cost/benefit ratios ranging from $0.76 to $3.43 and from $1.15 to $5.52 when fitness programs are part of a comprehensive health promotion strategy. The major limitation of fitness programs, however, is overall low participation, mainly by those who are already reasonably healthy and active. What is not measured are the less visible organizational benefits, such as increased satisfaction, a sense of camaraderie, and the feeling that this is a fun place to work.

A final lifestyle program we will consider is stress management. Seminars on coping with job demands or work/family tension may offer useful personal tips. However, there is no evidence of real health and productivity pay-offs. Despite their popularity, stress management and other programs aimed at increasing an individual's coping skills generally are ineffective over the long run if they address superficial issues, not root causes. There are few, if any, lasting benefits for the organization and limited benefits for the individuals involved.[9] I am not suggesting that these types of program be scrapped. After all, they do address employees' information needs, and they may signal to employees that the company cares about their well-being. But unless such stress-reduction sessions launch further discussions about more systemic solutions, such as changes in workload or job redesign, any benefits will be transitory.

Addressing Chronic Health Conditions

A goal of some workplace wellness programs is to help employees better manage pre-existing health conditions. Increasingly, employers see these health management programs as one way to contain rising health-related costs and meet the needs of an older and more diverse workforce, which includes more individuals with disabilities and chronic health conditions. Depending on the size and demographic profile of the workforce, there could be substantial benefits to employees and the bottom line from introducing a chronic-disease management program.

Allergies are a common chronic condition that affects people's health and work performance. One study of telephone customer service operators at a large U.S. financial services corporation examined the relationship between allergies and productivity using data from a computerized productivity measurement system.[10] The productivity of workers with allergies decreased as much as 10 per cent during peak pollen season. Based on average daily compensation at the time, this represented a loss of $52 per affected employee per week. Employees using antihistamines were more productive than were those not using medication. The researchers calculated the return on investment of providing drugs to allergy sufferers (average cost of $18 per week) to be 2:1.

If a program focusing on chronic health conditions is an employer's main healthy workplace initiative, it will have little impact beyond the productivity and cost benefits just noted. The same goes for fitness facilities or smoking cessation. As I explain below, a single-issue approach using a stand-alone initiative is less effective than when it is integrated within a comprehensive set of measures to promote wellness as part of a company's broader commitment to a healthy and productive workforce. When positioned within a comprehensive health promotion strategy, each specific component reinforces the message that the company cares about the well-being of its employees.

Targeting High-Risk Employees

Professor Vic Strecher, a health behaviour expert at the University of Michigan, described to a workplace health promotion conference audience a U.S. manufacturer 88 per cent of whose health care costs went to a small group of seriously unhealthy employees who comprised only 8 per cent of the company's total workforce. Another 40 per cent of employees were considered 'at risk' of developing a range of serious health problems, such as heart disease or diabetes. Numbers like these make the case for designing workplace health promotion programs that target high-risk employees.

Indeed, there is solid evidence for targeting high-risk employees.[11] For example, one study used a randomized control trial method (considered the 'gold standard' design among medical researchers) to assess the impact of a comprehensive worksite health promotion program on full-time, blue-collar workers in a large, multi-location industrial firm.[12] Workers in the program received support and resources on healthy lifestyles, fitness, nutrition, stress management, smoking cessation, health risk surveys, safety, and counselling. Workers in the two-year program had 11,726 fewer disability days, compared with similar workers at non-program sites. This amounts to a return on investment of $2.05 for every dollar invested, just in terms of reduced absenteeism. Other studies tracking high-risk employees over several years find similar benefits from comprehensive programs aimed at health-risk reduction:[13]

- A University of Michigan study at Steelcase Corporation found that for every employee who had excessive alcohol consumption, the firm spent $597 more annually in health costs. For every employee who was sedentary, the cost was $488 and hypertension cost $327.
- The Employee Benefit Research Institute determined that Citibank reduced health risks and saved between $4.56 and $4.73 for every dollar spent on its health education and awareness program.
- Dow Chemical's workplace disease management programs, targeting mainly individual employees who have chronic conditions, resulted in median benefits over time of over $8 for every dollar invested.
- Eight organizations in Halifax, Canada, calculated an ROI of $1.64 for every dollar invested in a comprehensive wellness program designed to reduce the risk of heart disease and even more for higher-risk employees such as smokers.

These ROI levels may be the best we can expect. For one thing, employees are becoming sensitive to how much meddling by their employers in personal health matters they will tolerate.[14] While the latest programs offer more powerful tools, they also lead to heightened concerns about privacy and individual choice. Sophisticated health-risk assessment (HRA) tools help high-risk employees to develop the motivation to change their behaviour and remove barriers, such as thinking they are unable to change. This requires 'smart' HRAs that personalize the information, resources, and approach depending on an individual's attitudes, strengths, and readiness for change. Because these tools require larger investments, employers expect more employees to 'voluntarily' participate. Some U.S. employers, such as courier service UPS, pay employees to complete the HRA. Others require it.

An Organizational View of Health and Wellness

We've seen that individual wellness – optimal physical, psychological,

Figure 2.1 Strategic impact of health and wellness

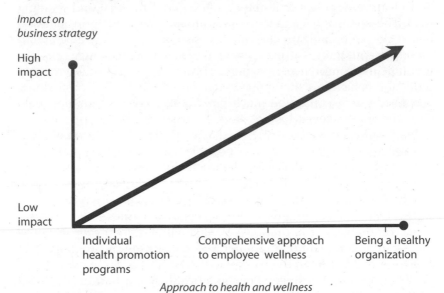

*Impact on
business strategy*

High
impact

Low
impact

Individual
health promotion
programs

Comprehensive approach
to employee wellness

Being a healthy
organization

Approach to health and wellness

and emotional well-being – is the goal of a comprehensive approach to health promotion. Wellness is promoted, whereas illness and injury are prevented. Wellness focuses on positive states of being, not simply the absence of illness, disease, or injury – although this, too, is a goal, as we saw in studies reviewed earlier. Individuals' overall quality of life depends in large part on whether they experience wellness.

A simple question can move us beyond this individual focus: what are the organizational benefits of wellness? To help in answering this question, figure 2.1 shows that as organizations expand their focus from stand-alone programs (occupational health and safety being the most common example) to a comprehensive health promotion approach, they can expect a modest impact on performance. Most of the managers and employees who have participated in my workshops locate their organization at or near the middle of the continuum in figure 2.1, because they take a comprehensive workplace health promotion approach. This would include, for example, a wellness committee, a wellness coordinator, and a range of programs and policies aimed at promoting healthy diets, weights, nutrition, lifestyles, and, increasingly, an emphasis on mental health promotion within the worksite.

Many of my workshop participants also aspire to a healthy organization ideal, recognizing that getting there may be a long and winding road. These managers and employees are looking for opportunities to realize deeper organizational benefits – such as more inspired employees and a reputation as an excellent workplace – from healthy workplace investments. Comprehensive wellness programs target underlying attitudes and behaviours that influence an individual's lifestyle: smoking, being sedentary, eating too much junk food, or not getting adequate sleep. Fewer, however, look at work environment influences on individual health and wellness. That is why workplace health experts have concluded that further progress is possible only through expanding the individual health promotion model to include workplace cultures, relationships, systems, and structures. As one workplace fitness expert stated: 'Positively influencing behaviour in the workplace requires a shift in focus from individual/personal behaviour change to more strategic, comprehensive approaches ... This will require a shift in thinking, so that "interventions" are not seen as short-term programs, but as part of the culture of the workplace.'[15] Adopting this expansive approach is a natural next step beyond a health-promotion focus. If you are looking for opportunities in your health-promotion programs to energize a healthy organization strategy, you must be clear about how they reflect the organization's values. And you also must show how a healthier work environment will support employees to implement the corporate strategy.

In this regard, consider using health promotion programs to strengthen culture and leadership, two of the building blocks of a healthy organization. Look for ways to maximize the non-health spin-offs from any workplace health initiative. Meeting employees' health and wellness needs becomes easier if they are active participants in the entire process, not merely end-users of health resources. In this way, employees take ownership – in other words, leadership – for the means and the ends. And as managers and employees work together to make the work environment healthier (and safer, too), the trust this establishes will result in more cooperative workplace relationships. Over time, higher levels of trust will foster a wider range of workplace improvements. For example, in unionized settings, the joint design and implementation of comprehensive health promotion programs has yielded more than reduced employee health risks and benefit costs. Positive results also flow from how the program is developed. Both the United Auto Workers in the United States and their Canadian counterpart, the

Canadian Auto Workers (CAW), have addressed workforce wellness issues through union-management cooperation, collaborative problem solving, and front-line employee 'ownership.'[16] Programs had active employee involvement through worksite committees and consultations to identify areas of need. What is especially innovative about the CAW-Chrysler wellness program is how it reaches out to the community. In fact, the local public health unit was a partner in a program called 'Tune Up Your Heart,' aimed at individuals at high risk of heart disease. While at first glance, these health-risk reduction programs resemble others in large worksites, this observation is based only on the 'what' of the program. An organizational health perspective provides useful lessons on the 'how,' highlighting the importance of shared leadership and a culture of cooperation.

Limitations of Workplace Health Promotion

In more general terms, putting in place the building blocks for a healthy organization requires that you recognize the limitations of workplace health promotion initiatives. With this recognition comes a shift in thinking, from an individual to an organizational focus. There are four basic limitations:

- Workplace wellness often is stand-alone, not fully integrated with other human resource management policies and practices to enhance the work environment.
- A narrow focus on individuals' health-related attitudes and behaviour often excludes workplace factors that affect employee health and well-being.
- Productivity benefits come mainly from reduced absenteeism and lower employee health care costs – and we know there is more to productivity.
- There is an accounting focus on ROI, rather than on attempts to broaden corporate thinking in ways that place wellness at the core of an organization's strategy.

For thinking to shift, senior managers must come to view employee wellness as a strategic goal. Currently, employee health promotion typically is viewed by management as just that – a health issue. Yet many experts propose what amounts to a seamless integration of health into a company's business strategy. As the editor-in-chief of the *American Journal of Health Promotion* explains: 'human performance is higher when people are physically and emotionally able to work and have the desire to work. Higher levels of human performance lead to higher levels of productivity, which in turn can lead to higher profits.'[17] The healthy organization of the future will infuse health promotion into all corporate functions, from human resources, benefits, employee assistance programs, occupational health and safety, workers' compensation, organizational development, and business operations.

Comparing Health Promotion and Organizational Perspectives

Let us look in detail at the differences between the workplace health promotion and healthy organization perspectives. I compare these approaches side by side in figure 2.2. Try using figure 2.2 as an assessment tool for identifying where your organization lies on the dimensions listed down the left side of the table. On each of the dimensions, assess whether your workplace is closer to one column than to the other, noting how this position may vary for each of the dimensions.

. In short, workplace health promotion programs can be transformational. Change agents can use these programs to cultivate the holistic thinking, longer time horizon, and wider employee involvement that characterize a healthy organization. Most workplace health promotion initiatives can provide the momentum for an organizational approach. So the comparison between the two perspectives in figure 2.2 is not as cut and dried as it first may appear. You may lean more to one side than the other on specific dimensions. Knowing where your workplace has moved to on the organization side of the continuum is an important piece of information for planning change.

Studies have tested the healthy organization framework, with encouraging results. For example, a study at a large manufacturing firm in the United States identified a cluster of management practices – a commitment to continual improvement, having a well developed HR strategy, and fair pay and rewards – that predicted both organizational effectiveness and employee stress outcomes.[18] In addition, organizations whose cultures are characterized by innovation, cooperation, and a sense of belonging are higher on both effectiveness and wellness measures. Indeed, many of the job and work environment factors directly related to health and well-being reflect an organization's entire approach to human resource management. These include physical working conditions, ergonomics, work schedules, work content, work group relations, supervision, training and development, economic rewards, and organizational culture.

Figure 2.2. Comparing key dimensions of workplace health promotion and healthy organization perspectives

Dimension	Workplace health promotion	Healthy organization
	⟶	
• Target	• Individual	• Organizational
• Change model	• Health promotion	• Organization development
• Scope and focus	• Program based	• Systemic and holistic
• Time frame	• Short and medium term	• Ongoing and long term
• Individual benefits	• Reduced health risks	Improved quality of work life and capabilities
• Organizational benefits	• Lower health benefit costs and absenteeism, improved morale	• Higher performance, effectiveness, and sustainability
• Community benefits	• Enhanced reputation and employer brand	• Tangible and sustainable benefits
• Links to strategy	• Part of people strategy or HR plan	• How the business operates
• Links to culture	• Reflects organizational values	• Embedded in corporate philosophy and values
• Responsibility	• Formal roles (e.g., Wellness Committee, Workplace Health Coordinator)	• Shared responsibility and accountability
• Leadership	• Usually top down	• Distributed throughout organization

Beyond this evidence, the idea of a healthy organization has strong intuitive appeal and this is sparking innovation in workplaces. The health care sector is adopting healthy organization thinking. In the United States, NIOSH's healthy organization model (introduced in chapter 1) has guided changes in health care work environments as a way to improve the quality of patient care.[19] This plan requires expanding continual quality improvement to include the quality of the work environment. In Canada, a coalition of professional and employer groups formed the Quality Worklife – Quality Healthcare Collaborative (QWQHC). It defines a healthy health care workplace as 'a work setting that takes a strategic and comprehensive approach to providing the physical, cultural, psychosocial and work/job design conditions that maximize health and well-being of health care providers, quality of patient outcomes and organizational performance.'[20] Making an explicit connection between working conditions and quality health care marks a significant shift in thinking, given that health care providers traditionally have put patients' needs ahead of their own health and wellness.

Leveraging Workplace Health Promotion

Husky Injection Molding Systems is a global leader in high-speed moulding injection systems that produce plastic bottles as well as products for the packaging, automotive, and telecommunications industries. Husky's comprehensive approach to wellness provides employees with incentives to participate in nutrition and fitness programs. Husky has documented cost savings such as reduced absenteeism, low injury rates, reduced drug costs, low turnover, and higher productivity.[21] Its corporate headquarters, located in Canada, has a Wellness Centre staffed by professionals, its manufacturing centres around the world have fitness facilities, and company cafeterias offer healthy foods.

Robert Schad, the company's founder, personally believes in a holistic approach to health. Employee wellness grew beyond a health focus, however, becoming a corporate goal associated with innovation, competitiveness, and profits. Husky belongs in that small but growing group of organizations that give new meaning to a 'comprehensive' approach to healthy workplaces. The company's guiding principles provide a road map for its employees around the world to innovate and act in customers' best interests. Specifically, employees strive for honesty and integrity, open communication, environmental responsibility, and improved quality of community life where the company operates. Not that every CEO needs to embrace personal wellness as the founder of Husky does. But a corporate commitment from the top goes a long way towards realizing this part of the strategy and culture.

One of the guiding principles is 'people are most productive in a safe, high-quality work environment.' This principle is put into practice not only via wellness, but also in open-concept environmentally friendly building designs and people development practices. Health and wellness are part of a culture that values and nurtures many connections between people, performance, and community. As a result, Husky has been on the *Globe and Mail Report on Business* and Hewitt Associates' 50 Best Employers in Canada lists and on other '50 best' lists in Canada for corporate citizenship and environmental responsibility.

Companies like Husky view health as a long-term business priority. Practically, this attitude makes sense, because improvements take time and persistence. Workplace health promotion evaluations that track the two big pay-offs – absenteeism and employee health care costs – will require several years to show any results from a new program or policy change. Tracking a wider range of results, as companies like Husky do, requires equal patience. For example, the University of Michigan's Health Management Research Center has worked with various companies to gain a broader understanding of workplace health promotion costs and benefits.[22] To do this, the Center calculates an 'overall wellness score' that includes measures of job satisfaction, life satisfaction, and stress.

These examples show the potential for leveraging strategic, company-wide, long-term benefits from workplace health promotion. There is a positive upward spiral created as soon as a company moves from an individual to an organizational approach. Health promotion initiatives can have collateral benefits, such as improving employee satisfaction and loyalty and reducing turnover. Workforce performance can only improve.

Organizational Solutions for Wellness

It is useful, therefore, to apply an organizational health perspective to several major workplace wellness concerns: absenteeism, presenteeism, stress, and work/life imbalance. What becomes clear is that these issues have as much to do with organizational performance – or the capacity to successfully implement strategy – as they do with wellness. Furthermore, solutions depend on placing the four healthy workplace building blocks firmly in position.

Rethinking Absenteeism

Lower absenteeism accounts for the largest component of the workplace health promotion program ROI. Not surprisingly, absenteeism has caught the attention of many employers. It is on the rise, costly, and a widely used indicator of employee health and productivity. But a closer look at absenteeism shows that to uncover its root causes, the ingredients of a vibrant workplace need to be addressed. This puts workplace relationships, organizational processes, job designs, and total work rewards squarely on the change agenda.

High absenteeism imposes huge costs on employers and the economy. According to the Health and Safety Executive, work absences cost U.K. private and public sector employers £12 billion annually.[23] Estimates for Australia suggest that 3 per cent of the workforce takes unscheduled leave each day, costing $800 (Australian) per worker annually.[24] U.S. employers face estimated absenteeism-related expenses of $74 billion (U.S.) annually, including overtime and overstaffing to cover these costs.[25] In Canada, the monthly Labour Force Survey shows that absenteeism has been rising since the 1990s. Actual work time lost for personal reasons increased from the equivalent of 7.4 days per worker in 1997 to 9.7 worker days in 2006 – an estimated 102 million work days for all full-time employees.[26] This trend contrasts with a steady decline in lost-time work injuries, which no doubt helps to explain why more employers are moving beyond workplace safety to address a wider range of health and wellness issues.

Ironically, health care workplaces are among the least healthy of any industry, so employers have increasingly sought healthy workplace solutions to bring down absenteeism costs. The U.S. Veterans' Health Administration calculated the costs of absenteeism and concluded that a modest reduction in nurse absenteeism would save $17.8 million annually across all of its facilities.[27] In the Canadian province of British Columbia, absenteeism rates in health care are 73 per cent higher than the provincial average. Reducing absenteeism in British Columbia's health care workforce to the provincial average would save enough to pay for the equivalent of more than 500 full-time positions – which would benefit the public.

However, solutions to high absenteeism require more than absenteeism management policies. Such tactics focus on symptoms and are often viewed by employees as rigid and punitive. Cost savings can be best realized by addressing the root causes within the work environment. In health care, absenteeism among nurses and physicians is related to high levels of job stress and burnout.[28] A cluster of organizational factors drives up absenteeism and erodes the quality of work life. These include workplace relationships (especially teamwork), organizational culture, the quality of supervision, workloads, scope for autonomy and decision making, and professional development opportunities. Essentially, when employees have positive experiences of these features they have a vibrant workplace – one of the cornerstones of a healthy organization.

A holistic, organizational perspective on absenteeism also is guided by corporate values. A CEO of a financial services company described how moving from a traditional sick-day model to 'care days' improved employee wellness. Time off work declined under the new approach and contributed to employee perceptions of what the CEO called a 'thriving workplace.' Through discussions with employees the company realized that the old policy forced them to call in sick for an entire day when all they needed was a few hours to attend their child's school play or take their elderly parent to a doctor's appointment. Under the care days policy, employees took only the hours they needed to care for themselves or their family members. For the company, the goal was less about reduced absenteeism costs than it was about living up to its values, which included employees' wellness and family needs.

A truly comprehensive workplace wellness strategy needs to be grounded in an understanding of the complexities of absenteeism, including its organizational causes and costs. This sets the stage for solutions based on the kind of organizational culture and support systems employees need to experience mental well-being. As such, addressing absenteeism provides an opportunity to build a healthier organization.

Present but Not Productive

Focusing on absenteeism gives an incomplete picture of employee health and productivity. Most discussions of absenteeism use binary thinking: employees are either present or absent. But this assumption is flawed. In studies at Steelcase and Xerox, University of Michigan researchers discovered that 'not all absent employees are automatically nonproductive and not all employees present are automatically 100 per cent productive.'[29] Let us explore this last point, a phenomenon known as 'presenteeism.' Professor Deb Lerner, a work disability expert at the Tufts Medical Center in Boston, describes presenteeism as 'when you appear not to be absent.' In the past few years, presenteeism has caught the attention of senior managers. Paul Hemp, writing in the *Harvard Business Review*, describes presenteeism as a $150 billion hidden cost in the United States that reflects the health problems people bring to work, such as migraines, arthritis, and back pain.[30] Hemp makes the case for employer action, arguing that presenteeism reduces corporate performance.

Presenteeism takes several forms. It can occur when a worker who has been injured or is recovering from a medical condition returns to work after disability leave. The return-to-work process monitors the individual's work limitations, supporting recovery as close to full functioning in the job as possible.[31] Presenteeism also occurs among individuals with prior health conditions, such as allergies and migraines. According to a U.S. study, presenteeism costs (based on the level of self-reported work productivity) account for 61 per cent of total costs associated with ten common health conditions: allergies, arthritis, asthma, cancer, depression, diabetes, heart disease, hypertension, migraines and headaches, and respiratory disorders.[32] This type of lost productivity exceeds absenteeism, reinforcing the need for comprehensive wellness programs that include a chronic disease management component.

Presenteeism also occurs when employees experience work/life conflicts and heavy workloads. The causes are organizational. For example, one major study found that going to work when unwell was a consequence of high work/life conflict. More than four out of five employees with high work/family conflicts reported this behaviour, significantly more than other employees in the study. This form of presenteeism also results from employees with heavy workloads feeling compelled to put in long hours. It also reflects a sense of commitment to clients and co-workers. This is why nurses and other health care professionals show up for work even when they are sick.

In short, there are basically two perspectives on presenteeism, one focusing on working while sick or injured and the other focusing on work pressures. Actually, these perspectives are connected. That is because constant workplace change, increasing workloads, and growing job pressures have become standard features of working life and therefore health risks in their own right. To illustrate these links between worker health, work pressures, and absenteeism and presenteeism behaviour, I turn to a study I conducted in a government social services department. A survey asked employees to report absenteeism during the prior twelve months. Then it asked about presenteeism: 'during the past 12 months, how many days did you work despite an illness or injury because you felt you had to?' Those reporting presenteeism were asked to describe their main reasons for doing so.

Absenteeism in the department was double the regional workforce average. Employees attributed 43 per cent of all absenteeism to job stress. However, the typical employee also went to work 6.7 days when ill or injured in the twelve months prior to the survey because they felt they had to. Underlying this behaviour were a feeling of not wanting to fall behind in their work, heavy workloads or caseloads, and a feeling of responsibility to their clients. This was a stressed-out, overworked group of employees who exhibited multiple signs of poor physical and mental health. Most of these problems could be attributed to the cumulative impact of their working conditions. So it is not surprising that presenteeism was high, with roughly one day of presenteeism for every two days of absenteeism. ·

There are steps you can take to address the sources of presenteeism. First, it is important to diagnose the problem in your organization by adding questions to your employee survey on self-reported absenteeism and presenteeism. Second, ask employees to give their reasons for presenteeism. Third, designing proactive return-to-work processes can deal with this type of presenteeism, helping employees, their supervisors, and health professionals track functional improvements. And fourth, health experts are advising larger employers to provide on-site medical support for individuals suffering from the most common chronic health problems.

These are good initiatives, but equally important in the repertoire of solutions for presenteeism is improving the psychosocial work environment. That is the only way to address job stress, work/life imbalance, and other psychological pressures that have become all too common in twenty-first-century workplaces. Doing so is a precondition for a vibrant workplace.

Healthy Psychosocial Work Environments

This discussion of absenteeism and presenteeism highlights another weakness of workplace health promotion. Most employers are doing an adequate job of complying with occupational health and safety regulations and legislation. In North America, Europe, Australia, and other advanced industrial countries, lost-time injury rates have slowly and steadily declined over the past several decades. Yet despite the spread of workplace health promotion programs, the problems of stress, burnout, and work/life imbalance persist. The main reason is that most comprehensive workplace health promotion initiatives are not comprehensive enough. They do not adequately address the psychological and social dimensions of jobs and workplaces – what experts call the psychosocial work environment.

A healthy psychosocial environment enables well-being and performance. It also reduces employer costs. Employer-sponsored health care plans face double-digit rate increases over the next five to ten years, with prescription drugs the largest cost component.[33] Mental health-related pharmaceuticals are the biggest of these and a growing category of drug prescriptions. Much of the illness being treated is stress related.

Several decades of research pinpoint the causes of stress or, on the flip side, what is needed for a vibrant workplace.[34] People feel under stress when their job demands exceed their resources to respond to these demands. High psychological job demands – urgent deadlines, too much work, competing or conflicting goals – and a low level of control over these demands increase a person's exposure to 'job strain.' For example, a factory worker whose workday is controlled every minute by the unrelenting pace of an assembly line has a high-tension job. Over time, this strain can increase the risk of serious health problems, ranging from depression to heart disease. Among knowledge workers, persistently heavy job demands can result in 'burnout,' a psychological state where people feel mentally exhausted, cynical about their work, and professionally ineffective.

However, someone facing high psychological demands but who has the autonomy, job resources, and team support to manage these demands will have more positive mental health outcomes. This person has a healthy job, which enhances their quality of work life and contributes to organizational performance through increased initiative, learning, and collaboration. For instance, medical researchers who are expected by their employers and their colleagues to produce breakthrough treatments manage this pressure with the help of a great team, ample funding, a well-equipped lab, and the autonomy to set priorities and schedules. In such active jobs, employees can keep stress at tolerable levels. At the same time, they learn ways to do their job better and how to be resilient in the face of change.

Also important is whether a worker's job rewards – pay, job security, career opportunities, and satisfaction – match their mental and physical effort in the job. A lack of reciprocity in this regard is associated with increased risks of cardiovascular disease, depression, alcohol dependence, and poor self-rated overall health. Finally, social scientists have known for years that the support we get from the people around us – family, friends, and neighbours – influences our quality of life. So, too, in the workplace: supportive co-workers and supervisors are an important resource a worker can draw on to cope with pressure.

Work/life imbalance and job stress are close cousins. Balancing work

Figure 2.3 Relationship between work/life balance and job stress

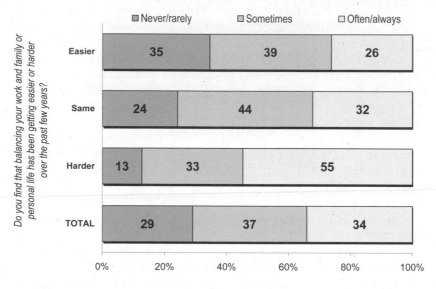

In the past 12 months, how often did you experience stress in your job?

Note: Differences between work/life balance groups are statistically significant. Chi-square test, $p < .001$
Source: *Rethinking Work*, EKOS Research Associates – Graham Lowe Group national worker survey, fall 2004

and non-work has become somewhat more difficult to achieve, according to Rethinking Work, a nationally representative study of Canadian workers.[35] The impact can be seen in an individual's health and well-being, job performance, and ability to be a good parent or spouse.[36] This is how work spills over into families and communities – either positively or negatively. For example, 55 per cent of Rethinking Work survey respondents who found it harder to achieve work/life balance reported often or always being under stress in their job. This compares with the 26 per cent who found work/life balance easier to achieve (see figure 2.3).

Solutions to stress and imbalance require a positive perspective, emphasizing the benefits of active jobs and work/life balance for achieving employee and organizational health. For the organization, these benefits are indeed significant. Employees who experience low job stress or who have work/life balance will contribute more and cost

Figure 2.4 Organizational impacts of job stress

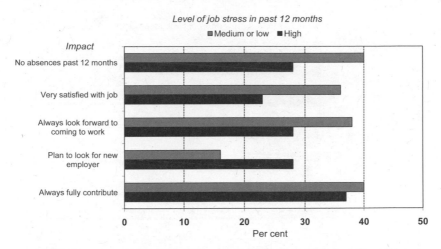

Level of job stress in past 12 months
■ Medium or low ■ High

Impact

No absences past 12 months

Very satisfied with job

Always look forward to coming to work

Plan to look for new employer

Always fully contribute

Per cent

Note: All differences between the hgih and the medium-low stress groups are statistically significant. Chi-square test, *p* < .05

Source: *Rethinking Work*, EKOS Research Associates – Graham Lowe Group national worker survey, fall 2004

employers less than workers who lack these positive psychosocial job conditions. Key indicators of these benefits are lower absenteeism; higher job satisfaction; stronger commitment; lower turnover; and fully contributing skills, knowledge, and abilities. Many studies confirm this finding; figures 2.4 and 2.5 offer supporting evidence from the Rethinking Work study.

Stress and work/life imbalance are organizational problems that require organizational – not individual – solutions. When the Rethinking Work survey asked employees who experienced stress to suggest solutions, a reduced workload and better people management practices were at the top of the list. Additional suggestions covered economic rewards, hours, and schedules; relationships with co-workers; and more input and job resources. Furthermore, among those employees whose work interfered with their personal life, reduced workload also was a sought-after change, followed closely by more flexible work arrangements.

Employees know what makes a workplace vibrant. Their suggestions for improvement push beyond health promotion programs into this broader terrain – which I explore in chapter 3. A vibrant workplace

Figure 2.5 Organizational impacts of work/life balance

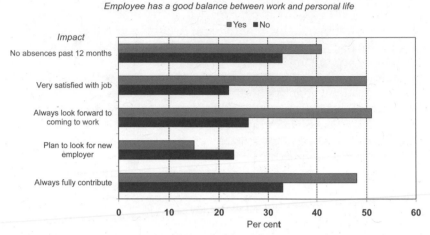

Note: All differences between the yes and no groups are statistically significant. Chi-square test, $p < .05$
Source: *Rethinking Work*, EKOS Research Associates – Graham Lowe Group national worker survey, fall 2004

does not dwell on the negatives of stress, burnout, or work/life conflict. Rather, it sets positive goals. Work design, workplace relationships, and management practices are aligned around the twin goals of wellness and performance.

Talking about Health and Performance

To summarize, I've argued that when it comes to employee health and well-being, there is much more to productivity than reduced employee costs. Managers who understand this are more likely to introduce organizational systems, policies, and practices that support employees to flourish in their jobs and lives outside work. For these people innovations to take root in an organization, you will need to find a common language for talking about health and performance. This language must resonate internally. Eventually, it will be reflected in your operating philosophy about what contributes to responsible, long-term business success.

Actually, you may not use words such as *health* or *wellness*. Change agents must therefore take every opportunity to link employee health and safety to the organization's performance and its business goals.

When discussing employee health and wellness, try to expand the conversation beyond employees' health-related attitudes and behaviours to include their capacity to contribute to team and organizational success. And encourage others to think of healthy work environments as the enabling contexts for developing employees' capabilities. This can be achieved by talking about learning, collaboration, and innovation as by-products of a healthy workplace.

Conversations about performance often raise awareness of the importance of having vibrant workplaces. Describing the health/performance connection in terms that make sense to senior managers and business owners will, I believe, reposition employee health and wellness as effective and responsible business practice. Here are three brief examples:

- A senior manager in Xerox Global Services used the image of 'islands of floating knowledge' to describe the knowledge management challenges large organizations face. In a climate of mistrust and disrespect, nobody will want to share their good ideas. From an organizational health perspective, we are talking about basic requirements for a vibrant workplace.
- A growing number of industrial employers are now championing a safety culture as a way to reduce lost time injuries to zero. A safety culture focuses on the workplace fundamentals of a healthy organization, such as open communication, trust, collaboration, and shared responsibility for workplace improvements.
- An insurance company executive told a conference that long-term disability often is caused by stress resulting from interpersonal conflict with a boss or an overwhelming dissatisfaction with the job. In other words, what looks like a personal health issue is symptomatic of how the organization is managed and the quality of relationships between individual employees and their supervisors.

I'm encouraging you to view all parts of your organization through the wide lens of health. By doing so, you will be able to see the multiple advantages that flow from work environments that nurture employee well-being. You also will be better able to use what your organization has been doing to promote employee health to launch deeper improvements in the work environment. As a senior manager put it during a conference discussion about how to achieve healthy outcomes, 'we need to build great workplaces, not talk about health.' Subtle shifts in thinking and language can move you forward. That is why I have chosen to discuss vibrant workplaces that inspire employees. You need to find your own way to describe what lies beyond health and engagement in tomorrow's workplace. The next chapter challenges you to do just that.

3 How Vibrant Workplaces Inspire Employees

What does a healthy organization look and feel like? The most accurate way to answer this question is to ask your co-workers or employees. Most employees and managers I have posed this question to have their own shortlist of what defines a healthy workplace and why achieving this vision is important for them, their employer, customers – and society as a whole. Usually, the discussion also revolves around what makes people look forward to coming to work each day. What I have learned from these conversations about work experiences is that there is no difference between what really inspires them about their jobs and what makes the office, hospital, factory, store, or other setting in which they spend their day a fulfilling work environment.

This chapter looks at a healthy organization through the eyes of employees. I focus on individuals' personal work experiences, needs, and values to describe what makes a workplace more than just healthy and how these factors do more than just engage employees. I believe that the aspirations people carry into workplaces provide a larger common vision of a vibrant workplace. The big difference between a vibrant and a healthy workplace is that the former seamlessly connects well-being and performance, with the potential for greater benefits than are possible using stand-alone health promotion or HR programs.

While meeting the aspirations that workers carry into a workplace may be a desirable end in itself, it falls short of a business case for investing in an organization's human resources. So we also need a longer answer to the question about what a healthy organization looks and feels like. By taking action to address employees' aspirations for vibrant work environments, managers and other change agents are putting in place the cornerstones of a healthy organization. A vibrant workplace energizes the entire organization by inspiring employees to continually find better ways to meet customers' or clients' needs. The result is a talented, motivated, and healthy workforce able to sustain higher levels of performance. The healthy organization idea, used in this way, is an integrating framework that helps to 'connect the dots' of health, workforce capabilities, and performance.

My main objective in this chapter is to encourage readers to think about using employees' experiences in their workplace as a basis for change and improvement. Here, then, is a summary of the main action insights the chapter offers:

1. Just as companies focus on enhancing the 'customer experience,' they also must find ways to improve the employee experience, because these goals are connected.
2. By understanding what truly inspires employees, you can identify how a vibrant workplace develops employees' capabilities and promotes well-being.
3. Involving employees in crafting a vision of the kind of workplace they want provides a blueprint for improving the drivers of well-being and performance.
4. A vibrant workplace vision also can help you find solutions to human resource challenges, particularly retention, recruitment, engagement, and development.
5. Employees' assessment of whether they have a healthy workplace also gauges how well an organization is developing capabilities for future success.

I invite you to use the ideas in this chapter to stimulate discussions in your team, unit, department, or organization about a shared vision of a vibrant workplace. Once this conversation begins, you soon will be talking about what really inspires people to do their best work. That is how you can forge strong links in the healthy organization value chain.

How Employees Experience Healthy Organizations

At the Gaylord Palms Hotel and Convention Center in Orlando, Florida, the senior manager who opened the facility in 2002 implemented a culture-based strategy to achieve service excellence.[1] The manager expected that a customer-driven culture would have a competitive advantage over other hotels in attracting customers and employees. What is more, the culture would be a substitute for traditional management controls such as rules, procedures, and direct supervision. The first step was to define the hotel's mission, goals, and seven corporate values (service, citizenship, integrity, respect, excellence, creativity, and passion). The acronym STARS (smiles, teamwork, attitude, reliability, and service with a passion) defined how employees would perform their jobs. Then the mission, goals, and values were used to hire, train, and motivate employees who would be 'the STARS.' This sounds corny, but by common hospitality industry performance measures, it succeeded. The cultural dynamic operates at the emotional level of how employees experience and live the culture: 'positive emotional content is infused and mirrored in the behaviours of employees to themselves, to each other and to guests, customers and owners.'[2] Among all employee groups, even those who did not have direct customer contact, positive work experiences contributed to high job satisfaction and high customer satisfaction.

Like Gaylord Palms, many companies are striving to create the ultimate customer experience. They want every detail of how the customer receives services or buys products to be as genuinely positive as possible, providing what customers value most. Designing the right experience for the customer has become the ultimate goal in managing customer relationships. Outstanding experiences breed customer loyalty – and higher future revenues and profits.[3]

The public sector has picked up these ideas, developing client-first strategies of their own. In 2009 the state of Queensland, Australia, launched the Queensland Health Awards for Excellence to showcase high performance in the state's health system and recognize staff contributions to patient-centred care.[4] Among the award winners were projects to improve indigenous people's access to health care, a mobile women's health service, and initiatives to break down language barriers – all of which improved the overall health care experience of clients. Queensland Health also awards excellence in supporting and developing staff. The state includes workplace culture measures in its annual quality report on health care organizations, using measures obtained from its state-wide Better Workplaces Staff Opinion Survey. The survey measures the climate of the workplace – including what I have called vibrant workplace ingredients.

In examples as diverse as a Florida luxury resort and an Australian public health system, we see current efforts to link employee and customer or client experiences. I further explore this theme below, showing how employees' experiences of their job and work environment have an enormous impact on performance-related work attitudes and behaviours, as well as on their overall sense of well-being. That is why it is so important that these experiences are as positive as possible as often as possible.

Employers ignore at their peril employees' perceptions, just as it is a mistake for businesses to ignore their customers' opinions about their products or services. Hence the need for an employee-centred view of a healthy organization. Indeed, an accurate way to gauge what makes employees feel satisfied and committed – or, even better, to be inspired – is to ask them to describe the ideal workplace. Taking this positive approach, rather than starting with workplace problem-solving, mobilizes employees and managers around a shared vision of a vibrant workplace. The result is a collective aspiration that can be a powerful energizer for change and improvement.

My emphasis on employees' experiences may sound too subjective, particularly for managers who like numbers and measureable outcomes. These sceptics need to be reminded, however, that decades of employee research by academics and consultants – and some large employers – have been able to accurately quantify the impact of attitudes and values on well-being. It is well established that at the top of the hierarchy of human needs are two that can be met in large part through people's work. One is self-esteem, which flows from a combination of respectful relationships, recognition and feedback for contributions, and the sense of accomplishment from a job well done. Another basic need is to develop potential by having opportunities to learn, grow, and apply innate abilities. Both needs are essential for personal well-being and job performance, and both needs depend in large part on the work environment.

Research on psychological needs now focuses on the sources and benefits of happiness. Happiness is a positive state of psychological and emotional well-being. Martin Seligman, a University of Pennsylvania psychologist who launched the positive psychology movement, believes that finding authentic happiness instils meaning and purpose in life. He has developed an Authentic Happiness website with tools and resources to help people to make themselves and the world happier.[5] Work is central to happiness. Two University of British Columbia researchers discovered that 'happiness' (overall satisfaction with life) is strongly influenced by non-financial aspects of a job. Especially important is the level of trust in workplace relations, which depends on the quality of workplace communication.[6]

Employees' experiences are based on their assessments of many aspects of their work situation, including choices, trade-offs, and preferences. Such personal calculations are not like a mathematical formula. Rather, they are filtered through what each individual, or group, considers most important. In this way, values and perceptions shape our individual and collective definitions of a healthy organization.

Envisioning Vibrant Workplaces

I like to begin a workshop on creating healthy workplaces by inviting participants to think about what the 'ideal' healthy workplace looks and feels like for them. I ask participants to spend a few minutes writing down their personal vision of a healthy workplace, one in which they can imagine experiencing an excellent quality of work life. Sitting in small groups at round tables, they are then asked to share their personal visions with others at the table. It takes about fifteen or twenty minutes for people at each table to agree on the ingredients of a healthy workplace. And when the table visions are presented to others, it is remarkable how much convergence there is around what people consider most important in the ideal workplace – and how far beyond 'healthy' these visions move the discussion.

Indeed, absent from how employees and managers envision the ideal healthy workplace is an emphasis on individual health promotion or wellness programs. That is because in the minds of employees the fundamentals of a healthy workplace transcend personal health and wellness activities. This insight is important for managers and workplace health and wellness professionals, many of whom still operate within the health promotion mindset described in chapter 2.

This is a recurring theme in the examples I provide below of how front-line employees, professionals, and managers from a variety of organizations envision a vibrant workplace. A group of employees in an industrial facility stated that a healthy workplace means much more than 'management giving us gym passes or fitness programs.' It wasn't that they opposed what they called 'lifestyle programs.' They wanted more fundamental changes in the workplace. These workers went on to talk about the things that needed fixing, such as cleaning up dirty and cluttered workspaces, supervisors using respectful language when talking to their employees, and a variety of small changes that would give production workers a greater sense of dignity in their jobs. Later discussions with managers and workplace health and wellness staff in the same company acknowledged that launching a wellness program that did not address working conditions considered to be unhealthy would be a waste of time and money.

The examples below show how employees' visions of healthy workplaces go directly to the levers that managers are trying to pull to improve retention, engagement, and performance. These actions build an organization's reputation as an exemplary employer, fostering employee loyalty and sought out by talented job seekers. The following visions are about achieving these goals.

The five examples below of healthy workplace visions, like those from numerous other workshops, form a composite picture of the essential ingredients of a healthy organization that supports overall employee well-being. As noted in chapter 2, good mental health contributes to positive physical health, as well as to job performance and a sense of belonging to the organization. People's perceptions of the quality of their job and workplace put a premium on basics, such as self-worth, positive relationships with others, making a contribution, and developing personal potential. In a healthy organization, these conditions are continually encouraged and reinforced.

- *Municipal managers and professionals.* At a workshop for about 200 managers and professionals in a large municipality, the participants liked to imagine a 'healthy, high-quality' workplace. For them, this vision was broader than a healthy workplace. The use of 'quality' raised all sorts of issues about people being able to do their jobs well and make the city a better place to live in. It did not take long for this large group to zero in on the top two ingredients of a healthy, high-quality workplace: excellent working relationships within and between departments and excellent two-way communication. Discussion of these features identified a close connection: people cannot have good working relationships without honest and constructive communication.
- *Industrial managers.* Senior managers at an industrial processing facility reflected on what they had learned through consultations with managers and employees about a healthy and safe work environment. These leaders decided to state in their own words a more encompassing 'people vision.' This vision described a workplace resting on four pillars: clean, safe, and healthy; enables employee involvement and input; supports skill development and career growth; and values trust, cooperation, and open communication. The managers went on to say that achieving this vision has to be a shared responsibility requiring constant effort.

- *Health care managers and professionals.* At another workshop a large group of middle managers and front-line supervisors at a health care organization created a shared vision based on three primary goals. The first goal was teamwork. These health care managers and professionals imagined teamwork that cut across the existing silos created by departments and disciplines. Positive and respectful working relationships were seen as the basis for cooperation. The second goal concerned employees' connection with the organization. Making this stronger depended on recognizing everyone's contributions to patient care and cultivating staff involvement in and ownership of this mission. The third goal was the pay-off: staff would be healthier physically, mentally, and emotionally; they would be happy, satisfied, and excited about their work; and over time the organization would gain a reputation as an excellent place to work.

- *Laboratory scientists.* A group of forensic scientists working in several lab facilities configured their vision of a healthy workplace, beginning with how they wanted to feel each day at work. Above all was a sense of excitement and enthusiasm, so that they could not wait to go to work and would arrive with positive attitudes. They would be able to contribute to the goals of organization. Everyone could be a leader, having a balance of autonomy and responsibility in their job and being able to seek out opportunities to deal with change and to be innovative. Perhaps as a comment on perceived current gaps in the organization, the scientists viewed key enablers as 'managers who lead by example' and who would trust them to be innovative in their jobs. Labs as healthy workplaces also would have friendly co-workers and respectful working relationships. Excellence would be promoted through continual learning and time for reflection. Finally, there would be support for healthy lifestyles.

- *Community social service workers.* The following vision was created by several not-for-profit agencies providing similar services to persons with disabilities in dozens of communities. The group described healthy workplaces in two ways: 'Heard, happy, healthy, and here (i.e., present and eager to work)'; 'Appreciated, connected, dedicated, and satisfied.' Respectful relationships were considered foundational, as were trusting and caring relationships – which also extended to clients and their families. Other healthy workplace elements included valuing, recognizing, and celebrating people's contributions. One important way that healthy workplaces would value employees would be through fairness, especially in pay and benefits, which were below average in the sector, owing to funding not keeping up with rising service needs in communities. In addition, a healthy workplace also meant open communication, a strong collective voice for staff in planning change, and flexibility in work arrangements.

Envisioning an Inspired Workforce

At this point, managers with a bottom-line focus may be asking, 'so what?' Scepticism about how employees (including managers, unless they also are business owners) envision a healthy workplace should evaporate once the connection with improving employee engagement is clear. In my experience, employees and managers see an engaging work environment and a healthy one as part of the same organizational fabric. Indeed, when asked to envision the ideal future workplace, what most often comes up sets the bar for employee well-being, performance, and passion about work much higher than it is today. All the more reason to think in terms of vibrant workplaces that inspire employees.

Let us consider what workshop participants in two different organizations had to say when asked for their vision of engaged employees or an engaging workplace. As above, I am providing the actual words used by these groups to express what this abstract concept of 'engagement' means to them. I encourage you to compare these descriptions with the words used in visions of a healthy workplace. You will see the similarities with engaging workplaces; in fact, they are the same thing.

- *Natural resources professionals.* A natural resources organization I worked with wanted to create a culture of engagement. To senior management, this meant a workplace that personally involved each and every employee in providing excellent service. A team of professional employees was brought together from across the organization and asked by senior management to create a vision and an action plan for increasing engagement. At a workshop, the team came up with an 'engagement vision.' By creating its own vision of engagement, the team realized where shifts in the corporate culture were required. Higher levels of engagement depended on a work environment with the following eight attributes:
  - Everyone feels as if they belong to one big team with common objectives and understands how their job contributes to these objectives.

o All interactions are meaningful and positive.
o Communication is open and based on trust.
o Knowledge is gained and shared effectively.
o Employees feel empowered to be innovative and take risks.
o Managers support employees, bring out the best in them, and recognize their contributions.
o Employees are motivated to do better and to embrace change.
o Employees achieve a sense of accomplishment, work/life balance,
   and well-being.

• *Health care senior managers*: A world-class, research-intensive health
  care organization also developed a vision of engagement. At a
  workshop I conducted with its senior management team, discussions explored what an engaged employee actually looks like. The
  hospital had set as a goal increased employee engagement and now
  had to define what that meant in operational terms. The result was
  an 'engaged employee vision,' which the executive team used to
  guide its decisions and actions on a wide range of human resource
  issues. Ideally, the qualities of an engaged employee are as follows:
  o Collaborative.
  o Respectful.
  o Communicates openly and listens well.
  o Knowledgeable and open minded.
  o Sees the 'big picture.'
  o Solution-focused and problem-solving.
  o Caring and compassionate.
  o Dedicated, reliable, and accountable.
  o Flexible and adaptable.
  o Excited by results.

Notice how this vision describes personal attributes. The other visions
I use as examples focus on workplaces, presenting the same factors in
terms of what workplaces should support and encourage. In the end,
they amount to the attitudes and behaviours of individual employees
and teams.

These visions provide important practical lessons. First, the visions
underscore the need for change agents in any position to focus on fundamentals, such as workplace relationships and supporting employees
to grow and to do a good job. Second, the visions reinforce the need
for individual managers to practise the most frequently mentioned features of healthy and engaging workplaces: open communication with

employees and showing respect for them as individuals. Third, one of
the most effective ways for senior managers to fine-tune the organization's strategies for engagement, wellness, and talent development is to
take seriously employees' experiences.

One sign that some companies are moving in this direction is that
exit interviews with employees who quit have given way to 'stay' interviews. Stay interviews are proactive consultations with existing employees, asking about the most positive feature of their experiences as
an employee that keeps them with the company and feeling engaged.
Yes, this is ground-up people strategy development. But it is no different from asking customers what they want and improving products or
services to meet these evolving needs.

How Vibrant Workplaces Inspire Employees

The visions above describe the main ingredients of a vibrant workplace
and how employees are expected to experience this sort of work environment. Now we can pull them together into composite visions that
offer a ground-up perspective on the workplace conditions and employee experiences that describe the healthy organization of the future.

The vision summarized in figure 3.1 captures what many people want
in their work environment. These factors combine personal and group
visions of a healthy workplace. Similarly, figure 3.2 describes what
people working in this kind of environment will experience – which is
nothing short of inspired. The inspired employee vision describes work
experiences that generate well-being and performance. Terms such as
'excited,' 'passionate,' 'happy,' 'enthusiastic,' and 'dedicated' describe
the possible goals for a healthy organization.

Interestingly, 'promotes a healthy lifestyle' is the only specific reference to employee health promotion in figure 3.1. All the other ingredients describe characteristics of people's jobs, relationships, and
organizational processes and systems. While not mentioning health,
these ingredients have everything to do with it, providing the conditions for people to thrive at work. That is clear from figure 3.2. Again,
mental and physical well-being, or health, is but one of many outcomes.
Yet all the other results contribute to high levels of physical, social, psychological, and emotional well-being.

You can use these summary visions as checklists of potential improvements needed in your work environment and the expected benefits to co-workers or your employees of making these improvements.

Figure 3.1 Vibrant workplace vision

Relationships	• Respectful relationships • Friendly co-workers • Caring and compassionate • Open, honest two-way communication based on trust
Job	• Understand how your job fits into strategy • Employees are empowered to be innovative and take risks • Involvement and ownership
Team	• Cooperation and collaboration • Feel part of a team with common objectives • Gain and share knowledge effectively, learn from each other
Supports	• Supportive managers who bring out the best in staff • Value, recognize, and celebrate people's contributions • Fairness, including in pay and benefits • Promotes a healthy lifestyle

Figure 3.2 Inspired employee vision

- Experience mental and physical well-being
- Experience a sense of accomplishment
- Passionate, involved, enthusiastic and happy
- Positive attitude about work, co-workers and management
- Can't wait to go to work
- Flexible and adaptable in dealing with change
- Innovative, inquisitive, proactive and creative
- Self-driven and directed – a leader
- Excited by results
- Solution-focused and problem-solving
- Dedicated, reliable and accountable

In practical terms, addressing the workplace vision elements requires an assessment of your organization's component parts. That is where healthy workplace advocates must focus their energies if they want to move beyond the limits of individual health promotion.

Focusing on Work Experiences

What I am proposing is an employee-centred perspective on organizational success. The best route to excellent customer or client experiences is through excellent employee experiences. Or, according to the healthy organization value chain: vibrant workplaces = inspired employees = sustainable success.

Improving organizational performance by putting employee well-being first may sound counter-intuitive. But it works. This point is emphasized by Isadore Sharp, the founder and CEO of the Four Seasons luxury hotel chain.[7] Sharp describes how every employee focuses on one priority – pleasing customers – because every manager focuses on pleasing employees. Four Seasons' management trusts and empowers staff to do what is best for customers. As a result, employees are passionate about providing a quality of guest experience far superior to what is available in other hotels. Four Seasons' success comes down to a strong but simple corporate philosophy based on the Golden Rule – treat others as you want to be treated yourself.

Other companies express the same idea in their own terms. For example, FedEx's Purple Promise – people, service, profits – is grounded in the same thinking found at Four Seasons. Vancity, Canada's largest credit union, located on the west coast, makes a corporate commitment to creating a great workplace, which reflects the corporate philosophy that excellent customer experiences begin with excellent employee experiences. Clive Beddoe, former CEO of Canada-based WestJet Airlines states the people-performance connection in another way: 'Many years ago, I heard a story that said the people who suffer the most stress in life are front-line personnel who are charged with responsibilities but not given any authority. That, to me, is almost like an abuse of people. How can you ask someone to be responsible for something and yet not give them the authority to make decisions when confronted with an issue? Recognizing that, we empower our people and trust them to make decisions on the front line. And for them, a job that would otherwise not be particularly satisfying becomes very satisfying. When you empower people and trust them, you'll be amazed what they can do.'[8]

Good examples also can be found in the public sector. Britain's National Health Service (NHS) looked at its performance through the eyes of employees. Despite much effort, building quality into health care organizations has been an elusive goal, especially high-quality work experiences. Yet the NHS took an innovative approach to measuring and improving health care work environments.

In 2008 the Department of Health dug deeper into the drivers of NHS performance in a research project called *What Matters to Staff*.[9] This study took a ground-up approach to identifying the determinants of satisfaction and performance. Employee interviews and focus groups identified what makes NHS staff feel motivated and fulfilled at work. The language used by staff became the descriptors for the qualities and the management actions that staff considered most important for delivering each of the factors. A subsequent survey validated the factors identified in the staff consultations. Staff experiences of ten factors contributed the most to four key outcomes: staff motivation to provide high-quality patient care; staff advocacy of the NHS; patient satisfaction; and public satisfaction. Here are the ten factors that matter most to staff, grouped into four themes:

- Theme 1: The resources to deliver quality care for patients:
    - I've got the knowledge, skills and equipment to do a good job.
    - I feel fairly treated with pay, benefits and staff facilities.
- Theme 2: The support I need to do a good job:
    - I feel trusted, listened to and valued at work.
    - My manager (or supervisor) supports me when I need it.
    - Senior managers are involved with our work.
- Theme 3: A worthwhile job with the chance to develop:
    - I've got a worthwhile job that makes a difference to patients.
    - I help provide high-quality patient care.
    - I have the opportunity to develop my potential.
    - I understand my role and where it fits in.
- Theme 4: The opportunity to improve the way we work:
    - I am able to improve the way we work in my team.

The NHS staff survey was revised to reflect the factors identified in the *What Matters to Staff* research. These are now part of annual performance reporting and management accountability for improvements. The parallels with the vibrant workplace vision, above, is indeed striking. It is fair to say that in the highest-performing NHS organizations, staff are more than motivated and satisfied – they are inspired.

Defining Good Jobs

While these examples are useful, I also want to put the vibrant workplace-inspired employee link into an even broader context, so we are able to widely apply the visions outlined earlier. Based on input from hundreds of participants in my workshops, we now have a fine-grained picture of what a healthy and engaging workplace looks and feels like. I now will use survey data representative of a national workforce (Canada) to explore more precisely how peoples' experiences of high-quality jobs and healthy work environments are shaped by the vision elements in figure 3.1.

Some years ago, I conducted a study with Canadian Policy Research Networks (CPRN), a social and economic policy think tank, designed to answer a basic question: 'What's a good job?' The answer to that question is relevant today for the building blocks of healthy organizations. The study's goal was to provide decision-makers in government, business, unions and professional associations, and non-government organizations dealing with workplace and labour market issues with new insights about how the workforce downsizing and restructuring of the 1990s had transformed employment relationships. Several national roundtables convened by CPRN sparked heated debate about the end of loyalty – and job security – as employee-employer relationships weakened. Employers were worried that it would become more difficult to find and keep talent as the wave of baby boomer retirements gathered momentum.

This focus on employment relationships displays a panorama of positive workplace features, confirming the relevance of the factors listed in figure 3.1. Researchers had shown that workers' perceptions of the quality of their work environment are critical for outcomes such as job satisfaction, organizational commitment, absenteeism, and job performance. A growing number of human resource practitioners wanted to act on this evidence. But it was difficult for HR managers to convince their executive team that performance pay-offs logically flowed from higher-quality work environments. The study's report, *What's a Good Job? The Importance of Employment Relationships*, addressed this gap. It provided solid evidence that the strength of employee-employer relationships mattered for employees' quality of work life and for their employers' human resource goals and organizational performance.[10]

We knew more could be done to make an evidence-based case for workplace improvements. Also important, therefore, was clearly showing the connection between the defining features of 'good jobs' and the growing field of workplace health promotion. In short, the work-health connection provided a new avenue for convincing decision makers that investing in people and their work environments was the best recipe for organizational success.

During the 1990s occupational health researchers made progress unravelling the connections between work and health. The storyline they developed went as follows: workers who have autonomy, adequate job resources, appropriate levels of economic and psychological rewards, supportive managers with good people skills, are consulted on organizational changes, and have a sense of economic security will be healthier than workers who lack these conditions. And the same conditions benefit employers, because healthy workers are ready, willing, and able to do a good job.

The new information-based, global economy of the late twentieth century was not particularly healthy, even though fewer people did strenuous manual labour in factories, mines, forests, and other industries historically associated with occupational risks and hazards. New-economy jobs had their own musculoskeletal risks, such as repetitive strain of retail cashiers, back and shoulder pain caused by poorly designed desk chairs, and overuse problems from keyboarding. But the emerging health risks seemed mostly to be in the psychosocial domain – which, as we saw in chapter 2, lies beyond most workplace health promotion programs.

Healthy Workplaces through Employees' Eyes

Against this backdrop, two colleagues and I used the CPRN survey on changing employment relationships to answer a question that was foremost in minds of workplace health practitioners and researchers: 'What do employees perceive to be the ingredients of a healthy workplace?'[11] The answer, we hoped, would guide the design of healthier and more productive workplaces, as well as provide a bigger window for viewing healthy workplaces.

The *Harvard Business Review*, the leading publication for managers, has published dozens of articles on strategy, leadership, and innovation. In contrast, there are only a handful of articles on health and wellness topics, such as emotional intelligence, presenteeism, and 'extreme' work hours. Health remains at the margins of business strategy. Yet most executives consider employee capabilities a key business success factor. Capabilities are best developed and applied in the context of optimal quality of work life. So clearly there is an opportunity here to address what matters for managers through an exchange of ideas that bridges well-being, human resources, and performance.

Everyone stands to gain from eliminating silos of organizational practice and knowledge. Researchers and practitioners still live in separate worlds. And there is a lack of interchange between practitioners in occupational health, human resources, organizational development, training, and learning – not to mention line managers. Workplace health promotion practitioners could benefit from a broader understanding of work contexts and organizational systems. Human resource professionals could benefit from a broader understanding of how HR goals intersect with health and wellness. Managers could benefit from a 'health' lens that would help them to see the impact of decision options on individual and organizational health.

Social scientists have confirmed that ultimately it is the worker who judges job quality. Using this approach, we set out to understand a critical dimension of job quality: experiencing the work environment as healthy. We explored the links between workers' perceptions of a healthy work environment and outcomes that matter for employees and employers alike. In this regard, job satisfaction is the most widely used indicator by organizational researchers of a person's quality of work life. Moreover, HR professionals use job satisfaction measures in employee surveys to gauge employees' work experiences. From an employer's perspective, we also considered outcomes related to employee performance and costs: organizational commitment, morale, absenteeism, and intent to quit.

Why Some Workplaces Are Healthier Than Others

To summarize why some work environments are considered healthier than others, I draw on the Changing Employment Relationships Survey, described earlier. Perceptions of a healthy workplace were documented by asking: *To what extent do you agree or disagree that this describes your job*: 'The work environment is healthy.' In addition, respondents were asked how strongly they agreed or disagreed with a similar statement: 'The work environment is safe.'

Both measures are consistent with epidemiological research on health status among adults. Population health surveys in many countries use global self-reports of overall health as accurate indicators of health status. For example, Statistics Canada's Canadian Community Health Survey uses this type of measure, which correlates consistently with other, more specific, self-reported and clinical measures of health status. It does not mean we can do away with detail, but rather that such single self-reports are efficient and accurate key indicators of work experiences.

We first looked at the relationship between employees' perceptions of their work environment as being healthy and safe. Workplace health promotion practitioners do not focus on safety, assuming that the organization has safety systems and practices in place. However, we discovered that in employees' experience of their workplace, healthy does not necessarily mean safe, and vice versa. Just over two-thirds of employees surveyed reported that their workplace is both healthy and safe, based on the proportions of respondents who agreed or strongly agreed with each statement. Another 17 per cent reported that their workplace is safe but not healthy, and 4 per cent reported it to be healthy but unsafe. This means that only 15 per cent did not perceive their workplace to be safe, while 28 per cent did not perceive it to be healthy.

These findings resonate with the high priority many employers now place on removing safety hazards and preventing injury. This safety emphasis has grown over the decades, as employers responded to occupational health and safety regulations, financial incentives created by workers' compensation rates, and the professionalization of safety. Clearly, safety belongs within a broader set of health and well-being goals. Safety goals are best achieved within the context of a healthy work environment. Managers and professionals in health and safety, HR, and workplace wellness need to join forces for an integrated approach to supporting overall employee well-being.

Viewed even more broadly, the survey results corroborate the vibrant workplace vision outlined above. After considering many possible factors that could shape perceptions of a healthy workplace, including employees' demographic characteristics and their industry and occupation, we discovered that five distinct clusters of working conditions were most influential in this regard. Figure 3.3 summarizes this analysis (which isolated the 'net' effects of each factor, after taking into account the influence of all the other factors). I have provided the wording of the survey questions, so anyone designing or updating an employee survey can see if their measurement tool includes these indicators of healthy work experiences.

Communication and social support are central to one's work experiences. In practical terms, this tells us that good horizontal and vertical communication in a workplace, friendly and helpful co-workers, a positive relationship with one's supervisor, and receiving recognition are key enablers of a healthy work environment. Thus, perceptions of healthy workplaces reflect the relationships in which workers participate daily and that facilitate their job effectiveness. This certainly is one of the key messages coming out of the workplace visions presented ear-

Figure 3.3 The most positive and negative influences on employees' perceptions of a healthy work environment

---

Most positive influences

Communication and support
- Communication is good among the people you work with.
- The people you work with are helpful and friendly.
- You have a good relationship with your supervisor.
- You receive recognition for work well done.

Job resources
- How frequently have you lacked the necessary tools needed to do your job?
- You get the training needed to do your job effectively.
- You have access to the information you need to do your job well.

Job rewards
- The benefits are good
- The pay is good.
- Your job security is good.
- Your chances for career advancement are good.

Job autonomy
- You can choose your own schedule within established limits.
- Your job allows you freedom to decide how to do your work.
- You can influence decisions that affect your job or work life.

Most negative influences

Job demands
- Your job is very stressful.
- Your job is hectic.
- How often have you had difficulty keeping up with the workload?
- Are you free from conflicting demands that other people make?

Notes: This table summarizes the results of statistical analysis. Actual wording of survey
questions are provided.
Source: Lowe, G.S., Schellenberg, G., and Shannon, H.S. (2003). Correlates of employees' perceptions of a healthy work environment. *American Journal of Health Promotion*,
17, 390–9.

lier. And it provides convincing evidence of the importance of a high-quality psychosocial work environment for employees' well-being.

This emphasis on communication and social relationships was echoed in a series of employee focus groups we conducted in four cities across Canada. Focus group participants described the quality of workplace relations and communications as indispensable for a 'good job.' Furthermore, the importance of communication also stood out in responses to an open-ended survey question, which asked people to state in their own words the single most important change they would like to see in their relationship with their employer. Of those seeking improvements in their employment relationship, the single most important change they wanted was improved communication, broadly defined. Typical suggestions included the following:

- Better communication; there's a lack of communication between the senior people and their employees.
- Better communication in the organization as a whole with everyone involved.
- I would like to see more clarity in the direction the company is headed.
- More personal evaluation.

The factors defining a healthy workplace transcend demographics. Characteristics such as age, gender, ethnicity, and education do not help to explain whether an employee experiences their workplace as healthy. Thus, employers need not waste time trying to devise specific workplace improvement strategies for young, or older, workers, for example. Three other sets of working conditions, while not as influential as communication and support, also are associated with positive perceptions of the work environment: having adequate resources, extrinsic job rewards, and job autonomy or 'having a say.' Job demands have a negative impact on healthy work environment experiences. Having job autonomy helps in addressing job demands. But none of the other factors offsets the negative impact on employees of having a stressful and overloaded job – a finding that resonates with our discussion in chapter 2 about the causes of stress, burnout, and work/life conflict.

Why Employees' Perceptions Matter

One additional piece of information from this study should encourage managers to pay careful attention to employee's work experiences. We also discovered that perceptions of a healthy work environment impact performance and costs. The more that employees viewed their work environment was healthy, the higher their level of job satisfaction and their commitment to their employer. Employees in the healthiest environments also had the lowest rates of absenteeism and were planning to stay, rather than quit. The positive effects of healthy work environments can be seen at the team or group level, too. Employees who believed they had really healthy workplaces also reported the best morale among co-workers.

These findings confirm that the summary visions in figures 3.1 and 3.2 of vibrant workplaces and inspired employees indeed are connected. Given managers' ongoing concerns about employee engagement, the commitment measure we used is worth examining more closely. It actually goes to the heart of what many managers define as engagement. Specifically, we measured commitment by a scale comprising four questions on personal identification with the organization's values, loyalty to the organization, willingness to work hard to help the organization succeed, and pride in working for the organization. These are attitudes and behaviours that almost every senior management team today wants to cultivate in its workforce.

What I've just presented are correlations, so they may not fully describe cause and effect. However, the strength and consistency of the links between perceived healthy environments and organizational performance certainly suggests that when management teams rethink their employee engagement strategy, or try to be more proactive in retaining employees, the goal of a healthy work environment should be high on the agenda.

Closing the Inspiration Gap

There are basic steps you can take to improve the work environment and provide more inspiring work experiences. I am speaking directly to managers, who have considerable power to ensure that vibrant workplace ingredients are in place. Actually, one of the most effective steps in this regard is relatively inexpensive in financial terms, but may require a major psychic investment.

To venture in this direction, a manager would have to make a determined effort to understand the filters employees use for assessing their jobs and work environment. These filters are peoples' work values – what is fundamentally important to them in a job, workplace, and career. That manager also would need the will to address major gaps between employees' work values and what they actually experience on a daily basis. I call this discrepancy between what employees want and what they have the 'inspiration gap.' Closing the gap will move an employer much further down the path to a truly healthy organization.

Specifically, closing the inspiration gap requires three pieces of information:

1. What workers value most in a job, an employer, and a career.
2. How they assess the specific features of their current job.
3. Where the biggest gaps are between what they value and what they have.

Most employee surveys conducted by employers provide only one of these pieces of information: assessments of various working conditions. So I would encourage HR professionals and others who manage internal employee surveys also to find out what really matters to their workforce by tapping into basic work values. It then will be possible to calculate the third piece of information: the inspiration gaps you need to close.

Earlier, I identified positive influences on employees' perceptions of whether their work environment is healthy. As for the negative influences – stressful and hectic jobs, heavy workloads, and conflicting demands – they obviously require remedial action. You can readily diagnose these problems in your workplace using an appropriately designed employee survey, or through focus groups, employee forums, or other consultation techniques. Doing so will address some of the biggest concerns employees – and employers – have voiced about unhealthy psychosocial work environments.

However, removing these toxic factors from a work environment does not make it healthy, never mind vibrant. But certainly it is a first step. There also must be a range of positive factors put in place, such as those listed in figure 3.3 or in the vibrant workplace vision in figure 3.1. Employee input on where to start is critical. A useful source of information in this regard can be gleaned from a basic gap analysis of employee survey results – assuming you have asked parallel questions about work values and work experiences.

Here is how to do this sort of gap analysis and what you might expect to find. Using the list of positive influences on perceptions of a healthy work environment in figure 3.3 as an illustration of this procedure, imagine that you also have employee survey data on the importance or 'value' your employees place on each factor. By comparing their assessments of these factors with how important each one is, you can calculate an inspiration gap score.[12] Most employee surveys use rating scales on a negative to positive continuum. The most common would be a five-category rating scale that goes from 'strongly disagree' to 'strongly agree.' The same statements used to assess jobs and the work environment also can be used to ask employees what they consider most important. A similar five-category rating scale is employed, but ranging from 'not at all important' to 'very important.'

When you have the survey results, compare the answers with the assessment and importance questions for each job or workplace dimension. Put them side by side in an Excel spreadsheet, and simply subtract the percentage who answered 'strongly agree' on the assessment from the percentage who answered 'very important' on the values version of the same question. This procedure will give you the gap score.[13] Look closely at the relative size of the gaps and then create a ranked list of priority issues you can address by discussing solutions directly with employees.

The Changing Employment Relationships Survey (used in figure 3.3) also asked about work values. This work value question included most of the positive factors identified in figure 3.3. I summarize the findings here to prompt you to think about what you might find if a similar assessment tool were used in your workplace. We discovered that the greatest room for improvement is in the following features of jobs and the work environment:

1. Career advancement opportunities.
2. Being able to choose your own schedule.
3. Freedom to decide how to do your work.
4. Receiving the training needed to do your job effectively.
5. Receiving recognition for work well done.
6. Good communication among the people you work with.

The gaps are rank-ordered above and range from 32 to 14 percentage points.[14] To revisit a prominent theme in this chapter, note that none of these workplace characteristics refers directly to health and wellness. Furthermore, all of them are already in the strategies and annual work plans of many HR departments. The implication, then, is that employers can make considerable progress in closing the inspiration gap by doing better what they already are doing.

Also important to point out is that there were gaps of about 20 percentage points for benefits, pay, and job security. HR professionals know that it is critical to have the right mix of economic rewards and, equally important, the perception that these rewards are 'fair.' However, decades of job satisfaction research tells us that extrinsic rewards are a source of dissatisfaction if perceived by employees to be deficient. Rarely are they a major source of satisfaction. So the six factors listed earlier are more important for the overall quality of one's work experience.

The Dynamics of a Healthy Organization

Managers and human resources professionals often make decisions based on assumptions about how higher-quality job and workplace conditions contribute to positive employee experiences and improved productivity. This is exactly what the healthy organization value chain proposes: talented and motivated employees in a supportive, well-resourced work environment will contribute to better results for customers and communities that can be sustained over time. Numerous studies show this to be sound thinking. Indeed, the quality of an employee's job and work environment has an influence on her or his overall quality of work life and job performance.

To fully appreciate the dynamics of a healthy organization we need to further unravel its inner logic. In this regard, it is useful to know how the defining characteristics of quality jobs and healthy work environments are related – and how they are shaped by other parts of the organization's systems, culture, and operating environment. Many practitioners assume a logical sequence, whereby quality jobs in healthy and safe work environments enhance an employee's quality of work life and well-being and, as a result, contribute to the organization's success. It is the ideal triple-win, because employees and their families, the company and its shareholders, and customers or clients stand to benefit. At least, that is the common assumption and what is implied in the summary visions I provided earlier.

However, organizational life is more complicated, because this neat chain of cause and effect can be influenced by many factors. Growing concerns over this decade about recruitment and retention, employee engagement, productivity and innovation, and controlling rising employee benefit costs has given new urgency to sorting out how all these job and workplace factors influence employees' work experiences and behaviours. The late-decade recession highlighted just how fragile are the gains in morale, well-being, and performance made by companies committed to becoming exemplary employers.

I would encourage you to examine these issues in your workplace, using your data and with the benefit of input from your employees or co-workers. Test out some of the ideas presented in this chapter. For example, are your most satisfied workers also highly motivated to innovate and collaborate – and if not, why? For your workforce, what are the vibrant workplace conditions that are most likely to stimulate employee and customer satisfaction? What would excite your employees or team members so they feel passionate about their work and how it contributes to making others' lives better? The point is, you need to explore ways to put in place two building blocks of a healthy organization – vibrant workplaces and inspired employees – in your unique context.

Now is the time to consider the role that the two other building blocks of a healthy organization play. The healthy organization value chain in chapter 2 depicted culture and leadership as foundational, because of their enabling role. The centre of the value chain is a vibrant workplace, and its most immediate result is cultivation of an inspired workforce. But change agents – whether senior managers, HR professionals, or an employee wellness committee – have to step forward to raise the issues, initiate a conversation about the potential for improvement, and find opportunities to implement solutions. Perhaps even more critical as an enabler of improvements to work environments is culture. This point has been illustrated in organizations as diverse as Gaylord Hotels, the Four Seasons, health care organizations in Australia and England, and airlines such as WestJet. Chapter 4 examines how a positive culture builds healthy organizations by the strength of its people values.

4 Positive Cultures

In 1995 Canadian National Railway (CN) was privatized after many decades of government ownership. To survive in the private sector and return shareholder value, CN had no choice but to shake off a low-productivity, bureaucratic culture. Typical of the old culture was the widespread practice of 'early quits' – workers going home early on a full day's pay. Under the leadership of CEO Hunter Harrison, CN adopted a high-performance business model. Called Precision Railroading, this model focused on customers' needs and delivery goals. Precision Railroading is more than a management or operating system; it is a way of thinking and behaving that became embedded in a customer-focused culture. Intensive effort to shift the culture included rebuilding the corporate strategy around Five Guiding Principles – service, cost control, asset utilization, safety, and people – against which every decision was tested.[1] Culture change brought behaviours in line with these principles. Front-line employees were empowered to meet customers' needs and were recognized for these efforts. The practice of 'early quits' disappeared, and CN became the best-performing, most profitable railroad in North America.

Toyota is famous for its relentless pursuit of product quality and customer satisfaction. The company's success is rooted in The Toyota Production System (TPS), an integrated model of 'lean' manufacturing that touches on all aspects of corporate strategy, systems, structures, and culture. TPS is a way of thinking – the fabled Toyota Way: it emphasizes long-term thinking over short-term financial goals. Customer value is added at every step of the production process through continual improvement and learning. The same approach eliminates waste and reduces costs in the production process. And the organizational culture respects, develops, and challenges employees and external suppliers. Most important, the cultural foundations of the TPS support all workers to continually improve production processes and product quality through skill development, learning, teamwork, and individual initiative.[2] (Toyota's massive safety recall in 2010 to fix gas pedals in its vehicles is putting the TPS under intense public scrutiny, creating an unprecedented test of the resilience of the company's culture.) A model of operational and product excellence, Toyota has influenced the global diffusion of lean production methods in manufacturing in the past two decades; however, few other companies have been able to replicate the unique cultural features of the Toyota Way.

In the early 1990s New York was one of the most crime-ridden cities in America. To bring down the crime rate, Mayor Rudy Giuliani appointed William Bratton police commissioner in 1994.[3] Bratton recognized that because police policies rewarded effort rather than results, crimes went unsolved. Consequently, morale was low, absenteeism rates were high, and public perceptions of the NYPD were negative. Change required a shift in the culture, so that police officers would view citizens as customers whose needs came first. A 'cultural diagnosis' identified what police officers believed were major impediments to solving and preventing crime. The policing process was re-engineered to remove these impediments. Information reporting and sharing was improved with new technology. The biggest change, however, was sending officers out into the community. As more officers were assigned from administrative tasks to district precincts and from patrol cars to neighbourhood foot patrols, they responded better to community needs and anticipated the potential causes of crimes. Within two years, crime rates dropped and started a steady decline that continues today.

The cases of CN, Toyota, and the NYPD illustrate the critical role culture plays in supporting employees to succeed in their jobs. Relative to their peers, these organizations have become healthy and sustainable, in large part because of the strength of a positive culture. What makes these cultures positive is the way they support employees to benefit customers and communities and experience the sense of accomplishment and pride that flow from this process. Positive cultures cultivate the human capabilities required for the organization to thrive in the long term. For example, CN managers and employees became more 'passionate' – the company's word for an engaged workforce – about excellent customer service because they wanted to, not because they had to. Toyota nurtures a highly committed workforce because it trusts and respects its employees, challenging and enabling them to further develop their talents. As NYPD decentralized decision-making to local precincts, patrol officers took more leadership, were recognized for doing so, and found their work more meaningful.

This chapter focuses on the makings of a positive culture. I offer examples, insights, and suggestions that will help you to nurture and strengthen your organization's culture so that it can become a solid building block of a healthy organization. To summarize the action implications:

1. Positive cultures have widely shared, people-centred values that guide managers and employees to act with stakeholders' best interests foremost in mind.
2. Negative cultures are unhealthy, unethical, toxic, and potentially disastrous for employees, customers, and society.
3. Successful organizations view their culture as a strategic advantage, giving them a competitive edge and a rallying point for a talented and motivated workforce.
4. The sense of community in healthy organizations reflects a culture of trust and ethical responsibility, benefiting the organization's relations with stakeholders.
5. Cultures can be changed by energizing and evolving the best of the organization's existing values and including employees in the process.

What Is Culture?

I am frequently asked some variation of this question: 'why are some organizations better places in which to work *and* better performing for customers than others?' A big part of the answer is culture. Culture is the organization personified. It tells the company's story: who it is; how the actions of employees, managers, and external partners overcame challenges to bring it to where it is today; and the qualities that will take it where it wants to go. An organization's culture expresses its unique personality, character, and philosophy. If the culture is negative, employees will be disgruntled – as in an episode of *The Office* TV series or a *Dilbert* cartoon – and words such as indifferent, self-serving, and uncaring will be fitting descriptions of customers' experiences. In contrast, a positive culture is based on strong and authentic people values. It instils employee pride and loyalty, giving their work a greater sense of purpose and meaning. Top management set the tone and direction for a positive culture, but they will not be its keepers. Everyone in the organization 'owns' the culture and feels a responsibility for contributing to its ongoing vitality.

Organizations are like mini-societies. Anthropologists' insights about how societies operate highlight the fact that cooperation – necessary to survive and flourish – requires groups to have shared beliefs, customs, rituals, language, and myths. Organizations also have their own cultural systems, reflected in what managers and employees collectively believe, say, and do in their jobs. Essentially, culture is a set of shared assumptions and beliefs about how organizational life ought to be conducted. Culture is visible in how things get done by managers and employees inside and outside the organization. To understand the culture of an organization, we need to see through employees' eyes how they interpret their work activities and, most important of all, the values that guide them to behave as they do.

Organizations can have multiple and sometimes conflicting cultures, which results from groups holding dissonant values. A 'them–us' mentality found in some unionized workplaces essentially is a conflict of two internal cultures. In organizations that have undergone years of budget cuts, layoffs, and restructuring, negativity can pervade the culture. One professional in a human service agency described this to me as 'a culture of embittered entitlement.'

Not all strong cultures have positive consequences. Just think of the individualistic values – what critics call 'raw greed' – that dominated Wall Street investment banks and hedge funds leading up to the 2008 global financial crisis, blinding otherwise clever financial professionals to the inherent risks in mortgage-backed derivatives. The sub-prime mortgage fiasco was in large part a product of a culture that left no room for questioning and provided no moral incentive for thinking through the consequences of complex derivatives for investors or mortgage holders.

Perhaps more common is the sense of being socially disconnected that comes from working in an organization with a weak culture. Employees in such an environment lack clear guidelines for how to do their jobs. Left to their own devices, workers in weak cultures fall back on their own informal work rules. This becomes the default culture. Sometimes, a default culture taps into an employee's personal or professional sense of responsibility.

At other times, the default culture may breed indifferent service at a restaurant, unhelpful 'help line' employees, or more dire consequences. Early in this decade, 2,500 residents of Walkerton, a small town in

Ontario, Canada, became seriously ill, and some died, from drinking contaminated water, because the local water utility had tolerated years of incompetence and indifference over testing water quality. The provincial government launched an inquiry into the Walkerton tragedy, which later concluded: 'For years, the Walkerton Public Utilities Commission operators engaged in a host of improper operating practices, including failing to use adequate doses of chlorine, failing to monitor chlorine residuals daily, making false entries about residuals in daily operating records, and misstating the locations at which microbiological samples were taken. The operators knew that these practices were unacceptable and contrary to Ministry of Environment guidelines and directives.' [4] While these lax work practices are contemptible, they are symptomatic of a more widespread indifference about regulating and enforcing water standards. Without a strong ethic of competent public service – which would emphasize public safety and service quality – disasters like Walkerton are bound to occur.

To avoid such fiascos, senior managers must give high priority to shaping a durable culture that connects every employee with the goals of the organization, particularly the needs of customers, clients, and other stakeholders. As sociologists have shown, the more deeply ingrained and widely shared the values of an organization, the less that management has to impose formal rules and regulations to ensure that employees pursue common goals. In organizations where strong and positive values are widely shared, people can trust each other to do the right thing. In other words, values-based organizations can be far less bureaucratic. This no doubt is a change that employees and customers alike will welcome.

Edgar Schein, the MIT professor credited with coining the term 'corporate culture,' separates culture into three levels. The first and most visible level is the organization's artefacts, including the physical workspace and its furnishings, corporate branding, employee dress, how employee contributions are recognized, and styles of personal interaction. Travellers on WestJet airlines cannot miss the flight crew's casual uniforms, friendly banter, and folksy jokes, all intended to make customers feel like guests in someone's home and generate a team spirit among employees. The second level consists of the ways that the culture gets expressed in mission and vision statements, values, codes of conduct, corporate annual reports, and the like. GE's 'Imagination at work' tag line brands the company as an innovator on the frontiers of green technology as well as in its other longer-standing business arenas.

The third and least visible level includes the unwritten assumptions about how organizational life should be conducted. In one professional service firm, my conversations with managers and employees revealed a tacit rule: be polite to each other. This politeness resulted in pleasant, if superficial, interactions. But the unintended side-effect was an inability to honestly challenge each other's ideas in planning sessions, which was a problem in a knowledge-based organization that needed a flow of fresh ideas. As the organization reflected on what it needed to do to become healthier, managers and professionals eventually brought this aspect of its culture into plain view and talked about the need for open and respectful debate as a way to make better decisions.

Organization experts also distinguish between corporate culture and organizational culture. The former is imposed from the top by senior management and may or may not be carried around in the heads of employees. The latter is a more genuine expression of the shared beliefs that bring managers and employees together around common goals and how best to achieve them, especially through positive relationships with each other, with customers, and with outside stakeholders. While this distinction may seem like splitting hairs, the difference is subtle but useful for anyone wanting to strengthen the culture in their workplace. The foundation of a healthy organization is a culture that has been and continues to be co-created by the members of the organization, rather than imposed from the top.

Culture as Competitive Advantage

Today, more and more executives understand how culture affects business success. The once fuzzy notion of corporate culture has honed a sharper strategic edge. Furthermore, in the wake of the 2008 global financial crisis, the need for corporate ethical standards of honesty and accountability have taken on a new urgency. But an organization's culture must provide more than an ethical compass steering employees away from corrupt or criminal acts. A positive culture – defined broadly by its strong people-centred values – can help to address a range of common challenges any organization faces.

Figure 4.1 summarizes how an organization's culture strengthens the link between people and performance. The beliefs and values embedded in the culture guide the organization's approach to leadership, help to shape its HR policies and practices, and make the quality of the work environment a priority. Employees know that they are genuinely

Figure 4.1 The culture connection

Positive
employee
experiences

Inspired
performance

Vibrant workplaces

CULTURE

People leadership
and supports

valued. In turn, they value what they have in their workplace, feeling it is 'theirs.' When employees and managers learn from and celebrate what they have achieved, the culture is further strengthened. This is how culture can energize a positive upward spiral of quality of work life and performance. This is how a robust culture becomes a powerful competitive advantage.

Increasingly, business leaders articulate how their organization's culture helps them to outdistance competitors and cultivate a talented workforce. We can see this effect in 'best companies to work for' lists created by Great Place to Work Institute and published in *Fortune* magazine and *HR Magazine*. Here are some examples:

- Al Stubblefield, CEO of Baptist Health Care, in Florida, asserts that 'culture will drive strategy or culture will drag strategy.' He attributes the organization's turn-around success to a rebuilt culture that equally values patients and staff.
- Wim Roelandts, CEO of XILINX, a California-based maker of programmable silicon chips, observes that while competitors can offer the same benefits and pay, they cannot replicate a culture.

- As Isadore Sharp, the founder and CEO of the luxury hotel chain Four Seasons explains: 'A culture cannot be copied, it cannot be imitated. It has to grow from within over a very long time, based upon the consistent action of senior management. *That* is the barrier to entry for other hotels trying to compete against us. It isn't just having a fine building.'[5]
- The CEO of software firm Analytical Graphics believes that having fun at work is a catalyst for innovation. Chief Culture Officer Susan Schor's role at women's clothing retailer Eileen Fisher is to nurture 'a joyful atmosphere' that inspires people's best work, individually and collectively.
- Lee Lee James, COO and vice-chair of Synovus, a Georgia-based financial services firm, attributes continued growth and profitability to a strong focus over the past decade on creating a 'culture of the heart,' which puts people as the first link in the firm's value chain and guides decisions.
- Jeff Chambers, who headed human resources at software maker SAS, talks about three principles that inform the SAS culture: flexibility, trust and values. Above all, these principles guide the daily behaviour of managers because, as Chambers notes, 'managers are the hinge that swing the door between employer and employee.'

These examples highlight the benefits of positive cultures for business success. Al Stubblefield's comment that 'culture drives strategy' aptly summarizes complex organizational dynamics. Expanded, it means that a positive culture supports employees to implement the organization's strategy with a sense of pride and ownership in the results.

Some employers express this culture-people-strategy link using the language of health. Take, for example, ArcelorMittal Dofasco (formerly Dofasco), a steel producer in Hamilton, Ontario. Founded in 1912 and one of the corporate pillars of the local economy, Dofasco developed its own style of employee relations, called 'The Dofasco Way.' The Dofasco Way defines a corporate culture supported by programs such as profit-sharing, extensive training, and employee well-being. Senior management attributes a low voluntary turnover rate and productivity increases double the Canadian manufacturing sector average to a culture that has as its centrepiece health, safety, and wellness. When Dofasco received the National Quality Institute's Healthy Workplace Award for excellence in these areas, Don Pether, the president and CEO at the time, stated: 'From the top down and the bottom up, the health, safety and well-being of people is a deeply ingrained aspect of our corporate culture ... In addition to our shared responsibility for health, safety and well-being, it is a business advantage to have employees healthy and at work. Our responsibility as an employer is to create conditions where all Dofasco people can achieve and contribute to their full potential, work safely and remain in good physical and mental health.'[6]

Unhealthy and Healthy Cultures

ArcelorMittal Dofasco's success in a turbulent global industry attests to the strategic value of a healthy culture. But most organizations are not there yet. In fact, cultures range from healthy and robust to unhealthy and downright toxic. So the ongoing challenge that managers, employees, and HR professionals face is how to minimize the negatives and maximize the positives in their particular culture. To understand this, and also to appreciate the vital role of culture in an organization's effectiveness, a comparison of cultures in healthy and unhealthy organizations is instructive.

Unhealthy Cultures

Robert Sutton's refreshingly frank book, *The No Asshole Rule*, provides guidelines for creating a civilized workplace.[7] Sutton describes the 'culture of fear' that engulfs workplaces when managers and employees get away with bad behaviour, demeaning others, and generally acting like jerks. The repercussions can immobilize an organization. People retreat and/or quit, usually in that order, often at considerable personal and organizational costs. Sutton describes how a new CEO at a Fortune 500 company fixed a broken culture. The CEO purged about two dozen toxic senior managers by applying the performance management system the way it should have been used, to prevent bullying and harassment. The moves by this new CEO restored a large measure of humanity to the organization, benefiting both customers and employees. Sutton's candour about how jerks rob workplaces of civility and co-workers of their dignity strikes a chord for many of us. He spotlights jerks' behaviour: a repertoire of insults, threats, public humiliation, rude interruptions, dirty looks, passive aggression, and more. But workplaces do not have to be populated with jerks for their cultures to be negative.

At the extreme, an unhealthy culture can be disastrous, like the Walkerton contaminated water tragedy. Take the fatal end in February

2003 of the Space Shuttle Columbia, which was torn apart over Texas at a speed of Mach 19.5 just minutes from landing, killing the seven astronauts aboard. The world's attention focused on a chunk of foam dislodged from the shuttle's left wing seconds after take-off. However, the Columbia Accident Investigation Board concluded that there were deeper organizational causes – specifically NASA's 'failed safety culture.'[8] Three critical goals for successful space missions – safety, system reliability, and quality assurance – were jeopardized by communication breakdowns. Contrary to NASA's official line that employees were empowered to stop an operation if they detected even the hint of a problem, the margin for risk tolerance and error had grown perilously wide in the space program.

As a result, foam problems were accepted when there was no engineering rationale for doing so. Budget cuts, staff shortages, thick bureaucracy, and intense pressures to meet deadlines contributed to this complacent attitude about safety. Professionals who were supposed to be operating the best safety and quality engineering programs in the world over the years had become unable or unwilling to communicate openly about potential hazards that space missions faced. Communication breakdowns also were a failure of professional responsibility. While the inquiry report does not address working conditions or employee experiences, we can only imagine how it must have felt to be an engineer or manager connected to the Space Shuttle Columbia, knowing that corners were being cut and things could go wrong.

A less extreme but more common example of a negative workplace culture is one that encourages overwork. A culture that tolerates and even rewards overwork is counterproductive, eroding employees' quality of work life and their ability and commitment to perform their jobs well.

I saw such a culture at the head office of a large energy company, described by one of the HR managers as 'a hard-driving place.' One division alone had accumulated millions of dollars in unused vacation time liability. With sixty-hour work weeks being common, turnover was a revolving door and morale was sagging. Employee cynicism increased when the company was named one of the city's top employers. The company also had gained a public profile for social and environmental responsibility. While charitable contributions showed generous corporate philanthropy, employees saw a huge disconnect: few of them had any time to do community volunteer work, given their demanding work schedules. When asked for explanations, professional employees described an 'engineering and accounting culture' that focused on operational results, a lack of people skills among senior managers, and a leadership team that believed hard work was a virtue. Some senior managers paid lip service to employee concerns about workload and how it interfered with their personal lives, but these issues did not make it onto the executive team's agenda. Meanwhile, talented employees – especially up-and-coming female professionals – left in search of a better quality of work life.

Even more extreme was what I witnessed at a non-profit professional organization that provides a wide range of services to members. Many employees of this organization saw their work as more than a job. For them it was a personal calling, because they believed in the service mission of the organization – improving the lives of members, their families, and communities. Over the years, the organization developed work norms and values that put member service ahead of employees' needs, even if their health and well-being was at risk. For professional member-service staff, fifty-hour work weeks were usual, plus extra time spent travelling and working out of the office. These employees attributed a chronic culture of overwork – a fact of organizational life that had been documented in employee surveys over many years – to increased service levels expected by members, more complex work, and rising management expectations for job performance.

In this unhealthy culture, work pressures and job dedication resulted in relatively low absenteeism but very high presenteeism, as workers felt they could not afford to take time off even when sick. This practice had become institutionalized as a cultural norm, but with significant costs. Feeling demoralized, employees had little trust that management would take their interests into account. Employees' personal health suffered, and surveys revealed above-average rates of major health risks, such as smoking, high blood pressure, diabetes, and obesity. Even though the organization was saddled with escalating long-term disability costs as more employees burned out, remedial action was slow to come. Employees told tragic stories about the human toll, recounting how co-workers had died on the job from complications arising from chronic health problems because they did not have time to care for themselves.

An unhealthy culture triggers a downward negative spiral. While this may not spell the end of an organization, it likely results in chronic underperformance, avoidable employee costs, and reduced quality of work life for employees, unless, of course, executives, line managers,

HR, and rank-and-file employees take decisive steps to expose these negative consequences and, at the same time, present a positive alternative.

Healthy Cultures

The biggest difference between healthy and unhealthy cultures is their values. Healthy organizations value respect, responsibility, honesty, fairness, and integrity. Indeed, these are the qualities most people want in any relationship. The power of these values lies in how they influence day-to-day interactions among co-workers; between managers and employees; between employees and their customers or clients, suppliers, and business partners; and between the organization and the larger community. The result is a positive upward spiral of improved quality of work life and performance.

Strong core values generate trust, which is a good barometer of the overall health of an organization. People need to trust each other in order for their work environment to be healthy and productive. Trusting someone means being comfortable taking risks in the relationship. One is more likely to open up and share ideas, reveal confidential information, ask for advice, offer help, willingly cooperate, and in other ways be vulnerable. Being vulnerable is safe only if there is confidence that the other person will behave in expected ways and that their actions will take others' interests into account. It is at the micro-level of personal interaction that trust is built. As philosopher Robert Solomon and business consultant Fernando Flores comment in their book, *Building Trust in Business, Politics, Relationships and Life*: 'Without trust, the corporate community is reduced to a group of resentful wage slaves and defensive, if not ambitious, managers. People will do their jobs, but they will not offer their ideas, or their enthusiasm, or their souls.'[9] The picture presented is poles apart from a healthy organization.

It is telling that some of my examples of healthy organizations are on the best workplaces lists produced by the Great Place to Work Institute in different countries. The assessment for these lists uses the institute's Trust Index employee survey, which measures what the institute identifies as three drivers of trust: management credibility, respect and fairness. As noted earlier, high-trust organizations have superior performance. Employees benefit, too. An analysis of Trust Index results for organizations on the 2007 list of 50 Best Workplaces in Canada, compared with those of organizations that applied for the list but did not make it, shows that employees in the 50 best workplaces are far more likely to experience their workplace as psychologically and emotionally healthy. This no doubt reflects the fair and respectful treatment they receive from managers and co-workers.

Researchers also have documented the personal and organizational benefits of trust. A research team at the University of Florida compared results from 132 studies of the relationship between trust and two big outcomes: risk-taking and job performance.[10] This research, published in the *Journal of Applied Psychology*, makes a useful distinction between trust and trustworthiness. Trust in a relationship between two people depends on the trustworthiness of each person in the eyes of the other. Trustworthiness refers to the qualities that must be present for someone to trust you. These qualities include loyalty, openness, caring, fairness, availability, receptivity, consistency, reliability, and discreetness – all of which can be learned. So trustworthiness can be incorporated into leadership training and development as part of efforts to build a healthier organization.

There is good reason for employers to do so. The more that managers are trustworthy, the more that employees feel committed to the organization, perform their jobs well, take risks in their work, and are 'good citizens' by helping others and contributing to a positive work environment. When trustworthiness is widespread among managers, employees are less likely to partake in counterproductive behaviours. These include disregarding safety procedures, making threats, tardiness, absenteeism, and other actions subject to discipline. From the employees' perspective, these examples of trustworthiness add up to a more vibrant workplace.

To be meaningful, corporate values and ethics must extend from the inside out. Internal relationships based on trust will foster stakeholder trust in the organization. Unfortunately, public confidence in corporations, governments, and other large institutions has steadily declined over the past several decades, reflecting an erosion of trust. It has not helped, of course, that the opening decade of the twenty-first century is book-ended by corporate scandals, from the likes of Enron to the entire global financial system teetering on the brink. Unsurprisingly, the average person feels that whoever makes decisions in these organizations does not care about their interests. Corporate ethics, ideally, should ensure that an organization and its employees can be trusted by external stakeholders to consistently 'do the right things.' That is, dealings will be honest, transparent, accountable, fair, and respectful of others' rights and interests. The almost total absence of these qualities explains the public outrage over the implosion of Northern Rock and Lehman Brothers and government bail-outs of other huge financial institutions.

In a healthy organization, the culture naturally encourages mutually beneficial relationships with stakeholders. The idea of 'community' aptly describes a healthy organization's internal and external worlds. For example, I recently facilitated workshops with professionals who provide health services to Aboriginal communities in Canada. The shared vision of a vibrant workplace crafted by the group ranked 'a sense of community' as the key ingredient. For them, community meant two things: a feeling of collegial support and common values within each worksite and the organization as a whole; and a strong connection with the individuals in the Aboriginal communities with whom they worked. When discussing what constitutes a vibrant workplace, these workers believed that the bonds they had cultivated within their teams enabled them to contribute to healthier Aboriginal communities. Or, in more general terms: healthy workplaces support healthy communities.

These connections between internal and external communities can be described in terms of citizenship. Organizational citizenship refers to the altruistic behaviours that workers engage in to support each other. This goes beyond being a team player, requiring employees to proactively think of ways to help co-workers succeed in their tasks and personal lives. These are the good citizens noted in the University of Florida study, described above. For example, corporate citizenship could be displayed as helping a colleague deal with a family medical emergency, sending a co-worker relevant articles or websites for a new project, offering to pitch in and help others who are overloaded, or volunteering to organize work group social events. In some organizations, employees contribute their unused paid sick days to an employee who is off work for several weeks or months recovering from an operation or illness. These are the small ways that individuals rise above their own immediate needs and interests, putting co-workers first.

Similarly, corporate citizenship describes the stance of a healthy organization towards society (see chapter 7, below, for more on this topic). Responsible corporate citizens provide financial support for arts, culture, community services, and a host of charitable causes from operas and art galleries to food banks and cures for cancer. But they also go beyond philanthropy. For example, each year TD Financial makes generous donations to community causes. What is more, the bank's employees select charities and community events to fund and in which to volunteer. As a result, less mainstream and more diverse charities receive support, such as local gay/lesbian/bi-sexual/transgendered pride events and help for people with HIV-AIDS. This community involvement supports TD's commitment to diversity and inclusiveness within its workforce, 25 per cent of whom are visible minorities. According to the bank's manager of diversity, all of its actions on diversity align with the corporate value of respect. Ed Clark, TD's CEO, states that 'diversity is how we do business,' and therefore it is central to the bank's long-term business strategy. For the bank, the goals of supporting diversity among both customers and employees are mutually reinforcing.

Culture Change

My point is that a positive culture enables all the organization's relationships to be rewarding. That is how culture helps to build healthy organizations. The attributes of a positive culture transcend values and beliefs about employee well-being. Indeed, positive cultures have values that run broad and deep – such as trust, which as we have seen is fundamental to business performance and responsible dealings with customers and communities. Even if the ideal culture is labelled healthy or positive, it is necessary to minimize some things on the negative side of the cultural ledger and maximize other things on the positive side. In other words, the culture may need to change.

Cultures Can Be Revitalized and Can Evolve

How do you change a culture to make it more positive and values based? The answer to this question depends on how you approach organizational change. One approach advocates transformational change: reinventing the organization, shaking it up, ushering in a new era, and radically altering how people work together and how the business operates. A contrasting approach claims that culture change happens incrementally. Based on my interpretation of the research on change and my consulting experience, I find myself in the latter camp. In reality, successful cultural change is more evolutionary than revolutionary. Over time and with persistent effort, it is possible to incrementally strengthen a culture in ways that look and feel transformational.

The operative word here is 'evolve.' As management expert Henry Mintzberg explains: 'You don't change cultures – you revitalize existing cultures. You can't take a company that has existed for years and just throw out its culture and drop a new one in place. What you do is bring back the energy that is still there.'[11] Change agents can take some comfort from this view. Surely, moving into place the culture building block of a healthy organization becomes a less daunting task if approached as step-by-step improvements, rather than having to orchestrate a radical make-over.

As you consider options for revitalizing your culture, here are some points to keep in mind. The examples I used of organizations at their cultural worst point to four cultural features that are incompatible with a healthy organization:

- Not meeting employees' human need for dignity and respect.
- Pursuing operational goals in ways that sacrifice the health, safety, and well-being of employees.
- Not understanding, or reflecting upon, the unintended consequences of your organization's culture for the businesses' long-term sustainability and success.
- Weak accountability for the consequences of actions.

At the other end of the continuum, positive organizational cultures meet all the following criteria, setting the standard for culture as a healthy organization building block:

- There are deeply held core values that define the basic operating philosophy of the organization, particularly how all individuals will be treated and are expected to treat each other.
- Employees see their personal values reflected in company values.
- There is wide recognition, continually reinforced by senior management, that the organization's culture is a foundation for its success.
- From the top of the organization down to the front lines, everyone actively is involved in living the core values daily.

The Culture-Strengthening Process

Let us examine how cultures can be strengthened. As you undertake this important task, bear in mind the systemic nature of culture. You cannot isolate culture as a target for change. Nor can you afford to ignore it when trying to change other parts of your organization. As such, culture can be elusive. Its features cannot be grasped in a concrete way, as, for instance, putting your hands on a marketing plan, an employee benefits handbook, or an organization chart. The practical implication, then, is that it is not always easy to pinpoint what needs changing in a culture. A few examples follow that will help you to identify culture's connections throughout your organization.

Positive cultures are modelled by the actions of senior management. This observation is based on a recurring theme in my conversations with HR and OD practitioners: their diagnosis of a need to 'transform' the organization's culture. Transformation is the solution, they explain, because the existing culture blocks the path to becoming a healthier and more highly performing workplace. Yet further discussion reveals that the changes sought have more to do with aligning senior managers' actions to existing organizational values, such as respect, integrity, and learning and innovation. For example, senior managers at a public agency participated in a values assessment, which showed that they believed operational efficiency and cost control were most important for the success of the organization. In contrast, all the organization's espoused values were about people. To address this disconnect in values, HR facilitated discussions with the senior management team about how they could better achieve operational goals through the application of corporate values.

Culture cannot be taken for granted. Doing so creates a blind spot when management implements a new organizational system, structure or process. To illustrate, a large telecommunications company wanted to notch up its customer service levels. New service standards and incentives focused on customer service quality, rather than on the volume of calls handled. In preparation, supervisors and managers were trained to coach call centre customer service agents to be more responsive to customers' needs. But the existing culture placed more value on supervisor behaviours that boosted call quantity rather than on customer service quality. A values shift was required to support the new customer service objectives and coaching. By not putting this issue on the table for discussion during training sessions, elements of the existing culture actually held back progress.

Organizational restructuring requires careful attention to culture. This is especially evident in mergers and acquisitions. For example, a health care organization providing rehabilitation services was created through the merger of two successful and well-established institutions, each with distinctive cultures. Little time was invested in creating a blended culture, other than developing statements of the new entity's

mission, vision and values. Senior managers and HR-OD professionals who led a new strategic planning initiative recognized that a unified culture would make it easier to successfully implement the plan.
These change agents did not want to signal to staff that the existing
culture was broken. Rather, they wanted to build on the best of the old
culture, while at the same time focusing everyone on the future. Timing was good, given a recent move from two separate facilities into a
new, state-of-the-art building, and senior managers initiated an organization-wide conversation on the organization's future that included
revitalized values.

Progress on culture change may be uneven. A large regional health
service organization had clearly committed to becoming a healthy
organization. The organization combines several facilities, each with
a distinctive history and culture. The overall vision is healthy people
in healthy communities, and a healthy workplace is a priority in the
strategic plan. A Healthy Workplace Council was established to coordinate actions on healthy workplace goals. People volunteer to be on the
council so membership is diverse, from front-line employees to senior
executives and union officials. As a member of the council put it, their
work injected 'more humanity' into how staff are treated. As the council
became a catalyst for regenerating the culture, it accepted that progress
would be uneven across departments and sites – a reality that fit its
community development approach to change. From this perspective,
the council cultivated work-unit leadership and empowered teams to
act on issues they consider important.

Strengthening Values

I recently gave a talk on how vibrant workplaces inspire employees at a
corporate educational forum. Forum organizers had chosen quality as
the theme – quality improvement, quality client services, and quality
workplaces. I asked the employees attending the forum how well they
knew their organization's values. Someone in the front row admitted
that, while she could not recite the values, she 'knew where to find
them.' This was a good opener for what turned out to be a frank discussion about how the values support the organization's quality goals.
What became clearer to these employees during a seventy-five- minute
interactive session is that they personally need to see their own values
reflected in the organization's values. This point was driven home by
a number of participants, who explained how they feel most inspired

about their job when, at the end of the workday, their personal values are reaffirmed because they and their team have done something they truly believe makes a difference for clients and society.

The Importance of Values

Values act as cultural glue, holding together the people and groups in an organization. The *Oxford English Dictionary* defines values as 'the principles or standards of a person or social group; the generally accepted or personally held judgement of what is valuable and important in life.' Sociologists refer to values as the beliefs that guide the behaviour of individuals and groups. Or, more simply, values act like social glue. In organizations, values often appear alongside the corporate mission (its purpose) and vision (its aspirations). The mission expresses 'what are we in business to do' and the vision articulates 'where we want to go,' while its values express 'how we will run the business and go about achieving our goals and aspirations.' More specifically, an organization's values should do these six things:

- Influence relationships with all stakeholders.
- Guide decision-making and priority-setting.
- Link employees to the mission and vision.
- Inspire and empower employees in their jobs.
- Provide the foundations of the organization's culture.
- Stand the test of time.

Rosabeth Moss Kanter, a Harvard Business School professor, studied some of the world's largest organizations to discover how they were able to quickly develop creative solutions to major social and environmental challenges.[12] The agility of these huge multinational companies – IBM, Procter & Gamble, Omron, CEMEX, Cisco, and Banco Real – defied conventional thinking about lumbering bureaucracies. As Kanter explains: 'In the most influential corporations today, a foundation of values and standards provides a well-understood, widely-communicated guidance system that ensures effective operations while enabling people to make decisions appropriate to local situations.' This echoes the conclusion that Jim Collins and James Porras reached in their best-selling book, *Built to Last: Successful Habits of Visionary Companies*.[13] Companies featured in this study had strong core values, which guided their adaptation to massive economic, political, and social changes in the twentieth century. Collins and Porras refer to core values as enduring principles that keep everyone focused on long-term viability as opposed to short-term financial expediency.

I will present three cases that illustrate the importance of values to an organization's success. The first, the Vancouver Organizing Committee for the 2010 Olympic and Paralympic Games (VANOC), is a new organization with a short lifespan. The second is IBM, which recently adapted its early twentieth-century founder's values to the twenty-first century. The third is mining company Teck Cominco's smelter operations, where senior managers launched a values exercise that led to guiding principles with clear behavioural expectations.

New Values

Achieving a successful Olympic and Paralympic Games presents huge organizational challenges in full public view. People from very different backgrounds – administrators, lawyers and accountants, engineers, former elite athletes, media experts – have to be forged into a high-performing team, knowing that the team will disband soon after the last athletes leave the games venue. The Vancouver Organizing Committee for the 2010 Olympic and Paralympic Games rose to this challenge by crafting a clear vision, mission, and set of values.[14] The vision and mission are appropriately lofty for the games but realistic, given the potential spin-offs:

- VANOC's vision is: A stronger Canada whose spirit is raised by its passion for sport, culture and sustainability.
- VANOC's mission is: To touch the soul of the nation and inspire the world by creating and delivering an extraordinary Olympic and Paralympic experience with lasting legacies.

However, it is the following explicit values that unify a diverse and expanding group of employees at VANOC:

- *Team* – We recognize that success and excellence can only be achieved and sustained by a deep commitment to working as a team and the practice of focusing on collective rather than individual effort and rewards.
- *Trust* – We act consciously to inspire the trust of everyone whose lives we touch by modeling the highest standards of honesty, integrity and ethical behaviour at all times.

- *Excellence* – We model individual and collective performance by working as a team with our partners to promote social cultural, health and sport excellence. Improve the sport performance of Team Canada and deliver on our vision.
- *Sustainability* – We proactively consider the long-term interests of all stakeholders in the Games, both here in Canada and throughout the World, to ensure that our impact is positive and our legacy sustainable for all.
- *Creativity* – We embrace new ideas, encourage input to foster breakthrough thinking and solutions that will allow us to amaze even ourselves in our ability to exceed expectations and deliver on our vision.

By following each single-word value with a description of how it plays out in practice, VANOC provides existing and prospective employees with a clear set of behavioural expectations. Because the organization has been in a steady recruitment mode, the values have provided a useful tool for screening applicants and orienting new recruits. Indicative of the importance VANOC places on values fit, its website provides a Values Assessment that prospective applicants are encouraged to use to determine if they share VANOC's values. The message: do not apply if you do not already believe in our values. As the website states: 'At VANOC, we have a vision, mission, and a set of values to which we are 100% committed. As a potential member of our team, you would need to fully ascribe to these values as well.' Overall, VANOC has created a simple checklist for a healthy culture:

Team
1. Do you enjoy working as part of a team, or are you a person that likes to work on your own?
2. Do you believe there are benefits to working as part of a team? If yes, what are the benefits?
3. What would you do if a member of your team was falling behind and needed your help?

Trust
1. Do you trust others easily?
2. Do you value honesty in others and in yourself?

Excellence
1. Do you aspire to excellence in all that you do?
2. Do you expect to be held accountable for all that you do?

Sustainability
1. Do you link your personal interests and values for creating healthy natural environments and social well-being with some of your work activities?
2. Are there ways you link your purchasing choices with your values?

Creativity
1. Do you enjoy thinking 'outside of the box'?
2. Do you enjoy working in a continually changing and fast-paced environment?

Renewed Values

IBM provides a good illustration of a well-established organization with a distinctive brand and culture that stood it in good stead for decades. Thomas Watson, the company's founder, laid down what he called Basic Beliefs in 1914: respect for the individual, the best customer service, and the pursuit of excellence. These proved enduring, but when the digital information revolution took off in the late 1980s, the company faltered. It struggled to find a new footing in a global information technology market, where its dominant role as a manufacturer of mainframe and then desktop computers had been eclipsed by low-cost newcomers. IBM had to reinvent its business model, moving out of manufacturing and into information technology, business consulting, and outsourcing services.

In 2003 IBM's newly appointed CEO, Samuel J. Palmisano, sought to re-energize employees. He launched an ambitious project to redefine the company's values using a high-tech, high-involvement process. IBM had developed an intranet-based tool that facilitates and summarizes discussions across all IBM's operations on key business issues. Palmisano presented four concepts – respect, customer, excellence, innovation – to a meeting of 300 executives to test the idea of values renewal. 'Respect' was jettisoned because of negative connotations (IBM had gone through a painful period of layoffs). The result was three draft values – commitment to the customer, excellence through innovation, and integrity that earns trust – that were proposed to employees in the 'Values Jam' online forum. There was lively debate and reflection on issues like internal silos, trust, integrity, and respect. After the Jam, Palmisano told an executive committee meeting: 'You guys ought to read every one of these comments, because if you think we've got this place plumbed correctly, think again.' An employee team sifted through the voluminous transcripts and results from pre- and post-Jam surveys. The result was three new values:

- Dedication to every client's success.
- Innovation that matters, for our company and for the world.
- Trust and personal responsibility in all relationships.

In 2004 another Jam was conducted in which more than 52,000 employees exchanged best practices for seventy-two hours. This event was focused on finding actionable ideas to support implementation of the values identified previously. A new post-Jam ratings event was developed to allow IBMers to select key ideas that supported the values. This values renewal at IBM is significant for its process. The new values were not imposed from the top but were the creation of employees from across the sprawling company. IBM has since adapted this grassroots approach for business development. In 2006 it launched 'Innovation Jam' to bring together employees, their family members, and IBM customers to discuss future products. IBM's use of executive blogs and its active encouragement of its staff to discuss in open forums the future direction of IBM products show how it lives the corporate values – and stays ahead of its main competitors.

From Values to Behaviours

Canadian mining giant Teck Cominco's operations in Trail, British Columbia, is one of the world's largest fully integrated zinc and lead smelting and refining complexes. The sprawling facility also produces other specialty metals, chemicals, and fertilizer products and generates its own hydro power. Mining and smelting have a long history in the mountainous Kootenay region of British Columbia. The Trail operations have become a global leader in smelting and refining technology. Several years ago, senior management developed and implemented a comprehensive 'People Strategy' to ensure that the facility maintained its competitive positions in global commodities markets. The strategy responded to its human resource challenges, which included sustaining the highest standards of workplace safety and health, unprecedented retirements due to an aging workforce, and recruitment and retention pressures created by a very competitive labour market especially for skilled trades.

Like IBM and other companies with long histories, the Trail Operations had a values statement, but it no longer resonated with managers or employees. So, as part of developing the People Strategy, senior managers also revisited the old values and came up with a draft of new values, with the idea of consulting with line managers, supervisors, and employees to consolidate them. The People Strategy's specific action items were implemented. They included improvements in new employee orientation, strengthening a safety culture, a wellness initiative, service recognition, enhanced leadership development, and profit sharing. But the discussion of values was put aside for more than a year.

The senior management team returned to the draft values that the People Strategy had successfully launched. A candid discussion identified concerns that are often voiced when executives scrutinize the meaning of specific values: they are too vague, they do not get close enough to explicit behaviours, they need to reflect what managers will actually do, and they are not really values but operational goals. For example, references to 'excellent results' were seen not as values, but rather as operational goals. This realization led the Trail Operations' top management to think in terms of guiding behavioural principles rather than values. They agreed that, first and foremost, any values statement had to be a meaningful guide to how they worked together and showed leadership. Here is what they developed and subsequently rolled out to managers, supervisors, and non-union professional and administrative staff:

> These guiding principles define what we value, how we behave, and what we expect of others. Living by these guiding principles will ensure Trail Operations' future success.
>
> - We act with *integrity*, treating all with *dignity, fairness*, and *respect*.
> - We commit to everyone going home *safe* and *healthy* every day.
> - We take *personal responsibility* for our actions and results.
> - We *support* each other to achieve our fullest potential.
> - We *act responsibly* to support a sustainable future for the *communities* and *environment* in which we operate.

An important step in developing the guiding principles was for the senior management team to agree upon specific behaviours that reflected how the principles translated into effective leadership. They went one step further. In order to communicate the importance of the guiding principles, not as abstract concepts but as explicit criteria for good management practice, they also illustrated each value with examples of how a member of the senior management team had followed one of the principles when making a decision or taking an action. As I show in chapter 5, these guiding principles became the basis for strengthening leadership skills across the Trail facility.

Revitalizing Your Organization's Culture

To summarize: healthy organizations consistently treat employees as *the* core business asset and the key to long-term success. Managers in these organizations are guided in their decisions and actions by strongly felt, people-oriented values. A positive culture requires more than just high ethical standards. Culture comes alive in the relationships that bind employees with each other, with managers and with customers. In this way, culture reinforces ethical imperatives, reaching deeper into the foundations of performance excellence. Positive cultures will help to address an organization's people challenges, especially by finding better ways to encourage employees to excel in their jobs and supporting them to meet their personal needs and professional goals. In short, an organization's cultural qualities may be decisive in shaping its future.

Senior managers must face the fact that their organization's culture is critical to attaining the high quality of work life employees want and the high performance shareholders and customers want. So it is important that culture be openly discussed and reflected upon, starting with top management. These conversations may not come easily, but you must look for opportunities to raise the issues we have just discussed. For some senor managers, talking about culture is far outside their comfort zone – the organizational equivalent to personal counselling. I have been inside organizations where the senior HR manager specifically asks that the word *culture* not be used in discussions with the executive team about developing a healthy workplace strategy. I also have been asked by managers to remove slides from presentations for leadership development workshops that list the corporate values, because the values are 'dormant' and showing them could provoke questions about why this is the case.

This chapter has provided various examples of organizations at different stages of cultural evolution. My intent is to help change agents to plan next steps that can contribute to a healthier culture in their workplace. Some organizations already are cultivating a positive culture. Indeed, on numerous occasions, I have heard employees and managers enthusiastically describe a culture of mutual respect, in which people trust one another and everyone's contributions are valued and recognized. Conversations about culture in these workplaces have a different objective: how to keep the culture fresh, alive, and 'owned' by everyone in the organization.

When you are considering how to revitalize your culture, it helps to recap key points about culture change. It is more useful to talk about revitalizing positive aspects of an existing culture that are critical for the organization's future direction rather than about creating a different culture. As one newly appointed CEO of a financial services firm put it reassuringly at an all-staff conference, 'I'm not here to change your culture but to help you to harness its strengths.' Harnessing the strengths of your culture requires collective reflection on the values that are going to guide you into the future. A way to kick-start the process of revitalizing your organization's culture is to find ways to breathe new life into its values – which may be relevant but dormant. This revitalization takes time and commitment from the top. View cultural change not as an end in itself, but as an evolving process that connects with any type of change in the organization. And strive to involve, consult, and empower employees to strengthen the culture so that it becomes theirs. The last point underscores why inclusive leadership also is a healthy organization building block – and it is the subject of chapter 5.

5 Inclusive Leadership

Emile is a health and safety coordinator at a large manufacturer. Several years ago, he was asked by the company's HR manager to look into wellness programs. The human resource plan for the year included a wellness program feasibility study. Emile had fixed parameters in which to work. A thorough needs assessment of thousands of employees was out of the question. And any plans would need the blessing of several unions. So his approach was to convene a series of focus groups representative of professional, administrative, and production staff and also invite key union reps. Focus groups identified current strengths in occupational health and safety that could be expanded to address wellness and agreed that a wellness initiative was needed. In the following year, a union-management wellness committee was launched. Emile was a member of the committee, but not the chair. Off to a slow start, the committee moved into action after making site visits to other unionized worksites that had comprehensive wellness programs. These visits showed what union and management cooperation could achieve. The committee's work opened the door to address a wide range of people issues as vital to the future of the business.

Lin is the vice-president of human resources in a large health care organization. The organization offered a long menu of programs in safety, workplace health and wellness, learning, and career development. Some showed success, such as reduction in lost-time injury rates and improvement in the return to work process for injured staff. Yet employees faced a bewildering array of support services, often not well understood and therefore underutilized. Lin and her team saw the need to consolidate and streamline these people initiatives, so the team developed a healthy workplace framework that tied them together. The framework grew out of a vision of what a healthy workplace looks like, developed by the HR-OD team at a retreat. The executive did not accept the need for what it saw as yet another HR initiative. Undeterred, Lin and her team adopted the framework as their internal guide, never losing an opportunity to communicate to the executive the strategic value of taking a holistic and integrated approach to workplace and workforce issues. After several years and a new CEO, a revised corporate strategy recognized that fostering healthy employees in healthy work environments is a key to health care excellence.

These real cases illustrate that the actions required to create healthier organizations can be led from many places and positions. In this chapter, I suggest that positive cultures and vibrant workplaces – two basic healthy organization building blocks – are products of combined efforts by many people. Healthy organizations do not result when a few lead and others follow. Certainly, it helps when senior managers make a commitment to improving the workplace and strengthening the culture – and to 'walking the talk.' But top-down leadership is not sufficient. In quite different ways Emile, Lin, and their co-workers show that even without executive-level commitment, progress still is possible with adequate time, determination, and patience. In fact, the greater the number of healthy organization champions there are in a workplace, the more likely it is that these changes will put down roots and become sustainable.

Whether your goals focus on elements of a vibrant workplace, supporting employees to be more inspired in their jobs, or refreshing your corporate values – the change agenda has to be 'owned' by everyone. In this way, healthy organizations are co-created through the ongoing and coordinated actions of all members of the workplace community. Impetus for a healthy organization can come from the bottom, middle, and top of the organization. Even if the full support of senior management is lacking, others in the organization have considerable scope to make improvements, often more than they might think. Any employee should feel motivated and enabled to make the organization healthier.

The key action implications flowing from my discussion in this chapter of the leadership required to build healthy organizations can be summarized as follows:

1. Achieving healthy organization goals requires an inclusive approach to leadership. Improvements have to be a shared responsibility.

2. Everyone in your organization has the potential to play a leadership role in achieving healthy organization goals. They need to be enabled to do so.

3. Each employee can show leadership in day-to-day relationships through values-based behaviours that contribute to a vibrant and inspiring workplace.

4. Inclusive leaders motivate by inspiration, are caring and connected, are trustworthy and trusting, are action-oriented, involve others, and are self-aware.

5. The tone, direction, and support for widespread leadership on healthy organization goals depends on the behaviours of supervisors and managers.

Leading the Way to Healthier Organizations

Adopting an inclusive approach to leadership invites others to participate actively in shaping their work environments. This point will resonate for anyone with a health promotion background. It enshrines the proven principle that people thrive in environments that they have intentionally created to be health promoting. This also is sound organizational development practice. The impetus and ideas for improving the organization's systems, structures, and culture spring organically from within. Each member of an organization has the potential to positively influence its healthy trajectory and should not have to wait for permission from top management to take initiative.

Leading at the Micro Level

Inclusive leadership extends our earlier discussion of vibrant workplaces. Recall that vibrant workplaces depend on the quality of relationships among co-workers and with managers. So we need to think about leadership at this micro level. It is through daily working relationships that you contribute, collaborate, support, and learn with others. Every time you pitch a new customer service idea to your team, acknowledge a co-worker's contributions, step forward to help others deal with a crisis or solve a new problem, or take initiative to improve the way you do your job, you are contributing to a vibrant workplace. When multiplied across an organization day after day, these small actions and values-based behaviours add up to a more vibrant and inspiring workplace.

Micro-level leadership also energizes the culture. This happens every time you consciously strive to live the organization's core values in your dealings with co-workers, staff who report to you, customers, and community stakeholders. These are small acts of leadership, simply because you are setting a positive example for others. As we saw in chapter 4, what distinguishes healthy cultures from unhealthy ones is the extent to which employees' behaviour is guided by strongly held common values. In positive cultures, behaviours are responsive, supportive, and constructive because people are highly valued. These behaviours are evident in how people plan and implement decisions, go about their tasks, and relate to each other, customers, and other stakeholders. It is through values-based behaviours that an organization realizes its vision. Some would argue that living the organization's core values should be like a habit – you do it simply as a matter of routine. But I believe it also requires intentional leadership. You must be proactive, anticipate others' needs, take initiative, be a role model, and more.

Micro-level leadership actions will become more frequent if the constraints of positions are loosened up. People will collaborate across functional boundaries and think beyond their job description. As the organization becomes more fluid, it is better able to tap into the skills, ideas, and knowledge of all employees. Employees feel more empowered to learn and contribute. Work experiences move to the positive end of the scale in terms of improved levels of satisfaction, commitment, and inspiration. This does not mean dispensing with defined roles and responsibilities or layers of management. These remain basic requirements: people need to know what is expected of them and how their efforts will be coordinated with others. But there is untapped potential for employees to take more leadership within their own roles and working relationships. Senior managers therefore must actively encourage others to do so.

Previous chapters described how senior managers enabled others to help move the organization towards a healthier ideal. The personal convictions of the executives at IBM, Teck Cominco's Trail Operations, and Trillium Health Centre set in motion what would become much wider discussions about the organization's values, vision and goals. These examples illustrate an inclusive approach to leadership, one that challenges others to be actively involved in shaping a better collective future. Inclusive leadership breaks through bureaucratic rigidities and the tendency these structures impose for employees to passively follow or react to edicts sent down from the executive suite. In the spirit of shared responsibility, employees, too, must seek out new ways to contribute, leverage the knowledge of others, and improve the way work gets done.

Who Are the Leaders?

I am challenging the conventional view of leadership that it is a few people at the apex of an organization who lead and employees who dutifully follow. This outmoded view reflects a twentieth-century model of bureaucracy – a top-down chain of command and boxed-in job descriptions. The successful twenty-first-century workplace has to move beyond bureaucracy to become flexible and flatter, agile and collaborative. Surely, this calls for a different approach to leadership. As a start, we should clarify where to draw the line between leaders and managers – or if there even needs to be a line. Reflect on your personal views in this regard. Do you view leadership as exclusive or inclusive? Do you assume that the CEO and other executive team members are the organization's leaders? Or do you believe that all employees can and should be encouraged to take leadership? In your organization, are the words *leader* and *leadership* used mainly to refer to the CEO and the entire executive team, or does it extend to middle managers? How and when do front-line supervisors show leadership? Are the leadership attributes required in that role clearly defined and well understood?

As you attempt to answer these questions, you may run into a basic dilemma. Business writing on leadership leaves the impression that all leaders are managers, but not all managers are leaders – a gap that needs closing. I frequently see this disconnect when middle managers are expected to participate in 'leadership development' sessions. But, in practice, decision-making that sets the organization's future direction – and impacts their roles – is done by the executive.

Growing emphasis by businesses on employee engagement has raised the expectation that all managers and supervisors need to be good at leading people. In twenty-first- century organizations, functional management positions require 'soft' people skills to inspire, develop, and retain staff. Increasingly, these activities are no longer something HR does through programs and policies, but rather are being built into the roles of managers. One sign of the diffusion of responsibility for people goals is the popular idea that managers should be coaches and mentors. And managers indeed are taking on these supportive roles. I hear more managers today than five years ago talking about wanting to inspire their staff, which is another way of saying they want to be great people leaders. Inspired front-line employees almost certainly will display leadership in their jobs and teams, which, of course, is a necessity in any organization aspiring to high performance.

The answer to the question 'Who are the leaders?' is 'everyone in your organization.' A good number of leadership experts would agree. For example, management thinker Henry Mintzberg challenges the exclusive view of leadership – the cult of the lone executive whose personal vision and determination guide the company to greatness. As Mintzberg argues: 'let's stop the dysfunctional separation of leadership from management. We all know that managers who don't lead are boring, dispiriting. Well, leaders who don't manage are distant, disconnected. Instead of isolating leadership, we need to diffuse it throughout the organization, into the ranks of managers and beyond. Anyone with an idea and some initiative can be a leader.'[1] I am not proposing a new model of leadership. Rather, I am reinforcing the importance of prominent themes in existing leadership models for building healthy organizations. Combing through the leadership literature, we can find nuggets of advice for anyone, regardless of their position in the organization, who wants to take initiative to shape a healthier and more productive work environment. This advice is summarized below into six attributes of inclusive leadership.

Widely Distributing Leadership Responsibility

The approach to leadership I am advocating also is referred to as 'distributed leadership.' In practice, distributed leadership involves a large number of employees in setting the direction of the organization. This is accomplished by breaking down hierarchical barriers and enabling people at the front lines of an organization to influence decisions that affect their clients, their work environment, and their jobs. Distributed leadership fosters collaboration to solve complex organizational problems, going beyond the traditional roles and lines of authority. If collaboration is a hallmark of a healthy organization, distributed leadership is the approach to direction setting, planning, and problem-solving that best fits.

Distributed leadership has been applied in schools. Its use has been prompted by dissatisfaction with the traditional principal-as-leader approach, where a single administrator is responsible for 'running' a school. A distributed approach focuses on how staff can take leadership for achieving learning and teaching goals. It recognizes that the problems of providing quality education have become so complex that the best solutions will be collectively generated from a holistic perspective. Another advantage of distributed leadership is succession, because it builds a broader base of leadership capabilities and interest among junior teachers in moving into administrative roles. This is achieved partly by creating recognition that the stresses of being a school principal can be reduced if leadership is shared.

For example, a study of thirty-eight government-funded secondary schools in New South Wales, Australia, found that schools using distributed leadership achieved exceptional educational outcomes, compared with those that used a traditional principal-leader approach.[2] Schools that distributed leadership to all teaching staff encouraged innovation in teaching and supported a school culture based on trust, mutual respect, sharing of authority, and collegiality. This study shows that responsibility does not rest on the shoulders of one person to drive a school's performance and its students' academic success. The solution is not simply adding more leaders, but a holistic and collaborative approach to thinking about learning and teaching.

Similar ideas have been tried in other industries. In health care, Trillium Health Centre adopted distributed leadership with considerable success. Trillium has been recognized by its peers as a leading example in Canada of a healthy, high-performing health care organization.[3] In the late 1990s the board and senior management team moved away from a command-and-control model of management and set out to fully engage all staff. Reaching this goal required encouraging all employees, physicians, and volunteers to make decisions and take ownership for them. Trillium strives to achieve healthy outcomes for its people in a work environment that nurtures innovation and health service excellence. To communicate this thinking, the organization adopted the concept of '1001 leaders,' which identified and publicly recognized people who showed leadership in their own area. Over the past decade Trillium has evolved. It continues to find effective ways to develop leadership in everyone, recognizing that the ability to positively impact the lives of patients lies solely in the hands of the people who work and volunteer in the organization.

Qualities of Inclusive Leaders

Leadership means taking action to achieve a shared vision of a vibrant workplace, knowing that this will benefit you and your co-workers, customers, and the larger community. The features of a vibrant workplace depend on both personal and organizational leadership. Leadership is not something separate or special, reserved for specific times and places. To emphasize an earlier point, we all can show leadership by how we go about our daily work and in our relationships with co-workers, direct reports, customers, and external stakeholders.

Inclusive leadership happens at the personal and organizational levels. As I have emphasized, there are many micro-level actions you personally can initiate, regardless of your position. Individuals in any position need to make a commitment to be guided by personal and organizational values, develop relationships based on mutual trust and respect, take initiative in their jobs, be responsible for learning and for teaching others, offer suggestions and ideas for now to do things better, engage in open and honest communication, support their co-workers or direct-reports, and recognize others' contributions.

At the organizational level, managers and professionals can ensure that the right support systems are in place. These are the effective people practices referred to in the healthy organization value chain in chapter 1. Professionals in HR, organization development, learning, health and safety, and related areas become change agents by crafting the policies, programs, resources, and systems that support employees to succeed in their jobs. To help to determine the potential effectiveness of people practices, you can use this question as a filter for assessing the merits of plans and decisions: how will it contribute to making the workplace more vibrant, strengthen the culture, and inspire the workforce?

Some people may read this and conclude that it is 'not them' to be this kind of leader. The good news is that leadership skills can be learned. Leaders are made not born. The qualities of leadership are not innate characteristics that individuals bring into the workplace as part of their personality or character. Leadership skills are 'soft' people and personal skills, not 'hard' technical skills. Leadership experts James Kouzes and Barry Posner observe that leaders motivate others to act on values and make visions a reality.[4] They also argue that 'leadership is everyone's business.' Everyone, regardless of their position or level of formal authority in an organization, must take personal responsibility for showing leadership within their sphere.

According to Kouzes and Posner, 'Leadership is about relationships, about credibility, and about what you do.'[5] The action verbs Kouzes and Posner use to describe the practices of exemplary leaders in all walks of life are 'model,' 'inspire,' 'challenge,' 'enable,' and 'encourage.' Leading by example is showing others the way forward. Inspiring

employees with a compelling visions and clear collective goals is what
motivates teams. Challenging old ways of thinking and doing is what
leads to innovative solutions that propel organizations into the future.
Actions that enable collaboration, knowledge-sharing learning, trust-
building, and higher performance are, in fact, showing leadership. In
more personal terms, leadership also means showing you care about
co-workers in heartfelt ways, recognizing their work, and celebrating
their successes.

Now let us apply these ideas directly to healthy organizations, following the inclusive approach I outlined above. Six qualities define the
kind of leadership that anyone can bring to their roles and relationships:
inspire yourself and others; be caring and connected; be trustworthy
and trusting; be action oriented; empower others; and be self-aware.
By cultivating these qualities, you will become a healthy organization
change agent.

1. *Inspirational.* Inspire yourself and encourage and support others to
   set and achieve higher goals for quality of work life and performance. Employees who are not in management should focus on what
   they can bring to their own role and to their team or work unit.
   Simple things – such as a positive attitude towards one's job and
   clients or customers, seeking out opportunities to improve teamwork, and strengthening the workplace community by volunteering in the local community – all contribute to the bigger goals of
   a healthy organization. Managers have more scope in this regard.
   Studies show that managers who use genuine inspiration to motivate their employees achieve significant change.

   Some call this 'transformational leadership.' Transformational
   leaders rally others around a higher purpose, a big vision, and
   higher moral and ethical goals. And they show they care about
   others' well-being. Barack Obama in his 2008 presidential election
   campaign passionately communicated a vision of a united America.
   His great success was the way he used that personal conviction to
   reach out to diverse audiences and make his 'Yes We Can' message
   about them, not about him. This style of leadership contrasts with a
   more instrumental, traditional style of leadership that emphasizes
   the effective management of employees so they get their jobs done,
   telling them what to do and motivating them with rewards and incentives.

2. *Caring and connected.* Whether as a manager or a co-worker, you

need to care about and be connected to those with whom you work. This attitude extends to appreciating others' contributions and viewpoints, providing honest and constructive feedback, and validating the capabilities they bring to the organization. Creating a sense of connection among employees fosters a workplace community. It also helps individuals to feel connected to the organization's mission.

Part of fostering connection is helping others to keep the bigger picture in view, so they see how they fit into it. People need to execute tasks, meet deadlines, and achieve operational goals. But when these nuts and bolts are the sole focus of your workday, the potential for meaningful and connected work experiences diminishes. Leaders keep the big picture in view and understand how their actions contribute to the workplace community and the organization's mission. They look beyond these basics, connecting people to the bigger purpose and encouraging learning and reflection as part of the process of task execution and goal achievement.

3. *Trustworthy and trusting.* Effective leadership requires a high level of trust. In high-trust relationships, managers rely on employees to do whatever is needed to meet customers' needs and to act ethically and honestly at all times. And employees trust managers. Knowing their views are respected, employees are going to offer new ideas, even if they are not well developed, and point out mistakes and errors as ways to learn and improve. Everyone is more willing to take risks that can lead to innovation in internal processes, services, or products.

   This leadership quality is healthy because performance, pride, and satisfaction are internally generated as part of work processes. Such a work environment is diametrically opposite to that of old-style bureaucracies, where everyone was risk averse and everything was done by the rules. We know that these traditional environments stifled initiative and creativity and sucked the meaning and humanity out of work for many people. Stephen M.R. Covey, in his book *The Speed of Trust*, asserts that 'Leadership is getting results in a way that inspires trust.'[6] This comment applies to managers and non-managers alike. The corollary is that leadership is about inspiring others to pursue with you outstanding results because they trust you and everyone else in the organization.

4. *Action-oriented.* Talking about visions, values, and commitment is a starting point. The result is a common language that enables

a shared direction and change objectives. But this talk must lead quickly to action, or it becomes a waste of time. As leadership expert Michael Fullan puts it: 'The litmus test of all leadership is whether it mobilizes people's commitment to putting their energy into actions designed to improve things. It is individual commitment, but it is above all collective mobilization.'[7] Fullan warns that collective action will not have sustained results unless the actors pursue external goals with an internal, or personal, sense of moral purpose. The leadership mindset required in an environment of constant change, according to Fullan, is really an ongoing process of organizational development and performance enhancement. In his view, leading involves understanding the change process, fostering in others a moral purpose, making sense of the whole, creating and sharing knowledge, and, above all, building relationships. Again, it is not the goal that matters as much as the process for taking action to reach that goal together.

5. *Empowering*. Employee empowerment and autonomy have been promoted by management experts for decades and have taken on a tired ring. Yet people do want a say in their jobs and workplaces – regardless of the label placed on it. So a key ingredient of effective leadership is enabling others, especially your direct reports if you are a manager, to be actively involved in decision-making and, as Trillium advocates, taking ownership for their implementation.

   Margaret Wheatley, a respected authority on leadership, offers a view of leadership that taps into our deep-seated personal need to shape our own life and not be controlled.[8] For managers, this way of thinking opens up opportunities to harness people's capacity to figure out ways to do things better. As Wheatley puts it, this is not optional for today's leaders: 'We ignore people's need to participate at our own peril. If they're involved, they will create a future that has them in it, that they'll work to make happen. We won't have to engage in the impossible and exhausting tasks of "selling" them on the solution, getting them to "enroll," or figuring out the incentives that might bribe them into compliant behaviors.'[9] The guiding principle here is that if people create something, they will support it. That neatly expresses what a healthy organization is all about.

6. *Self-aware*. At a personal level, leadership also requires you to apply to yourself the values and principles of a healthy work environment and behaviours– and to be conscious of how and when you do so. It is important to take the time, which usually is not long, to

reflect on how your intended actions will affect others and contribute to larger goals, beyond getting the task at hand done. Strong leaders are self-aware. This is a major step towards being aware of others' needs, interests, and emotional experiences in the workplace. And it is why some workplace health promotion experts define a healthy workplace as encompassing physical, mental, and emotional dimensions of well-being.

As Daniel Goleman points out in his influential book, *Emotional Intelligence*: 'imagine the benefits for work of being skilled in the basic emotional competences – being attuned to the feelings of those we deal with, being able to handle disagreements so they do not escalate, having the ability to get into flow states [being totally absorbed in the task at hand] while doing our work.'[10] If managers are expected to model healthy behaviours, they need to have an adequate level of self-awareness about those behaviours in the first place. So managers need to hold a mirror up to themselves and ask: do I personally make myself accountable for the behaviours I expect from others?

Let these six qualities guide your roles and relationships in the workplace. After all, leadership comes down to behaviour and the conviction and skills needed to put it into practice. Learning to lead the way to a healthier organization involves cultivating behaviours consistent with these six leadership qualities. It also means practising the values of the organization and showing others how its vision for its customers, employees, and society is being achieved – even if by small steps. The next section provides examples of leadership behaviours that can be the basis for training programs aimed at developing broadly based leadership capabilities across an organization.

Leading with People Skills

Many workplaces suffer negative consequences when managers regularly say one thing and do another – or do nothing at all to follow up on a commitment. The wider the gap between what managers say and do, the more dysfunctional a workplace can become. Employees retreat into the narrowest confines of their jobs and grow cynical when senior managers fail to meet the behavioural standards set for all employees through corporate values, codes of ethical conduct, and vision statements. The workplace will lack a sense of common purpose if managers do not put words into action, and employees' sense of personal meaning in work will be diminished, along with their energy to do an excellent job.

Most managers know these facts – at least intuitively. In discussions with middle managers, the point often is made that employees interact not with organizations, but with their immediate supervisor and unit or department managers. As one manager put it, 'we are the face of the organization for the employee.' How individual managers and supervisors behave in their relationships with employees is the most concrete expression of an organization's character. For this reason, people skills are the critical ingredients of effective leadership in a healthy organization.

Gaps in People Skills

The importance of managers' people skills cannot be underestimated for establishing vibrant work environments and inspiring employees. For example, lots of employers now talk about the total rewards offered employees as defining the company's employee 'value proposition.' An employee value proposition describes the organization's unique appeal to talented employees. It includes tangible rewards, such as pay, benefits, and perks. Equally important are the intangible rewards. These include a sense of personal accomplishment, being challenged to develop abilities and having opportunities to advance in a career, feeling connected with the team, and knowing that contributions are truly valued.

Employees' experiences of these intangible rewards are central to the vibrant workplace vision summarized in chapter 3. Supervisors play an important role in this regard. For example, supervisors can help employees to see their job in the bigger picture of the department's and organization's goals, enable the pursuit of career development goals, foster team spirit, provide constructive feedback, and recognize work well done. I often hear employees and executives complain that if only supervisors and middle managers had these people skills, the organization would be a better place to work. Evidence from employers, employees, and supervisors themselves backs up this observation.[11]

Part of the problem is that supervisors are recruited more often on the basis of technical proficiencies than on people skills. Not enough is being done to rectify this deficiency. As evidence of this, the Rethinking Work survey found that only 44 per cent of a representative sample of Canadian employers said they emphasized people skills when hiring or promoting individuals to front-line supervisor positions. Close to 40 per cent of employers had given no training in people skills to their managers and supervisors in the year prior to the survey. Only about one in four had provided such training to more than three-quarters of managers and supervisors.

From an employee's perspective, investments in people skills training for managers is high priority. For example, the Rethinking Work survey of Canadian employees asked respondents 'what type of training do you feel that managers in your organization need most, in order for them to be the best leaders they can be?' In response, employees emphasized interpersonal relations and communication, including listening skills. In the same survey, supervisors were asked to list what support, resources, or training they needed to be effective in their role. In addition to more training in people skills and leadership, time to be a people leader also was high on the list of needs. A good number of supervisors said they do not have enough time to communicate with their staff or to coach and mentor them. As they also pointed out, the job of 'managing people' is a low priority in their organization.

This evidence actually provides grounds for optimism. Yes, there are gaps in supervisors' people skills. But it also seems there is recognition of this lack among supervisors themselves and a readiness to do something about it. However, supervisors often face too many demands and a shortage of time, or an organizational culture that does not value good people leadership. But important as supervisors are in fostering a vibrant workplace, senior managers set the tone and expectations for people practices. Without positive role models at the top, even the most committed supervisor will have limited potential to rally her or his team around healthy organization goals.

Follow-Through on People Commitments

The test for employees is senior management's consistent and real follow-through on its commitments. This adds substance to corporate rhetoric about being an employer of choice, socially responsible, and environmentally friendly. On paper, many large and medium-sized organizations have perfectly adequate human resource policies, ethics, and environmental and community codes of conduct. An organization's policies are only as good as its practices, so that is what we need to look at. That is where the will of senior managers to ensure effective implementation values, ethics, and HR policies becomes critical. For example:

- Learning and development programs are common now, so we need clear evidence that the learning process is incorporated into people's jobs. This is the hallmark of a learning culture. Google has spectacular benefits, such as free gourmet cafeterias, at its headquarters. But the company's efforts to nurture employees extend far beyond such perks. All Google engineers spend 20 per cent of their time thinking up new ideas that will benefit the company, which takes them outside their job and into other areas of the business. In addition to the satisfaction that comes from developing new marketable ideas, this presents a huge opportunity for personal and career growth.
- Ethical standards and codes of conduct are displayed on most corporate websites these days. You need to find out how rooted these standards are in everyday practices, by asking questions such as: What are the guideposts that the executive team uses in a difficult situation? What is a recent difficult situation that tested these values? Environics Communications illustrates this point. The Toronto-based marketing and communications firm has turned down new business that is inconsistent with its strong ethical standards – no matter how much the opportunity may have been worth.
- Industry leader Genentech is a San Francisco-based biotechnology firm. The company is renowned for its commitment to innovative drugs that benefit patients. One executive also described it as having a 'culture of caring for employees.' Senior managers understand that a non-hierarchical, caring culture with a strong spirit of team work is a huge ingredient in the company's success. It is continually seeking employee input, listening to their suggestions, and understanding their needs. One of the sure signs that employees are truly valued is that the company has no vice-president of human resources. Instead, each of the seven members of its executive team has responsibility for people leadership.
- Respect is a cornerstone of a healthy, high-performing workplace. Many healthy organizations have a corporate philosophy built around respect for employees' contributions as a driver of performance. For example, Coastal Pacific Xpress (CPX) distinguishes itself in the trucking industry by its employee-first philosophy, which rests on the basic principle of treating its drivers with respect. Evidence of this philosophy can be found in stories about customers the western Canadian company 'fired' (as CPX puts it) because they were disrespectful and abusive towards staff.

These companies, which have been recognized by the Great Place to Work Institute in its annual lists of outstanding workplaces, demonstrate how senior managers show the kind of leadership that puts people first. The results are concrete practices that signal to employees – as well as to shareholders, customers, and society – that a strong culture is critical for business success. But these examples do not reveal how such decisions and actions were taken. Clearly, the decisions and practices outlined above would depend on open communication during the development, implementation, and evaluation phases. They also benefited from the input of employees. Once the decisions to act were made, they had to be applied in an even-handed manner. It is at this more basic level of connecting with employees that good leadership by managers, especially executives, is either strengthened or weakened.

Setting the Tone

How, then, can senior management set the tone for an inclusive approach to leadership? Realistically, senior managers cannot expect line managers, supervisors, and employees to be inspired by a vision that does not include them. It falls to senior managers to signal to others in the organization that it is through their dedicated efforts that the mission will be achieved. Senior managers must regularly and consistently communicate the importance of the organization's people to its success, using language that resonates down to the front lines.

Organizations that do better than their peers have created values-based cultures in which managers at all levels connect to employees' sense of purpose. That purpose has to be expressed in the quality of services or products today and the potential for even higher quality in future. Employees are valued and supported because they are the key to service excellence. So these high-performing organizations have a clear vision of the kind of workforce and workplace they are striving to create and maintain.

Consider an example from the public sector. In my work with governments across Canada, I have come across subtle but quite different ways of expressing public service values and visions. Most adequately describe how the public service will strive to meet the needs of citizens. Just as private sector companies talk about putting customers first, governments increasingly have tried over the past decade or more to improve the delivery of public services – in other words, putting citizens first. But it is rare to see the employees providing those services mentioned in the visions or values.

The province of Alberta stands apart from other governments in this regard, speaking directly to its public servants. The Alberta vision for public service is 'Alberta's Public Service ... Proudly working together to build a stronger province for current and future generations.' What speaks to employees is the sense of collective pride. And the Alberta definition of the public service value of respect (a common value within public services) is 'We foster an environment in which each individual is valued and heard.' Again, for employees the emphasis that matters is knowing their contributions are valued and that they have a voice in this large organization.

My point is that Alberta's public service vision and values speak directly to the individual employee, certainly more so than general statements about providing more innovative, cost-effective services and being responsive to citizens' needs. The lesson is that these statements need to reach out to employees. The language used must not only set the tone for people leadership across the organization, but also put in motion accountability. In the case of Alberta, regular employee surveys track progress on these and other ingredients of an engaged public service. Senior managers are held accountable for ensuring that there is progress by tying some of their annual performance bonuses to progress on these people goals. And supervisory training includes the soft skills required to foster the pride, teamwork, respect, and input espoused in the vision and values.

Focusing on Leadership Behaviours

The six qualities of inclusive leadership described above offer an effective approach to workplace roles and relationships. Theses guidelines need to be fleshed out with specific behaviours relevant to your organization's situation. Once you have identified behaviours, training and development programs can be adapted to equip managers, supervisors, and employees with the skills needed to put the behaviours into practice.

I will provide two examples of how organizations used their values or guiding principles to develop specific behaviours relevant to managers and employees, then used these behaviours as the basis for skill development, a process that also reinforced the values as collective guideposts of behaviour. The first example is Teck Cominco's Trail Operations in western Canada. Senior managers there took their guiding principles, described in chapter 4, and created specific behaviours for each principle. The second example is the City of London, a municipality of some 350,000 inhabitants located in southwestern Ontario, Canada. The city used a managers' leadership development program and an employee appreciation week to collect input on what these groups saw as the behaviours required to live the organization's values. My intent is not to recommend the specific behaviours developed by these two organizations. Rather, I want to illustrate different ways that any organization can involve managers and employees in discussions about how to lead by example.

Living the Guiding Principles

In chapter 4, I described how the senior management team at Teck Cominco's Trail Operations created a set of guiding principles. The goal was to develop clear behavioural guides that the management team would commit to following and that would lead the rest of the organization to foster a more positive and productive work environment. This initiative was not a defensive reaction to problems. In fact, the Trail smelter had achieved record productivity, profits and safety levels. But the leadership team, under the guidance of a new general manager and including several new members from outside the organization, felt it could achieve even higher levels of performance and at the same time improve working conditions – as long as everyone was part of the process.

Through a facilitated discussion of revised values, the senior managers crafted five guiding principles that expressed what they individually and collectively believed could help to guide the organization into the future. Each manager then had the opportunity to reflect on the principles. They provided descriptions of the behaviours they felt were essential to actually 'live' by the principle every day in the workplace. In a follow-up facilitated discussion, the behaviours for each guiding principle were reviewed and consolidated into the statement presented in figure 5.1.

Reading through these behaviours, note that the descriptions are simply stated. For example: no hidden agendas; listen first, then speak; honestly give and accept praise; and set up others to succeed. Because the goal was to make the guidelines useable throughout the facility, all workers must be able to relate to these behaviours. The company has a lengthy involvement in the community as the area's largest employer and has a commitment to environmental sustainability. Community and environmental dimensions of the guiding principles link internal and external behaviours. Such is not always the case, as many compa-

Figure 5.1 Teck Cominco's Trail Operations: examples of behaviours showing how we live by the guiding principles

---

We act with *integrity*, treating all with *dignity*, *fairness*, and *respect*.
- Always respect others' opinions and viewpoints.
- Avoid negative, behind-the-back comments or gossip about others.
- Speak to a person directly if you have concerns about his or her behaviour.
- Have courageous conversations about performance (others and your own).
- No hidden agendas.
- Listen first, and then speak.
- Don't jump to conclusions.
- Be courteous. Use language you would use at home with your family.
- Be forthright and honest with everyone, regardless of their position.
- Show respect for others by showing up for meetings on time and prepared.
- Try to make tough decisions so they are 'win-win.'
- Be honest about mistakes, learn from them, and improve.
- Expect honest feedback from others.
- Act ethically and honestly with business partners, even if you don't think they are doing the same.

We commit to everyone going home *safe* and *healthy* every day.
- Always take time to do your work safely.
- Intervene immediately if you witness an unsafe act or situation.
- Continually look for ways to reduce risks in your job.
- Consciously include safety and health leadership and management in evaluation of direct reports.
- Directly communicate care and concern when witnessing potentially harmful acts or situations.
- Reinforce learning from each other's errors.
- Positively recognize successes.
- Reinforce the idea that every incident is preventable.
- Make safety part of as many discussions as possible.
- Remind people about this principle if they are not following it.
- Follow up on incidents directly with the people involved.
- Talk about safety with each employee at least twice a year.

We take *personal responsibility* for our actions and results.
- Avoid rationalizing, explaining away, or accepting poor results.

- Deliver on what you say you are going to do. Live up to your commitments.
- Stay focused and use available resources to overcome barriers.
- Don't give up ... find creative solutions to problems.
- Honestly give and accept praise.
- Pursue excellence where it really matters.
- Don't be afraid to ask for help to get the job done.
- Own up to errors or misunderstandings without rationalizing.
- Don't blame others when things get tough.
- If you see something wrong, stop and address it.
- When holding others accountable, first make sure they have been empowered to act.

We *support* each other to achieve our fullest potential.
- Set others up to succeed.
- Don't compete with peers and co-workers.
- Focus on building people's confidence by acknowledging their contributions, strengths, and successes.
- Team and company results are more important than your personal accomplishments.
- Make sure that employees have adequate resources and time to do their jobs.
- Think beyond your team or department. Look for opportunities to grow the greater good.
- Have an open-door policy with direct-reports.
- Actively offer assistance and advice to employees.
- Accept assistance or advice when needed.
- Hold regular meetings with your managers to review opportunities for improvement.
- Always look for opportunities to develop individuals' capabilities.

We *act responsibly* to support a sustainable future for the *communities* and *environment* in which we operate.
- Consider potential impacts on the community and environment when making decisions.
- Understand through ongoing dialogue how the Trail community perceives us and our impact on them.
- Be role models for environmental sustainability and stewardship.
- Personally act to minimize waste and pollution.

- Be a good neighbour. Be good citizens.
- Be proactive and do what's right.
- Personally participate in and support worthy community programs and events.
- Take time to attend community meetings to identify and understand others' perceptions of us.
- Be transparent about community donations and activities.
- Challenge yourself and others to improve the status quo.
- Take a longer-term outlook on business decisions.

---

nies treat environmental and CSR issues as separate from their internal working relationships. One of the behaviours aptly sums up what is needed on both fronts: 'Be a good neighbour. Be good citizens.'

To make these behaviours as concrete as possible, the senior managers also offered one or two personal stories about how they had recently used each of the guiding principles. Some of these stories are presented in figure 5.2. You can see their usefulness as a communication tool in discussions of the guiding principles with managers, supervisors, and staff. Through telling these stories, senior managers modelled how other managers could positively reinforce the guiding principles by telling their own stories and encouraging their team members to do the same.

Figure 5.2 Teck Cominco's Trail Operations: senior managers' stories about living the guiding principles

---

We act with *integrity*, treating all with *dignity*, *fairness*, and *respect*.
- 'At recent bonus reviews, a reference was made to some employees who were close to retirement as 'floaters.' I referred to our guiding principle of respect and suggested we not talk about older employees this way.'

We commit to everyone going home *safe* and *healthy* every day.
- 'I observed workers working on a suspended load while touring the WHS worksite. Three levels of supervision and [a] safety coordinator were present. Initially I felt that if this was a safety issue one of the supervisors or the safety coordinator would speak up, as they are all more experienced with this type of field work. On second thought, I quickly concluded that my level of experience was irrelevant. I started

walking over to talk to the workers. Before I opened my mouth they recognized the issue, stopped work, lowered the load onto the ground then resumed work.'

We take *personal responsibility* for our actions and results.
- 'I was recently overloaded with action items and did not have enough time to complete them. As a result, one item that I had committed to doing for an employee in my group was not done in the expected time and I knew I would not be able to get it done. I met with the employee and told him my situation, saying that it was my fault to commit I could get it done that quickly. He accepted and appreciated the communication and we agreed to a new date (that I better deliver on!).'

We *support* each other to achieve our fullest potential.
- 'Rather than judging and labelling some employees, I have been focusing more on trying to find ways to make them more successful by training, feedback, and different job opportunities.'

We *act responsibly* to support a sustainable future for the *communities* and *environment* in which we operate.
- 'White sturgeon living in the Columbia River have been listed as an endangered species. We have decided to voluntarily provide resources including funding and employee time to the white sturgeon recovery effort. We do this because our operations are located on or near the Columbia River and we benefit greatly from the river. Therefore we feel it is appropriate to put some energy into taking care of the river.'

Storytelling is a powerful way to sustain a culture. It is used by many companies on the best workplaces lists created by the Great Place to Work Institute. Whether it is telling new hires about the culture or recognizing at a weekly team meeting how an employee used one of the values to get through a difficult situation, stories are timely reminders of how organizational life ought to be conducted.

Leadership to Build Supportive Workplaces

Several years ago, the City of London, Ontario, embarked on a journey to strengthen the organization's culture by making it more supportive and values-based. As in Teck Cominco's Trail Operations, there was nothing 'broken' at the city administration. Instead, the challenge was getting managers, supervisors, and employees to do things a bit differently, at least enough to make a real difference in work experiences and service quality. Over time, these improvements also would enhance the city's reputation as an employer of choice.

The City of London's vision is to 'inspire pride and confidence in every Londoner.' In fact, 'inspire' was a theme that ran through most of the city's strategy for public service. Talking about inspiring Londoners in their city raised the obvious question: how can employees also be inspired to deliver even higher-quality public services? Part of the answer lay in finding ways to live the city's two corporate values: individual responsibility and collective accountability. These values are about as compact and as basic as an organization can get in defining its values. But they worked for the city. Rather than creating a longer list of values with descriptions, the city opted to use the values as broad guidelines for creating a more supportive workplace. In fact, this became a strategic priority.

A Supportive Workplace Committee, consisting of managers, led a variety of initiatives to implement this strategic goal. Most important, it consulted widely with employees and managers about the ingredients of a supportive workplace and the behaviours that were required to create and sustain this sort of culture (their term). Basically, everyone in the organization had an opportunity to contribute to these discussions. Two main sources of input were a leadership development program for managers, run in partnership with the University of Western Ontario's Ivey School of Business, and round-table consultations with employees and managers during an employee appreciation week. These consultations first asked people to identify the key dimensions of a supportive workplace. Then the discussions turned to specific behaviours consistent with each of the corporate values that contribute to a specific dimension of a supportive workplace.

I participated in the employee appreciation week consultations and heard the same words being used repeatedly to describe what employees and managers wanted in their jobs and workplaces. Prominent themes in the discussions of supportive workplace behaviours were pride, trust, and 'standing together' – which refers to a common purpose achieved through teamwork and a sense of belonging. Sifting through the mountains of transcripts from these consultations, the Supportive Workplace Committee connected supportive workplace dimensions, corporate values, and behaviours. Figure 5.3 lists some of the

Figure 5.3 Examples of leadership behaviours to build a more supportive workplace and live the values, based on City of London consultations

Supportive workplace dimensions	Examples of how to live the corporate values	
	Individual responsibility	Collective accountability
Honest communication	Practise open, honest, clear, meaningful, timely, consistent, respectful, two-way communication with all employees.	Communicate division and department goals and direction across the organization.
Support each other	Follow through with your commitments to employees.	Actively encourage collaborative workplace relationships in which people support each other to achieve division and department goals.
Fairness	Have a positive and welcoming attitude towards the diverse experiences, backgrounds, and personal characteristics of your employees.	Ensure that the processes for recruitment, promotion, job assignments, and training opportunities are fair and equitable across the organization.
Work/life balance	Model balance in your own work life.	Understand employees' work/life balance needs and support them to achieve balance.
Recognize and celebrate contributions	Help each employee see how their job contributes to the City's Mission and Vision.	Share stories about individual and team successes within and across departments.
Fun environment	Encourage and support actions by employees to socialize and have fun together.	Hold regular events that celebrate people's contributions, strengthen the 'standing together' feeling – and that are fun!
Opportunities for training and development	Openly and regularly share your knowledge, expertise and ideas with others.	Facilitate access to appropriate training and development for each employee in ways that best meet their job and career goals.
Freedom and empowerment	Trust employees to do their job and provide them the resources they need to succeed.	Expect each employee to decide how to 'do the right thing' to achieve department and corporate goals.

Accessible management	Be approachable and available for employees to talk with you about their ideas, concerns and suggestions.	All managers and supervisors are visible and accessible to front-line employees.
Pride	Care about your work and take ownership for doing the best you can to serve the citizens of London.	Expect other employees to be ready, able and motivated to do their job to the best of their ability.
Respectful relationships	Personally show that you value each employee's input and job contributions.	In every interaction, treat others how you would like to be treated.

behaviours that enable supervisors and managers to create and maintain a more supportive workplace. The figure also links these behaviours to the corporate values of individual responsibility and collective accountability.

The city took a sequenced approach to leadership development. The intent was to incorporate leadership behaviours, like those listed in figure 5.3, into the system used to annually evaluate the performance of individual managers. Over time, the behaviours would also be reinforced in policies and practices, including revised criteria for recruiting people into supervisory positions. In other words, the leadership behaviours in figure 5.3 are meant to be not prescriptive but developmental. More than anything, they are an invitation to further reflections and conversations about how managers, individually and as a collective, can live the values as they build supportive workplaces.

Leading Change

To recap, leadership in a healthy organization is a shared responsibility. Everyone has a role to play. While senior management support and actions are major enablers of progress, the quest for a healthier organization must provide opportunities for all employees to become involved in that process. We have seen how healthy organizations approach leadership in inclusive ways, empowering employees down to the front lines to take ownership of work environment improvements. Managers and supervisors set the tone and direction for this involvement to happen. Reflecting on how Teck Cominco's Trail Operations and the City of London used guiding principles and values to define behaviours – starting with leadership behaviours – you can find opportunities in your organization for managers to encourage others to lead.

As Michael Fullan reminds us, leadership is all about bringing people together to achieve purposeful change. But here is the catch: someone has to take the initiative. That is why leadership is one of the basic building blocks of a healthy organization. Otherwise, an organization is beset with inertia, suspended in a state of limbo where any talk of creating a more vibrant workplace and improving employee experiences remains just that – talk. To avoid this inertia trap, change agents at all levels of an organization must understand the change process itself. This will equip them to play the most constructive role possible, working with others to implement improvements. Chapter 6 takes a close look at the dynamics of change involved in creating healthier organizations.

6 Healthy Change

Several years ago, the Canadian government's department of health asked me to write a report on healthy workplace change strategies. I discovered just how little tactical information is available on the actual processes for successfully introducing changes leading towards healthier workplaces.[1] In the five years since writing the report for Health Canada, I have observed dozens of organizations in different industries and countries develop healthy workplace strategies. Each strategy, in its own way, sought to forge stronger people – performance links. Yet despite careful planning, results often were disappointing. Somehow, the strategy could not get traction.

These experiences gave me a better understanding about *how* to bring about healthy change. This chapter offers practical lessons from a wide range of organizations that are in the midst of creating more vibrant workplaces and positive cultures. What I do not offer is a step-by-step guide. Organizational change is too contextualized and complex to follow a straightforward, project-management, one-size-fits-all approach.

A relatively small number of organizations have achieved remarkable overall health. Indeed, these companies have been recognized for this achievement on lists of best workplaces, best employers, best-run and most admired businesses, and most environmentally and socially responsible corporations. While much can be learned from this top tier, their so-called best practices are not easily copied. So this chapter mainly is directed at the large middle group of organizations that are neither dangerously unhealthy nor exceptionally healthy in terms of the vibrancy of their workplaces, the resonance of their culture, or the level of inspiration experienced by their employees. Mostly, my examples are very good organizations striving to become truly excellent. Their journeys provide tips that you can use to help to seize opportunities, navigate twists and turns, avoid pitfalls, and make progress on your healthy organization journey.

There are many theories of organizational change. The one that I find most helpful for understanding healthy change is proposed by Richard Beckhard, a pioneer in the field of organization development (OD).[2] OD practitioners plan and implement system-wide changes in an organization's processes. They often focus on how people work together and with customers and community stakeholders. Beckhard suggests that it is possible to design change to improve organizational health, as long as the focus is on the change process as well as the change goals. The usefulness of an OD approach to healthy change has been reinforced through my work with managers and employees. As we will see in the examples below, many types of change can be designed to strengthen the organization's capacity to collaborate, learn, innovate, adapt, and live its values.

Watching many workplaces advance towards their vision of a healthy organization, I have taken away five basic lessons, which this chapter describes:

1. Get your organization on its own healthy organization trajectory that fits its needs, strategy and unique circumstances.
2. Most organizational change can be designed as a healthy experience for those involved and for other stakeholders.
3. Consistent with the idea of inclusive leadership, find ways to personally influence healthy trajectories and processes.
4. A healthy change process will provide opportunities to put in place two healthy organization building blocks: inclusive leadership and a positive culture.
5. Five principles can guide action: understand your organization's readiness to change; align structure and culture; link people initiatives to the business strategy; widen the circle of involvement; and make time for learning and innovation.

Getting on a Healthy Change Trajectory

There is no standard recipe for creating a healthy organization. Rather, your challenge is to co-create with others in your workplace the most suitable way to connect employee well-being, working conditions, and performance. A customized approach to the changes needed must be tailored to the unique circumstances, culture, and needs of your organization. This requires creatively mapping out an appropriate healthy change trajectory and taking steps to get on it.

Focusing on the Journey

Becoming a healthy organization is more of a journey than a destination. Yes, the 'what' is important, but so, too, is the 'how.' Indeed, you need to set specific goals for the short, medium, and long terms. Yet, as we have seen, the attributes of a vibrant workplace and positive culture emerge and take root over time. Thus, each organization will be at a different point along a healthy organization trajectory, looking for opportunities to take the next step. What healthy organizations have in common is a commitment by employees and managers to achieve optimal results for all stakeholders. Everyone understands that results depend most of all on a positive work environment that supports employees to thrive.

Consider the following examples of organizations in which change agents are making concerted efforts to move down a healthy trajectory. These first-hand examples show that different paths can lead towards similar well-being and performance goals.

- A telecommunications company launched a new customer service strategy in its six call centres. The call centre that went furthest to implement supportive coaching and team-based learning achieved the highest customer service performance ratings, lowest turnover, and highest employee satisfaction. Employees at this centre experienced less stress in their jobs because they had more autonomy to meet customer needs and more support from co-workers to get the information required to resolve customer problems. This approach to teamwork was encouraged by the regional vice-president, whose motto was 'do what ever you can to meet customers' needs, just don't give away the store!'
- Anticipating a wave of retirements, a city administration developed a detailed HR plan. But this was not enough to renew management ranks. Rising workloads, overly bureaucratic reporting structures, and difficulty in setting priorities had taken the fun out of work. Promising employees and supervisors turned down promotions

to avoid high levels of stress and burnout. After wide discussion, there was collective realization that the solution lay in more flexible career paths, giving employees and front-line supervisors authority and accountability for decisions, and a more supportive culture.

• A logistics company measured its performance by how long it took to pick up, ship, sort, and deliver a package. Work was fast paced. Consultations with employees identified stress and work/life balance as major concerns. Leadership training was revised to help managers address these issues. The director of health and safety saw an opportunity and championed a pilot project that added to the corporate report card organizational health measures, such as lost-time injury, short-term disability, turnover, and overtime utilization. These metrics caught the attention of operations managers because they saw how healthy work environments affected the number of workers available on any given shift.

Employees and managers in each of these organizations took decisive steps towards healthy organization goals. Keeping up momentum requires putting firmly in place two of the healthy organization building blocks we discussed earlier: a positive culture and inclusive leadership.

The Role of Culture and Leadership

The culture building block of a healthy organization supports ethically responsible behaviours, including how people should be treated. The same values also offer guideposts for any type of change in response to volatile business conditions. The recent global economic crisis pushed employers into uncharted waters with few navigational aids. Trico Homes, as we saw in chapter 1, relied on its five core values to find a way to survive the collapse of the housing market in 2008.

Some companies also responded to previous market shocks in healthy and sustainable ways. In the aftermath of the 9/11 terrorist attacks on the World Trade Center, businesses providing or reliant on air transportation were especially hard-hit and nobody knew at the time what the outcome would be. Two major companies directly affected – FedEx and Four Seasons Hotels – approached these tough business decisions guided by their core values. FedEx's philosophy of 'people, service, profit' has shaped its character, one that includes generosity, caring, and helping others. The company's 'no layoff philosophy' kicked into gear. While people were reassigned immediately after 9/11, nobody was let go. Similarly at Four Seasons, the hardest-hit resorts reassigned staff to redecorate the premises instead of laying them off. As CEO Isadore Sharp observed, the test of a culture and its values is not what it is like in good times, but what it is like in tough times.

Examples of healthy change reveal that what is needed is not better change management – an overly popular concept among managers – but change leadership from many groups and individuals. Healthy change requires considerable effort by numerous and diverse champions. Change agents need to till the ground, providing fertile conditions for new ways of thinking and acting to take root and eventually flourish. Improvements become a shared responsibility – what I described in the last chapter as 'inclusive leadership.'

If you have a personal commitment to a healthier workplace, then you are an agent or champion of healthy change. As such, you should always be on the lookout for the language, opportunities, and allies to help make this happen. You likely will have a personal vision of a healthy organization or workplace. You probably do not accept the status quo but, at the same time, you understand that positioning change depends a great deal on timing and organizational politics. You may even describe your approach as 'change by stealth.' This is a term one champion used in a healthy workplace strategy workshop, because he moved one opportunistic step at a time, without the benefit of an official healthy workplace strategy. I certainly have seen change agents quit their job in frustration. But in my experience, most people who truly believe in the importance of healthy organizations remain tireless advocates and influencers of change.

Groups also can be powerful engines of change, diagnosing workplace needs and proposing action plans. Groups can troubleshoot and solve problems that fall outside the scope, mandate, or resources of existing organizational arrangements. For example, a task force, committee, or project group can break through red tape, bridge functional areas, and do end runs around resistant managers. Organizational change experts recommend that groups leading change need a clear purpose, a design that fits this purpose, links to other parts of the organization, and a group culture that supports risk-taking and learning.[3] Change team leaders should coach team members to focus simultaneously on performance and culture. The goal of a change team is not to 'manage' a new project but to stimulate organizational development and innovation through the actions of others.

Let us take the case of a new wellness committee in a large police services organization. Members spent several day-long sessions fleshing out goals and timelines. What really energized committee members was a discussion of the benefits each of them wanted to see result from committee efforts. It also helped that senior management left it to the committee to come up with its own definition of 'wellness.' The committee put its own stamp on wellness by identifying five organizational benefits (reduced costs, team effectiveness, productivity, retention, and morale) and five individual benefits (satisfaction, engagement, individual effectiveness, personal health, and work/life balance) that its wellness-related actions should achieve. By communicating these wellness benefits to co-workers, the committee encouraged others to think more about organizational health goals rather than just individual wellness.

Five Principles for Healthy Change

My approach to healthy change can be summarized in five broad principles, a synthesis of my practical experience filtered through relevant research evidence. They highlight the issues that change agents will need to consider as they move from thinking to action:

1. Understand your organization's readiness to change.
2. Align structure and culture.
3. Link people initiatives to the business strategy.
4. Widen the circle of involvement.
5. Make time for learning and innovation.

   I launch this discussion by providing a change readiness assessment tool that can be adapted for use in your organization. It is intended to stimulate thinking and discussion among change agents about the best current opportunities to move forward, enablers of success, and barriers that will need to be addressed.

   I then use case studies of organizations that I have worked with as a consultant to illustrate principles 2 through 5. Actually, you can see most if not all of the four principles illustrated in each case. The principles are intended as guideposts for individual change agents, from executives to front-line employees. They also are useful discussion points for committees or working groups charged with designing and implementing a quality of work life, performance improvement, or healthy workplace initiative.

Understanding Change Readiness

A basic insight from the field of health promotion is the importance of a person's readiness to make changes in their health-related attitudes and behaviours. A person's readiness to change determines what will be realistic goals and timelines for them – and whether they will make any progress at all. Readiness assesses past actions, knowledge and awareness about change benefits, and the motivation to adopt new lifestyle practices.

Organizations also can be assessed for their readiness to change in a healthy direction. Use the basic model of a healthy organization presented in chapter 1 to develop a vision that you would like to see your organization aspire to achieve. Use language in the vision that suits the character of your organization (e.g., healthy organization, healthy workplace, employer of choice, inspiring workplace).

Now use that 'draft' vision (at some point you will need to validate it with co-workers) to assess your organization on the change readiness continuum using the twenty-five criteria listed in figure 6.1, as applicable. Not all criteria may apply, so you will need to adapt the assessment tool to fit your circumstances. Enter a check mark in the appropriate box to indicate if each of the organizational characteristics listed in figure 6.1 fits one of these criteria:

- A current or potential source of resistance to introducing changes to realize your healthy organization vision.
- A source of inertia created by the weight of tradition and/or indifference that will have to be overcome.
- Ready to be tapped as actual or potential sources of support for healthy workplace change.
- Already generating momentum for healthy improvements in the workplace environment, the culture, or organizational processes and systems.

If you checked either the 'Resistance' or the 'Inertia' boxes, think about what you can do to move this factor to either 'Readiness' or 'Momentum.' Use the assessment tool in a group or committee that has a mandate to implement change, discussing the results as a prelude to identifying a change process and setting change goals. This is a diagnostic tool, not a test – there are no 'right' answers. This type of assessment should be one of the initial steps in planning a healthy workplace intervention.

Figure 6.1 Healthy organization change readiness assessment

Organizational characteristics	Resistance	Inertia	Readiness	Momentum
1. Organization's values				
2. Organization's vision statement				
3. Organization's mission statement				
4. Organization's strategic plan				
5. Organization's dominant culture				
6. Your department, unit, or team's culture culture				
7. Organization's social responsibility commitments				
8. Performance management system				
9. Other rewards and incentives				
10. The Board				
11. The CEO				
12. Senior managers				
13. Line managers				
14. Your manager				
15. Your coworkers or team				
16. Your staff (direct reports)				
17. HR professionals/managers				
18. OD, OHS and labour relations professionals and managers				
19. The organization's structures and systems				
20. Corporate communication				
21. Work unit communication				
22. Employee consultation and feedback				
23. Local union representatives				
24. Union leadership				
25. Professional groups or associations				
TOTAL CHECK MARKS				

Tailor the change strategy – including the evaluation component – to fit the picture that emerges. Whatever your readiness profile, the objective is to leverage the sources of 'readiness' and 'momentum,' find ways to reduce resistance, and break free of the inertia.

Successful implementation requires putting in place enabling conditions to help make the organization change ready. Doing so first requires identifying and removing barriers. This is an important step towards closing 'the knowing–doing gap.'[4] A common barrier to change is inertia: the deadweight of traditional practices that have gone unchallenged. Lack of information about alternatives contributes to inertia. Remarkably, when larger organizations put employee development, engagement, and retention goals on their agendas, they often discover pockets of internal excellence. Lessons that help other units to improve can help to overcome inertia. Thus, shared learning is a vital part of healthy change.

Heavy workloads and time scarcity also are major change barriers. In my discussions with managers or employees, these barriers invariably are identified as holding them back from doing more to promote a healthy organization. Overworked employees won't embrace a new change initiative, even one aimed at improving their work environment. It will be dismissed as 'just one more thing on my plate.' For managers and supervisors, lack of time is reinforced by incentives that give priority to operational and business goals, not people goals. One way for managers to make time is to involve more employees in the process – in other words, practising inclusive leadership.

Resistance among front-line supervisors and middle managers can be the Achilles heel of organizational change. Historically, the greatest opposition to redesigned work systems came not from workers, but from supervisors who perceived a threat to their limited power base. Similar scenarios are played out today if supervisors read into the change greater responsibility, more accountability, and increased work demands. Supervisors also may lack the skills needed to enable change, so managers at all levels need to be equipped to make constructive contributions. The best way for supervisors and managers to become enablers of healthy change is to directly involve them in improving drivers of health and performance for themselves and their team.

With these considerations about change readiness in mind, we now turn to four case studies to describe the remaining healthy change principles.

Aligning Structure and Culture

University of British Columbia Okanagan (UBCO) is Canada's newest university campus. Located amid the vineyards and orchards of the scenic Okanagan valley, the university was founded in 2005, when the world-class University of British Columbia took over the academic programs previously offered by a local degree-granting community college. UBCO has what it takes to succeed: part of the highly reputed University of British Columbia, a mandate to develop innovative interdisciplinary programs, unprecedented enrolment growth and faculty recruitment, and a brand new campus in a spectacular natural environment.

UBCO illustrates a general principle of healthy change: the importance of aligning culture and structure. As a new institution, UBCO cultivated a culture that would support an intimate learning community, with the ultimate goal of becoming the best small university in Canada. Other features of what UBCO executives, HR professionals, and others guiding these changes called a 'healthy workplace culture strategy' show how one organization put the cultural foundation in place as a new organizational structure – in this case, a new university – took shape.

GETTING OFF TO A GOOD START

For UBCO to seize the opportunities created by location, size, and UBC connection, clear leadership and active participation of faculty and staff were essential. Leadership came from a number of change agents in administration, human resources, faculty, and from those at the executive levels at UBCO. The acknowledged challenge was to forge a distinctive culture that captured the spirit of a new, rapidly growing university. A 'healthy workplace culture' was how Dr Doug Owram, the deputy vice-chancellor (the head of UBCO), and other leaders described the workplace component of a larger vision of a healthy and sustainable organization. Solidifying the culture was all part of the process of building a campus community that connected staff, faculty, and students with each other and with the Okanagan region.

Those leading the culture-building took a participatory approach. Most staff were new to the organization, but some had worked for years at UBCO's college predecessor – which had its own culture. So it was critical that the entire workforce had opportunities to shape the future culture. A number of linked initiatives helped in this effort. A full-time workplace health promotion coordinator launched an annual health symposium that brought people together to share what they were doing to create health promoting environments. The executive created a Healthy Workplace Culture Strategy that set the direction and, over time, would brand UBCO's unique working and learning environment. A Healthy Workplace Culture Working Group fleshed out strategy, beginning with consultations involving academic and non-academic staff. These consultations were jointly led by the provost (a senior academic leader) and the campus health promotion coordinator.

The Work Group's consultation took two forms: an online survey and five consultation sessions. The survey asked about health and wellness activities and needs, the UBCO Academic Plan, and attitudes about the workplace. Results showed a high level of interest in participating in a variety of health promotion activities or issues, ranging from community service to fitness, health screening, charity fund raising events, future health conferences, and community organic gardening. This immediately broadened the scope of what healthy activities meant to employees. The survey also revealed a need to connect people with UBCO's goals as laid out in its Academic Plan. Finally, the survey validated what informal discussions had identified as the bedrock of a healthy workplace culture, including mutual respect, supportive co-workers, fair treatment, helpful feedback, and work/life balance.

The community consultations were facilitated, open-invitation, ninety-minute discussions on three questions: What would a healthy workplace culture look like at UBCO? What are its characteristics? and What are the key values? Two major themes emerged: the importance of providing people with the supports and resources they need to do their jobs well (a clear link to UBCO's mission) and strengthening the feeling of community on the campus. Other important themes were the need to create a strong UBCO identify; the importance of valuing, respecting, and rewarding people; and improved corporate communication.

The consultations helped to articulate and strengthen the features of UBCO's healthy workplace culture. Above all, the process helped to foster a sense of community. Faculty, administrators, and support staff identified many potential actions that would help a positive culture to evolve. Follow-ups to the culture consultations included installing more bike racks, more regional outreach, enhanced childcare options, and workplace health promotion resources.

INSIGHTS ABOUT THE PARADOX OF WORKPLACE CHANGE

The UBCO story highlights a basic paradox of workplace change. One of the great truisms of twenty-first- century workplaces is that change is relentless. But if this is accurate, then why does research show that most major organizational change initiatives fail to achieve their intended goals? What stands in the way of the workplace changes needed to foster innovation and productivity or to create the kind of vibrant work environments that drive well-being and productivity?

To resolve this paradox, it helps to view workplace change in terms of yin and yang, with complementary but opposing forces in constant tension. These forces are structures and cultures, the hard and soft sides of every workplace. Structures are visible in organization charts, head-counts, job classifications, information technology, and rules about how work should be done. Culture is the organization as a community – the workplace's social glue created by shared meanings of how life in the office, at the service counter, or on the production line ought to be lived. If you want your organization to get on or stay on a healthy change trajectory, changes in structures or operational processes must be balanced with the values and other elements of culture.

In practice, however, structural change goals usually trump cultural change goals. I often hear senior managers acknowledge, after the fact, the need to 'fix the culture piece' in the wake of disruptive restructuring or downsizing. I also hear managers describe their struggles to create better workplaces that deliver better results. Their goals vary – recruitment and retention, employer of choice, employee wellness, workforce development, employee engagement. But the big roadblock is designing a change process that balances the yin and yang, aligning structures and cultures so they become complementary, not opposing, forces.

A case in point is health care, a sector that has experienced much consolidation and organizational restructuring. The merger of different hospitals and other facilities can cause turmoil on the front lines of care delivery. As one hospital administrator described a government decision to redraw organizational boundaries for a second time, 'they just blew us up again.' No wonder the goal of creating better workplaces that support the delivery of better patient care gets sidelined when health care managers are preoccupied with figuring out how they fit into new structures. The 'culture piece' gets left aside as the dust settles and, with it, the chance to tap into the cultural energy that comes from each unit's distinctive values and history.

A good alignment between structure and culture also contributes to successful corporate mergers and acquisitions. Encana, Canada's largest energy company, took this approach. Calgary-based Encana was created in 2002 when Alberta Energy and PanCanadian Energy merged. The new company set out to create a new, high-performance corporation with a culture supportive of this vision, blending the best from its predecessors and adding some. The centrepiece is a corporate constitution, which, according to founding CEO Gwyn Morgan, would 'foster complete, transparent accountability' for acting out the values as a means of achieving Encana's vision. The new culture is rooted in a shared set of 'moral principles' defining specific values that guide behaviour.

Similarly, successful acquisitions must draw on the strengths of the acquired company. Take, for example, a Houston-based energy firm that was acquired by a larger multinational. The Houston company had a hard-driving entrepreneurial culture that encouraged employee recognition and fun. On the day a big deal was signed, the president threw an employee party, complete with a mariachi band and margaritas. While the new multinational owner's head office recognized the need for overarching corporate values, it also realized that Houston's exuberant culture contributed to the firm's growth – a major reason for the acquisition.

To emphasize: it is important to view your organization holistically as a finely balanced system. The next time your organization refines its mission or revises its strategy, synchronize structure and culture. UBCO provides insights about how culture and structures must mutually evolve. The initial momentum described above picked up recently when the entire University of British Columbia system implemented a 'Focus on People' HR plan, placing priority on developing sustainable and healthy workplaces. A new strategic plan, *Place and Promise*, included sustainability as one of its pillars.[5] This plan opened up opportunities to explore the university's role in shaping a desirable ecological, social, and economic future. One of the university's commitments is to create fulfilling, values-based work environments. Leveraging these developments, UBCO's vision of a thriving learning community now rests on a culture of health and embraces a wider conception of health and sustainability.

Linking People Initiatives to the Business Strategy

Preserve (not its real name) is a government agency providing services directly to the public in many locations. It employs several thousand people in a wide variety of occupations, some part time and/or temporary. Although government regulated, it has considerable scope to be flexible and innovative in its people practices. However, saddled with an expanded mandate for service delivery, rising public expectations for service access, and a reduced budget, the organization has struggled to rally its managers and employees around a renewed business strategy.

How Preserve approached this challenge illustrates another general principle of healthy change: the importance in any organization of closely linking all people initiatives to the business strategy. The agency faced three common issues. First was an urgent need to implement a new business strategy within budgetary constraints. Second, the executive team had a mindset and leadership style inconsistent with its newly espoused people goals. And third, Preserve had too many separate people initiatives, resulting in confusion and inefficiencies. From a healthy organization perspective, the solution is to incorporate people goals, supports and actions at the centre of the business strategy.

MOVE DOWN YOUR OWN HEALTHY TRAJECTORY

Preserve's CEO emphasized in her communications with employees the importance to the corporate mission of creating 'one community' that would have a 'positive culture.' Some of the pieces were already in place. For example, the organization had a human resources plan. At executive retreats and employee forums, lengthy discussions took place about strengthening the culture so that employees would feel more empowered to respond to new goals and service delivery requirements. And the organization had good data on where the greatest needs and opportunities for positive change were, having conducted an employee survey and followed up with focus groups to identify priority action areas.

But, like many other large organizations, Preserve was attempting to do too much at once to advance its human resources goals. There were too many separate 'people' policies and initiatives; each time a new one was 'rolled out,' HR staff in the field and line managers would baulk at the added work. There also was a profusion of terminology and change initiatives, with dozens of different words being used to describe the organization's people priorities and goals, and separate strategies on leadership, healthy workplaces, engagement, change management, and learning. As a result, it was difficult for even the 'champions' of these initiatives to see how all the strands tied together, never mind to convince line managers of their strategic relevance. So, while there was readiness and some momentum, finding a path forward required cutting through all this dense underbrush or language and initiatives.

Key members of the human resource group recognized these challenges. But they also were well aware an effective process for moving forward had to address the executive's traditional style of managing, rather than leading. As one HR staff member put it, the executive focuses on 'fixing not building' people and culture. However, at one of its retreats, the executive compared its current leadership style with the kind of culture it wanted to create in the organization. This raised awareness of the importance of being less operationally focused and directive and more supportive of line managers and employees taking initiative and using their creativity. At subsequent meetings, the executive settled on a way of connecting strategy, culture, and work environments, a solution that emphasized employee engagement, defined as 'the energy of employees and the strength of their connection to Preserve.' This definition prompted follow-up discussions at which managers identified the key 'drivers' of engagement, which all managers were expected to improve.

HR took this as a signal to do something it had wanted to do for years: mine the organization's human resource data sources, including the employee survey results, to identify a handful of meaningful indicators to help managers to track progress on the HR strategy. The mapping exercise also involved an analysis of employee survey data to validate the executive's intuitive model of engagement drivers and outcomes. The upshot was a small set of key indicators that could be used in future to guide management actions in areas that mattered most. The organization was on the path to a more coherent, integrated – and certainly more efficient – focus on people initiatives, with built in accountability for managers. The stage was set for what the executive team wanted in the first place: shared responsibility for a positive work environment and performance excellence.

INSIGHTS ABOUT LINKS TO THE BUSINESS STRATEGY

Preserve is not alone in struggling to find the best way to connect its people support system to the corporate strategy. I want to use Preserve's experience to revisit a point made in chapter 2: workplace wellness and health promotion initiatives can be springboards to a healthy organization if they become integral to the corporate strategy. In this regard, healthy workplace advocates should heed the advice of HR experts, who argue that people practices must be directly linked with business goals if they are to impact performance.[6] This insight is missing from the studies of workplace health promotion return on investment discussed in chapter 2.

Workplace health promotion and wellness programs can be effective launching pads for deeper change, especially if they have a comprehensive scope. These features enable practitioners to address underlying organizational and workplace conditions that are prerequisites for achieving employee health goals and productivity. A major hurdle is encouraging more expansive thinking among employees and managers about how intangibles, such as quality of work life, are powerful drivers of tangible results, such as productivity, growth, and profits. In a healthy organization, managers view employees' well-being as an important goal in its own right that directly contributes to business success. Thus, actions required to create a healthy organization must address all aspects of work design and people management. Programs that deliver measurable improvements in employees' work experiences and performance cannot simply be 'added on.' They need to be woven into the business strategy.

A strategy-focused approach to healthy change must address three issues head on. The first issue emphasizes the *risk factors*, or the underlying job characteristics and organizational conditions that enhance or impair health and performance. The second zeroes in on an integrated set of desired *outcomes*, in terms of employee health, organizational results, social and environmental impacts, and the organization's long-term sustainability. The third highlights the *actions* required to address these underlying factors and achieve the desired outcomes.

In terms of risk factors, healthy change must target as required the relationship, job, team, and support factors identified in figure 3.1. These would include physical working conditions, ergonomics, temporal aspects of the workday and tasks, job content, job autonomy, co-worker relations, quality of supervision, and financial and economic aspects.

Outcomes will vary by the scope and objectives of the planned change or intervention. Among the outcomes to consider are improved employee health, which may help to convince senior managers that investing in employee wellness makes business sense. Reduced absenteeism and utilization of employer-provided health benefits are common in this regard. If the focus is more comprehensive, looking at the performance of the organization as a whole, a balanced scorecard approach that includes employee experiences – such as job satisfaction, commitment, and morale – are worth considering. If your organization is ready to adopt its own version of a healthy organization value chain, then you also can link employee experience measures with your customer or client experience metrics. And, as we will see in chapter 8, assessing an organization's impact on society and the environment is a fast-emerging area of social responsibility reporting.

In terms of actions, even though the process of creating healthy workplaces is not well documented, we can identify common features, based on assessments of comprehensive workplace health promotion initiatives in various countries that attempt to address environmental conditions and individual health behaviours. In most instances, these reviews did not jump to the next level – the healthy organization – because health outcomes and organizational results were not directly linked. Making that leap requires a clear understanding of these success factors.

Looking at cutting-edge human resource management practices provides insights about what works. 'Best practices' were a major preoccupation in the human resource management community during the 1990s. Academic researchers thought differently, debating whether 'best practices' exist. Viewed as especially troublesome was the implication in 'best' that there are objective standards for judging the effectiveness of practices and, furthermore, that such practices are universally applicable. A more nuanced view emerged. While researchers agree on the features of high performance work systems, whether they outperformed traditional systems was viewed as depending on the strategic fit within a firm's context and goals. For healthy organizations, this 'fit' factor must apply to all people initiatives and programs.

Widen the Circle of Involvement

The National Research Council's Institute for Fuel Cell Innovation (NRC-IFCI) is at the forefront of clean energy research and development. The institute works in partnership with industry and universities to develop hydrogen fuel cells. Located in Vancouver, Canada, its new facility meets the latest 'green' building design standards and is home to over 100 scientists and support staff as well as several hundred students, visiting scientists, and guest workers, who spend some time in the facility each year.

The NRC-IFCI provides an instructive story about how senior managers' initial discussions with employees about what they needed to achieve new performance goals in a revised business plan opened the way for participatory workplace improvements. By designing a change methodology in which groups of managers and employees identified root causes of performance and quality of work life problems, jointly crafted solutions were easier to find. And a true sense of shared responsibility for the future success of the institute was embodied in the work-

Figure 6.2 Institute for Fuel Cell Innovation's workplace vision

---

We are committed to collaboratively creating a high quality and safe workplace that supports all employees to contribute fully to the Institute's success. Achieving excellence in our research and external partnerships requires an excellent work environment. This is defined by:

- *Team work* based on the values of respect and trust.
- *Communication* within teams, among teams and between employees and management that is open, honest, and two-way.
- *Decision-making and business processes* that are based on the values of integrity, flexibility, transparency and accountability.
- A *culture* that puts people first, embraces diversity, is inclusive and friendly, celebrates success through recognition, and builds commitment to the Institute.
- *Support* for success by ensuring each employee has the resources, equipment and training they need.
- An overall *employee experience* that is personally rewarding, enjoyable and motivating.

---

place vision that employee task groups presented to the organization as a catalyst for change.

MOVING TO HIGHER GROUND

With a new business plan that raised the performance bar, the institute's senior managers realized that the organization had to 'move to higher ground.' Critical to success were basic elements of a high-performing organization, such as team work, cooperation, clear priorities, and effective communication. Through employee consultations, senior management established five task groups that focused on what were generally recognized as priority issues: communication, safety, human resources, workload, and equipment. Each task groups was co-led by a manager and a front-line employee, whose role included coordinating their work with that of the other groups.

At a day-long planning session, group members discussed creating what several participants called a 'dream workplace' at the institute as a framework for future success. To provide a common reference point for group deliberations, task group co-leads created a shared vision of what this workplace looks like (see figure 6.2). It was intended as a tool for priority-setting, coordinating recommendations from the group, and keeping everyone focused on the actions that would most effectively contribute to workplace improvements. This vision was validated by other task group members, then communicated and discussed among all staff. It turned out to be an invaluable organization development tool.

The five task groups went on to make dozens of specific recommendations for improvement, with follow-up action sequenced over the coming months and years. But the workplace vision helped everyone to see the importance of the common themes in these recommendations: improved communication, coordination and cooperation, learning and development opportunities, and sustainable workloads. Perhaps the biggest contribution of the groups to moving the institute onto a solid healthy organization trajectory was the emphasis they gave to getting the improvement process right. What the groups demonstrated was that employees and managers could work together to set realistic goals and design change processes that would continually improve the institute's ability to help bring to market cutting-edge fuel cell technology.

INSIGHTS ABOUT INVOLVEMENT

The NRC-IFCI case highlights critical insights about the collaboration required for successful change. Healthy change processes move organizations forward because they provide ever-expanding opportunities for others to become involved. Change is an opportunity for employees to be engaged in solving problems and taking ownership for results. While leadership from the top of the organization is a big plus, employees throughout the organization can become change agents and contribute to making it healthier.

Like leadership, the topic of organizational change has sparked much talking and writing by management experts. One prominent model of change suggests that senior managers can manage change just the way they would any corporate project. The widely used term 'change management' implies that managers are the ones in the driver's seat. However, the major weakness of this traditional approach to change is a reliance on top-down, executive-driven plans. Avoiding the limitations of change management requires balancing top management support with employee involvement, in other words, combining top-down and bottom-up approaches.

Richard Axelrod, an organizational development expert, argues that when top managers are the change cheerleaders, negative consequences for the organization's structure and culture can result.[7] The main

drawbacks include greater cynicism, resistance, bureaucracy, and rein-
forcement of top-down control – what Axelrod calls the 'Dilbert organization,' named after the hapless character in Scott Adams's comic strip
about a seriously dysfunctional office. The failure of many change initiatives can be traced to the change management process used, because
it 'disengages the very people whose support is essential to success.' As
a solution, Axelrod recommends 'widening the circle of involvement'
by using democratic principles of participation that create the trust and
confidence needed for change to succeed.

Axelrod's observations are backed up by academic experts on organizational change, two of whom state: 'The more people are involved,
the more the change effort is their change effort. The more individuals
can see that they can succeed in the future state, the more empowered
they feel.'[8] It is on this key point that organizational change intersects
with health promotion thinking. People need to be involved in creating a health-promoting environment that supports improvements in
personal health and well-being. Applied to workplaces, this requires
designing change processes in ways that contribute to healthy workplace goals.

My assessment of award-winning healthy workplaces identified
strong commitment from top management, reinforced by their individual behaviour, as a key success factor. Equally essential is the
meaningful involvement of all groups – front-line workers, all levels
of management, unions, and professional associations – in the organization. This key ingredient of organizational change resonates with a
core idea of health promotion. The World Health Organization's widely
used definition of health promotion suggests that worker involvement
in the process of creating and maintaining healthier working conditions
is a prerequisite of a healthy workplace. As the NRC-IFCI example so
clearly shows, real progress is possible when the impetus for change
comes from the bottom and middle of the organization, not just from
the top.

People cannot become enthusiastic participants in a change process if
they do not know about it. Open and constant communication is a key
success factor in any organizational change initiative. Creating healthier workplaces is no different. One of the complaints I often hear from
workplace health promotion or wellness coordinators is the low level
of uptake in available programs. It usually reflects two weaknesses: a
lack of continual communication, using language that is meaningful to
the diverse demographic groups, and designing programs so that em-

ployees actually feel some ownership over them – through committees, councils, or active consultation mechanisms.

It is equally important to keep everyone in the organization informed about the goals, strategies, and progress milestones for change. Traditional change initiatives driven from the executive suite often suffer from communicating too little, too late. As change expert John Kotter warns, most corporate change initiatives under-communicate by a factor of ten.[9] If change is flowing from the front lines of an organization, change agents must keep senior management informed about the impact of the initiative and use multiple channels to communicate progress to co-workers. Also important is helping all managers to adjust their thinking about what drives performance, so that workplace and cultural factors become part of their thinking in this regard.

Shifting thinking is an important step in changing action patterns. Effective communication is the means to this end. New thinking can come about only if a common language can be found for talking about health and performance within your organization. After a recent workshop I facilitated on how to improve job quality, one of the participants, who was a workplace wellness coordinator at a mental health NGO, raised the importance of language. She noted that different labels – healthy organization, healthy workplace, quality jobs, engaged employees, health and productivity – all point to similar determinants and outcomes. Depending on the type of organization, one label will work better than the others, so change agents need to find language that fits the context of their workplace. Using local language, they will be able to expand the possibilities for how decision-makers think – and take action – about the impact of the work environment on organizational performance.

Words such as *collaboration, adaptability, capabilities, productivity*, and *innovation* need to be paired with words such as *wellness* and *health*. If you are a workplace health promotion advocate and a member of a healthy workplace or wellness committee, focus on finding language that resonates with front-line employees as well as senior management. That may include creating a committee vision of a healthy workplace that uses words such as *capabilities, collaboration, change*, and *innovation* to describe the benefits of having healthy employees working in a vibrant environment.

Make Time for Learning and Innovation

EnerProf (not its real name) provides professional services to the energy sector. Its workforce of several hundred is located at a corporate office and many employees spend considerable time working off-site with clients. The workforce includes engineers, project managers, lawyers, auditors, and IT experts. EnerProf is a revealing example of an organization that didn't rush into a healthy organization strategy. Instead, it took stock by auditing what worked well and what needed fixing in its people practices, culture, and work environment.

Conducting an audit may not suit your organization. However, it gave the engineers and professionals in this business time in their schedules to identify, share, and discuss lessons learned about effective people practices that could propel the organization to a higher level of customer service. An audit was a formal process, so it took priority on people's agendas, thereby overcoming what is one of the major barriers to healthy workplace innovation: a shortage of time due to heavy workloads and competing priorities. EnerProf underscores the importance of these basic activities – reflection, discussion, and learning – for making workplace innovation happen.

CONDUCTING A HEALTHY ORGANIZATION AUDIT

Several years ago, EnerProf was at a critical juncture. As one of the managers put it, many of his colleagues were asking: 'how can we energize the organization to bring it to the next level?' Nothing was seriously wrong with EnerProf's culture, working conditions, or performance, but there was a growing recognition that to fulfil its client service mission and renew its workforce, which included replacing many baby boomers who were retiring, it had to do much better in terms of both people practices and performance. Above all, the organization needed to tap into employees' creative potential.

Converging circumstances brought this issue to the forefront. In response, the executive team requested an 'audit' of the organization's health. This approach was consistent with how it did business. The audit was designed to assess opportunities to improve in two areas: organizational effectiveness and working conditions. As they discussed what it meant to be a healthy organization, employees and managers came to see how the organization's mission depended on its culture, people practices, and work environments. Through these discussions, the company was able to identify a future change trajectory that would more tightly connect people and performance.

The idea of a healthy organization audit was initiated by the CEO, who pointed out that he was responding to several changes and opportunities in the organization. EnerProf had launched a high-profile work/life balance program several years earlier to improve its hiring of and retaining female professionals. This initiative succeeded to a point, in terms of increased recruitment of females. However, a recent employee survey found that heavy workloads and high stress threatened to undermine work/life balance. Employees feared reprisals if they spoke out about these conditions, in part because of a few unsympathetic executives, who left the organization shortly after the survey. Furthermore, the survey also identified needs in the areas of recognition, open exchange of ideas, and an environment more conducive to learning and creativity. These issues were acknowledged at a board/ executive retreat and reinforced in employee survey follow-up committees within each department.

As they talked openly about these issues, managers and employees across EncrProf identified several barriers to progress. The corporate values were dormant and needed to be revisited and revived. Managers had too many priorities competing for their time and attention. The executive team's 'action tracker' was cluttered with over sixty items. The performance management system was ineffective at focusing people on the results that mattered most for the future success of the organization. The human resource unit was slow to adopt a strategic view of its role. One of the five strategic goals referred to people, but in a confusing way that was difficult to translate into action. This made it hard to measure and report progress on people goals in the same clear way as was used for other operational and client service goals in an annual report card.

The actual process of auditing the health of the organization was healthy. It gave employees and managers time to reflect, openly discuss solutions, and consider options for next steps. When the project was completed, there was general recognition that it was unlike other 'projects,' because the organization had gained greater collective understanding, clarity, and focus on how to simultaneously make progress on people and performance.

INSIGHTS ABOUT THE NEED TO LEARN AND INNOVATE

EnerProf created what was, for it, the ideal opportunity for collaborative learning and, through the process, set new directions for workplace innovation. This custom-designed approach is necessary because, as I have emphasized, there is no standardized model for healthy change. There is no easy-to-follow checklist or template for bringing about the changes needed to create a healthy workplace or the more ambitious goal of a healthy organization. Off-the-shelf programs may work in specific areas, such as smoking cessation, nutrition improvement, or employee assistance. However, a generic approach does not work for primary workplace interventions that address the underlying, systemic determinants of health and performance.

The big insight provided by EnerProf is to avoid a 'paint-by-numbers' approach to creating healthy organizations in which change is a step-by-step program. Successful implementation of change requires ongoing reflection and learning by the groups and individual change agents involved. This dynamic approach to change requires continual feedback loops and adjustments to the initial plan. In this regard, we can extract some useful lessons from research on the diffusion of innovation. Indeed, a healthy organization strategy is an innovation because it introduces something new, institutionalizes its use, and diffuses the healthy practices and their supporting values more widely. After all, the goal is to make healthy practices a routine part of daily workplace activities. In this sense, not only is the content of the change innovative, but the actual strategy for carrying it out also has to be innovative. Thus, the creative part is designing and implementing change that fits an organization's unique history, culture, market conditions, and employee characteristics.

Furthermore, the organization's learning capacity is critical for successful innovation. Learning and innovation go hand-in-hand as defining characteristics of a vibrant workplace. I have closely observed dozens of organizations develop and implement their own healthy organization strategies. To varying degrees, they linked a vibrant work environment with HR goals and bigger strategic goals, from customer or client service to operational excellence. I recall a learning network meeting, where managers and training professionals from major corporations agreed that 'getting results is what it is all about, but equally important is *how* you do it.' These companies acknowledged that more time was needed for 'collective reflection' on how the company goes about achieving its goals. Learning requires time to reflect on what has been done – a very healthy behaviour for any organization to encourage.

Experts on learning organizations generally agree that people learn in workplaces through a process that extends over time, is collaborative, and is based on continual knowledge acquisition and dissemination. Learning helps workers to avoid repeating mistakes and to reproduce successes. Management expert Michael Beer, using a health-related metaphor, argues that 'the capacity to learn and change' is organizational fitness.[10] Especially important in this regard is learning through ongoing and rigorous reviews of change initiatives. By reflecting on the experiences of implementing change, then refining and readjusting the action plan, it is possible to make change a process of continual organizational learning.

Effective bundles of healthy workplace practices are hard to imitate. Diffusion is limited because there is no easy-to-follow checklist or template for bringing about the changes needed to create a healthy workplace, or the more ambitious goal of a healthy organization. While standardized programs may work in specific areas, such as smoking cessation, a generic approach does not work for primary workplace health interventions that underlie drivers of wellness and performance. A healthy workplace strategy is an organizational innovation because it introduces something new, making it the new status quo. Learning and innovation go hand-in-hand; both are defining characteristics of a healthy organization. A healthy work environment contributes to business success by encouraging learning and adaptability.

Measuring progress is an essential component of learning and innovation. Your efforts to monitor and evaluate healthy workplace programs, changes, and interventions must be viewed in this light. Monitoring and evaluation are often weak links in the chain that connects organizational change interventions to desired outcomes. Yet the information gained through these measurement activities is critical to making change a dynamic learning process. Good measures can help decision-makers to view workplace health initiatives as investments in people that build the human capabilities needed for high performance. Change can provide learning opportunities for employees and managers about how to do things better, but only if evaluation data are converted to useable knowledge that can inform decisions and actions. Healthy workplace advocates also need to document the cost of inaction, as this could be a message that captures the attention of senior management. Chapter 8 pursues these issues. For now, the key point is that evaluation and measurement should be viewed not as separate activities, but as resources for learning how you are doing on your healthy organization trajectory.

Change as Renewal

This chapter has covered a sweeping landscape – change – from a healthy organization perspective. My intent has been to provide a practical framework and guiding principles that you can use in your workplace. I have emphasized that the change process itself must contribute to healthy workplace goals. In short, how people experience the journey is what builds towards your vision of a more vibrant and inspiring workplace. That experience must be positive overall, personally engaging, and clearly tied to a better future. If people experience change as stressful, imposed from the top, or inconsistent with the organization's people goals and values, then both the process and end results will be unhealthy.

Healthy organizations are built through gradual and cumulative changes over time. Ideally, look for that next step – however small – that with few resources can boost morale, well-being, and performance. There can be big pay-offs from small improvements. As management experts Felix Barber and Rainer Strack, writing in *Harvard Business Review*, observe: 'Because employees represent both the major cost and the major driver of value creation, people-management moves that lead to even small changes in operational performance can have a major impact on returns.'[11] The trick, of course, is to identify those small steps along your healthy organization trajectory. The suggestions in this chapter are intended to help you to find ways to do this.

The trap lies in getting stuck simply thinking and talking about a vision of a healthy workplace – or the label that best fits your trajectory. Almost every organization has strengths to build on and opportunities to take bold new steps forward. Building incrementally on these strengths and seizing present opportunities, however small to begin with, can start making the vision a reality. As we will see in chapter 7, the pressures for workforce and workplace renewal and for strengthening community relationships offer many opportunities to progress down a healthy organization trajectory.

7 Sustainable Success

Nexen is a North American-based independent energy company with operations in western Canada, the Gulf of Mexico, Colombia, West Africa, the North Sea, and Yemen. The company finds, develops, produces, and markets crude oil, natural gas, and power. Its philosophy is to 'build sustainable businesses.'[1] Nexen takes a long-term view of its energy assets, stakeholders, and the environment. Corporate decision-makers strive to balance shareholder value, social and economic benefits, and environmental impacts. In many ways, Nexen exemplifies how the healthy organization value chain introduced in chapter 1 actually works. The makings of sustainable success are found in Nexen's long-term focus, values-based approach to ethical business practices, and genuine concern for the well-being of employees, society and the environment.

Achieving a sustainable business requires the infusion of social responsibility principles into corporate operations, people practices and community relations. In this regard, Nexen is guided by its commitment to 'behave ethically and contribute to economic development while improving the quality of life of the workforce and their families as well as the local community and society at large.'[2] The company's annual sustainability report to stakeholders provides accountability for how well it is living up to this commitment. The company wants to do more than minimize its carbon footprint or further reduce lost-time injuries among its employees – although both goals are important, of course. So it builds social and environmental goals into its energy products, for example, by adopting the Canadian Chemical Producers' Association's Responsible Care approach to safe and environmentally sound management of its products over their entire life cycle.

Also central to Nexen's vision of a sustainable business is the belief that its future 'is in the hands of its employees.' This belief guides actions on many fronts. For example, an ethical work environment is one of the drivers of the company's sustainability vision. Its Integrity Resource Centre provides staff training on integrity and ethical practices and investigates reports of any breaches of company policies. Over the course of one recent year, almost all of its 4,000 employees attended a workshop on integrity. The company also has tightened the links between its health, safety, environmental, and social responsibility policies and practices. A member of the executive team provides oversight for this integrated approach. Employee safety and health are not a separate set of goals and practices, but are embedded in the company culture and work environment by valuing trust, respect and cooperation. Since one of Nexen's core principles is investing in people, during the recent global recession the company was financially able to commit to no layoffs and it actually recruited new talent critical to its future plans.

Now that we understand the building blocks of a healthy organization, we can turn our attention to the top of the healthy organization value chain: sustainable success. This chapter examines sustainable success and its implications for an organization's social, environmental, and human resource practices. I have argued that workplace health promotion activities can be launching pads for addressing the underlying drivers of well-being and performance. By the same token, as your organization articulates its social responsibility commitments, the stage is set for you and other change agents to pose a fundamental question: in the future, how can we thrive in ways that benefit all stakeholders?

I believe that sustainable success depends in large part on how organizations go about renewing relationships with stakeholders, including employees. In this chapter, therefore, I focus on these two big drivers of sustainable success. First, I examine the quality of the relationships with customers, business partners, local communities, and society as a whole. Then I consider how to develop the future workforce capabilities needed to achieve the organization's goals and realize its long-term vision. I expand the discussion of healthy change in chapter 6 by addressing issues such as revitalizing relationships with customers, other stakeholders, and communities; developing workforce capabilities for the long term; and tapping the synergies between socially responsible business practices and internal people practices.

To summarize, here are the chapter's key sights for achieving sustainable success:

1. Organizations become more sustainable by taking a long-term approach to success, balancing the needs and interests of all stakeholders.
2. Healthy organizations have strong core values that guide the treatment of employees, communities, and the environment.
3. Social responsibility commitments open opportunities to embed social and environmental goals into business strategy, inspiring employees in the process.
4. Human resource strategies such as workforce diversity and flexible work arrangements benefit employees, the organization, and society.
5. Long-range workforce planning is a useful tool for aligning workforce capabilities with the future needs of the business and society.

What Makes Success Sustainable?

What actions can you take today to ensure your organization's success decades into the future? This question is central to plotting an organization's healthy trajectory. To answer it, we need to think beyond financial health and consider the social, environmental, and human resource dimensions of an organization's sustainability. We need an integrated approach that unites internal and external practices. Whatever actions you decide will move your organization down a healthy trajectory, their implementation requires a values-based corporate philosophy that is applied rigorously in all relationships, inside and outside the organization. This is the basic lesson from Nexen, Four Seasons, Trico Homes, Teck Cominco Trail Operations, and other organizations I have described. At the heart of sustainable success is the integrity with which board members, managers, and employees apply the organization's core values in all decisions and actions. Consistency in this regard expands the possibilities for positively shaping the future of your organization – and society.

Social and Environmental Dimensions

Sustainable success connects the building blocks of a healthy organization to social and environmental responsibility. Because corporate social responsibility (CSR) has an external focus, its internal supports often get overlooked. I propose that a company's external CSR practices depend on an enabling work environment, culture, and leadership. Equally necessary is how employees themselves contribute to and perceive these CSR practices. When companies showcase their carbon neutral footprint or close monitoring of human rights among Third-World contractors, we also need to understand the role employees played in these accomplishments. And when an organization receives an outstanding employer award, we need to determine if this recognition squares with its treatment of external stakeholders. This chapter presents a unified perspective on human resource, social, and environmental practices as the basis for sustainable success.

Here is what is needed to achieve sustainable success. For a start, the gap between rhetoric and practice regarding social responsibility must be closed. According to a global survey of CEOs conducted by McKinsey, a consulting firm, most believe their companies should embed responsible approaches to environmental, social, and governance issues in their strategy and operations.[3] However, far fewer are able to report actually doing so.

One company that has made progress over the past decade is athletic gear maker Nike. It has taken significant steps to protect human rights throughout its global supply chain, which employs over 800,000 people, although it is the first to admit that challenges remain. Perhaps more significant for closing the gap I just referred to is Nike's increasingly creative environmental practices. The company uses 'considered design' in the manufacture of its running shoes, rating each model according to a sustainability index based on waste reduction, reduced use of toxins, use of recycled materials, and the environmental impact of each ingredient.[4] However, what is missing from these stories (but could be easily added) is how Nike's employees went about these innovations, the supportive internal conditions, and the results in terms of a heightened sense of pride, satisfaction – and future inspiration.

Providing an employee perspective on CSR applies the same approach I used to describe the building blocks of a healthy organization. This makes sense, given that workers increasingly want green and responsible employers. For example, in a recent online poll of young Canadian workers, most would consider leaving their current job for a more environmentally friendly employer.[5] The kinds of companies that will be attractive are moving at an impressive rate to 'embed' human and environmental criteria in their methods of conducting business and in every step in the product or service chain. Sustainability becomes a design feature. Design consultant Valerie Casey at the California-based design house IDEO has written a 'Designers Accord.' Companies such as Johnson & Johnson, Adobe Systems, and others who sign on are making a public commitment to sustainable design and to tracking their carbon footprint.[6] While recruitment, retention, and talent development goals may not be central to the Designers Accord, it surely will bolster these companies' human resource strategies.

Human Resource Dimensions

What is critical about the human resource dimensions of sustainable success is how the organization goes about cultivating people capabilities for the future. Capability is a person's actual and potential ability to do something and, at an organizational level, collective capabilities are greater than the sum of individual capabilities. Human resource experts Dave Ulrich and Norm Smallwood call capabilities intangible assets. 'You can't see or touch them,' they argue, 'yet they can make all the difference in the world when it comes to market value.'[7] In today's uncertain economy, an organization's future depends more than ever on its capabilities to adapt, learn, lead, innovate and be resilient.

Many managers view talent management as getting the right people into the right jobs, and doing it quickly. While this is important, also needed is a 'big picture' view of the capabilities that will be required in five or ten years. As IBM discovered from interviews with over 400 HR executives in forty countries, boards and senior executive are paying more attention to long-range workforce issues.[8] Three priority areas for improvement identified by the IBM study were predicting future skill requirements, identifying and using existing talent, and encouraging collaboration. The study concluded that future organizational success depends on agile and adaptable workforces. These are the very attributes required to anticipate and effectively respond to emerging social and environmental challenges.

Most large corporations now publish CSR reports to demonstrate accountability and transparency in the eyes of stakeholders.[9] After all, to do well by doing good – the basic principle of CSR – an organization not only must apply ethical principles and incorporate social and environmental goals into business strategies. It also must be seen to do so by investors, employees, and the public. Increasingly critical to a company's reputation in this regard are its internal people practices.

For example, Vancity has been widely recognized for how it has combined CSR and HR within an ethical business framework.[10] Vancity – a credit union on Canada's west coast – has three values: integrity, innovation, and responsibility. It defines the latter as follows: 'We are accountable to our members, employees, colleagues, and communities for the results of our decisions and actions.' Living up to this commitment happens each and every day through even the smallest interactions involving employees, customers, and local communities. Everyone in Vancity's world – employees, customers, suppliers, and communities – is a partner in shaping its future. The employee value proposition also is the community value proposition.

There is talk now of a 'sustainability advantage' flowing from environmental policies and practices that contribute to human resource goals.[11] As such, a company's brand and reputation are becoming an integral part of future workforce planning. I am suggesting that any sustainability advantage could just as accurately be called a healthy organization advantage, because it rests on workplace, cultural, and leadership foundations.

Ingredients of Sustainable Success

To summarize this integration of the social, environmental, and human resource dimension of sustainability, we can identify four ingredients of sustainable success:

1. Applying long-term, holistic thinking to what success means for the organization. This thinking shapes vision, mission, and strategic plans, providing greater value to stakeholders through ethically sound business practices.
2. Using strong corporate values and ethics to guide all relationships, whether among co-workers, between senior managers and front-line staff, with customers, or with the communities touched by the organization's products or services.
3. Adapting vibrant workplace attributes – particularly collaboration, employee input, open communication, developing potential, and encouraging learning and innovation – to external stakeholder relations.
4. Regenerating the organization's human capabilities by renewing employees' talents and creatively seeking out mutually beneficial relationships with customers and communities.

Renewing Relationships with Society

So far, I have illustrated the importance of a long-range and integrative view of the organization's success. As such, the organization's vision – its ideal future – is realized and sustained by balancing the needs and interests of customers, employees, and society. Calibrating this balance is ongoing. In this regard, what steps can you take to renew your organization's relationship with society? To help you answer this question, I want to highlight the potential to simultaneously strengthen external stakeholder and workplace relationships.

Corporate Social Responsibility Evolves

As labels go, corporate social responsibility (CSR) has been criticized as heavy on rhetoric and light on action. But the basic idea is catching on in the corporate world. A global survey by the *Economist* found that CSR is moving up as a priority for executives.[12] More companies are looking for ways to 'get it right' – and some are leading the way.

CSR has developed in three waves. The traditional, first-wave approach is corporate philanthropy. For example, Imagine Canada is a national registered charity that sets standards in this area on behalf of the non-profit and charitable sector. Imagine Canada's 'Caring Company Commitment' encourages organizations to lead in the community by example. This initiative has seen over 100 companies make a commitment to dedicate 1 per cent of domestic pre-tax profits to support charities and non-profit organizations. The commitment also involves a pledge to encourage and facilitate employee volunteering and giving, championing and sustaining at least one community investment project with CEO support that leverages the company's expertise to make a difference in the community, and publishing an annual report describing the company's community investments and citizenship actions.[13] Many good causes providing community benefits rely on this philanthropy.

Over this decade, risk management has become a second wave of CSR, as corporations try to mitigate the negative impacts of their practices on communities and the environment. Now a third wave is fast emerging, which uses a CSR lens to identifying new business opportunities that are socially and environmentally responsible. This more 'strategic' approach to CSR goes beyond an awareness of a business's impacts on communities and a willingness to change practices that have negative consequences. It moves the CSR starting line forward, beginning with the premise that businesses can operate in ways that build in social and environmental benefits.

The Changing Face of Social Responsibility

CSR's third wave aligns with a healthy organization perspective. It shows the potential for actively engaging employees in providing sustainable products and services. Yet earlier waves of CSR also can contribute to more vibrant and inspiring workplaces and demonstrate core values. Let us briefly consider some examples of how organizations are linking philanthropy, employee volunteering, and environmental practices in ways that build healthier organizations.

Home Depot's approach to social responsibility reflects its founders' personal values.[14] A core corporate value is 'giving back.' One way Home Depot does this is through its Team Depot program in all of its stores. Employees give their own time to work together on projects that benefit communities, and they address broader issues such as environmental problems, at-risk youth, and affordable housing. Each Home Depot retail outlet has one Team Depot representative who is assigned two hours per week to initiate projects in local communities and receive special training on how to hold and run successful projects and volunteer events. Each store selects the issues or projects that are of particular importance to their communities. Working on Team Depot projects helps to further the team spirit among employees at Home Depot and gives individuals the opportunity to develop or demonstrate skills that might not be apparent in their regular jobs. Many of Home Depot's managers who have risen through the ranks have developed their leadership skills through close involvement with Team Depot projects.

TNT Express, an Amsterdam-based global logistics and express company, has been recognized for its ongoing efforts to be socially responsible. The company's 'Moving the World' program involves a team of fifty employees on standby at its corporate headquarters in Amsterdam to respond within forty-eight hours to help out in disasters anywhere in the world. This is a partnership with the World Food Program (WFP), the UN agency that reduces hunger. It has responded to dozens of emergencies, including the Asian tsunami in 2004 and the floods that wrought destruction to Bangladesh in 2007. Volunteers also work around the world on secondment to WFP and raise money for the program. In a staff survey 68 per cent said that pro bono work gave them pride in working for the company and that it helps in recruiting new graduates. According to the director of the Moving the World program, 'It's providing a soul to TNT.'[15]

Environmental sustainability goals typically are part of an organization's social responsibility commitments. Toronto-based Environics

Communications Inc. launched a comprehensive program to reduce its impact on the environment – largely at the instigation of its employees. When the company committed to becoming carbon neutral by 2008, it switched to Bullfrog Power (which sources power from generators that meet strict environmental standards), reduced paper usage, and used recycled paper. Environics has sought out environmentally responsible vendors for catering and provided all staff members with a refillable water bottle to avoid unnecessary plastics in the office. And every employee is eligible to receive $250 towards the purchase of a bicycle. These environmentally friendly moves did involve extra (although not significant) costs, but there also were big investments on a personal level. An important lesson is that managers and employees need to get behind environmental initiatives, or they risk being dismissed as 'greenwashing.' This is how an inclusive approach to leadership can not only improve the workplace, but also directly benefit society.

Good Corporate Citizen, Outstanding Employer

Investors are scrutinizing corporate citizenship more closely than ever. A company's reputation on CSR issues can influence its market valuation. Public fury over executive compensation in the wake of massive job losses and government bail-outs essentially is a debate about corporate ethics. Some companies are trying to raise public and investor awareness of how their CSR efforts contribute to society and corporate performance. Jeff Swartz, chief executive at Timberland, the U.S. outdoor footwear and clothing company, stated that 'commerce and justice don't have to be antagonistic notions.'[16] Timberland was among the first to measure the impact of its social and environmental initiatives. Increasingly, companies such as Timberland understand that they must act responsibly in all areas to build a sustainable business.

For TNT Express, sustainability refers to the environment, while social responsibility refers to employees, customers, investors, and society. They are combined into corporate responsibility, which is how TNT presents its rigorous annual reporting of performance in these areas.[17] TNT was the highest-scoring company on the Dow Jones Sustainability Index in 2007 and 2008 within their industry sector. In 2009 it was awarded a CSR Leadership Excellence Award.[18] Actually, what the practices of companies like TNT show is that sustainability extends beyond environmental impacts to include the renewal of human resources and community connections.

Like Timberland and TNT, a growing number of companies are being recognized for their socially responsible employment, environmental, and community practices. For example, in 2007 and 2008 the following organizations (most are large publicly traded companies, as required by some of the CSR awards) were selected based on cross-referencing organizations that have made it onto the 100 Best Corporate Citizens and/or the World's Most Admired Companies and/or the Corporate Knight's 50 Best Corporate Citizens lists with organizations that have made it onto one or more of the following outstanding employer lists: 100 Best Companies to Work For In America, 50 Best Workplaces in Canada, and the 50 Best Employers in Canada:

- Adobe Systems Inc.
- American Express Co.
- Cisco Systems Inc.
- FedEx
- General Mills Inc.
- Google Inc.
- Herman Miller Inc.
- Microsoft Corp.
- Nexen Inc.
- NIKE Inc.
- Procter & Gamble.
- Starbucks Coffee Co.
- Texas Instruments Inc.
- Timberland Co.
- Vancity Credit Union

I recently chaired a panel at the Health, Work and Wellness Conference, a large annual gathering held in Canada. Executives from three companies – Ernst & Young, Trico Homes, and Environics Communications – participated on the panel. The panellists described the ways their companies support employees to give back to the community and protect the environment. The topic was a big step beyond employee health promotion, but it responded to growing recognition that healthy organizations also benefit communities and the environment. The three companies have common fundamentals. Each was recognized as among the 50 Best Workplaces in Canada in 2008 by the Great Place to Work Institute Canada. (None is publicly traded, so would not meet CSR award criteria.) They have strong, trust-based cultures that value employees' contributions to customers and the community. And they have made social responsibility central to their operating philosophy, business plans, and employee engagement strategies.

The panel theme was 'moving forward by giving back.' Here are some of lessons from these three companies on how to do so:

- Involve employees in selecting charity and community partners as a way to create engagement. Also provide opportunities for employees' families to be involved in community activities, and seek employees' advice on how to make these activities fun.
- Support employees to give back. Provide the policies, practices, and resources needed to encourage employees to take initiative, make the time, and fully benefit from volunteer experiences.
- Lead the way for the entire organization to get involved. Senior managers must provide ongoing support, actively participate, and regularly communicate how community and environmental actions demonstrate honest, ethical, and responsible business practices.
- Learn from the process of giving back. Volunteering, charity support, and reducing the organization's carbon footprint provide ideal opportunities for employees to learn, grow, and find innovative ways to work together and with partners.
- Embed the principle of giving back in the corporate culture as way of extending workplace values (such as respect, fairness, and integrity) into society. This is how social and environmental responsibility becomes part of a corporate brand that will resonate with prospective recruits, customers, and community partners.

Environics Communications, Ernst & Young, and Trico Homes have developed successful practices for engaging with employees, the community, and the environment. These practices are woven into their people strategies. All are open to new approaches to volunteering, giving, and environmental sustainability and no doubt will rely on employees' input for creative solutions.

Making Sustainability Strategic

I mentioned earlier that third-wave CSR dissolves the lines between social, environmental, and business goals. As business strategy experts Michael Porter and Mark Kramer explain, 'the more closely tied a social issue is to a company's business, the greater the opportunity to leverage the firm's resources – and benefit society.'[19] Social and environmental benefits are designed into products and services. And companies taking a strategic approach to CSR map the social and environmental impacts all along the value chain. Strategic CSR also can have positive implications for employees and people practices, although this dimension needs more attention. Ideally, a company must consider the social and community impact of all its people policies and practices.[20] Just think of the potentially positive community spin-offs from corporate investments in training and education, safety and health, diversity, and decent compensation.

In other words, strategic CSR raises the bar for good corporate citizenship at the same time as it sparks innovation. Porter and Kramer's example is the Toyota Prius, whose hybrid engine produces environmental benefits and a competitive edge. Two other global corporations practising strategic CSR are GE and Boston Consulting Group, and we can learn much about sustainable success from their approaches.

GE is one of the world's largest and most diversified corporations. Its website states: 'At GE, we consider our culture to be among our innovations. Over decades our leaders have built GE's culture into what it is today – a place for creating and bringing big ideas to life.'[21] GE believes that 'a company can do well even as it does good.' This belief guides the philanthropic work of the GE Foundation and employee volunteering. More significant for a sustainable future, however, is that GE is greening its business. Each business unit has to cut carbon dioxide emissions in order to reduce overall greenhouse gas emissions by 2012 to 1 per cent below 2004 levels. There is also a remarkable change in direction, reflected in a new strategy called 'Ecomagination.' Jeffrey Immelt, the CEO, has a vision of clean technologies as GE's future. GE now promotes clean coal technologies and wind power and is investing heavily in other breakthrough green technologies – no doubt offering inspiring challenges to the scientists, engineers, and other employees involved.[22]

Boston Consulting Group (BCG), a global management consulting firm, is ranked third on *Fortune's* 2009 list of 100 Best Companies to Work For In America. BCG created a Social Impact Practice Network to have a lasting positive impact on society.[23] The network's efforts are guided by the UN's Millennium Development Goals of combating poverty, disease, illiteracy, and other problems afflicting the poorest individuals. Through partnerships and projects, 11 per cent of global employees participate in the network. This activity helps society, enriches the professional experiences of BCG staff, and helps the firm to attract and retain talented staff. BCG's community knowledge also gets transferred to its corporate clients, to meet its CSR objectives, and benefits BCG's ongoing philanthropic work with NGOs such as World Food Program, Bill & Melinda Gates Foundation, and Save the Children. The network is open to any employee and a global staffing team ensures that opportunities are distributed across the organization's locations. BCG also offers longer-term opportunities, such as six- to twelve-month secondments with a global NGO partner while remaining a BCG employee as well as social impact leaves of absence for up to twelve months. These socially responsible corporations place a high priority on open channels of communication with stakeholders. Toyota listens to its customers, GE consults with its partners and communities about wind power, and BCG plays an important information broker role. Interestingly, open communication is a pre-eminent quality of vibrant and high-performing workplaces, so here is a good example of how sustainable success results from applying the same effective people practices internally and externally.

Vibrant Workplaces Support Social Responsibility

The examples of CSR I have provided clearly show the opportunities in CSR to build more vibrant workplaces, positive cultures, and a shared responsibility for success. Authentic CSR is not a public relations exercise; it has real substance and credibility in the eyes of all stakeholders. When authentic, CSR has the potential to instil pride and foster team spirit among employees. It also can provide new outlets for employees' creativity, further demonstrate core values, and reinforce the organization's reputation as caring and responsive to community needs and concerns. Indeed, CSR and HR goals converge. Evidence of this can be found in the research for Great Place to Work Institute Canada's (GPTW) 2007 list of 50 Best Workplaces in Canada, published in *Canadian Business* magazine.

A major part of the Best Workplaces assessment process involves surveying a random sample of employees using GPTW's fifty-seven-question Trust Index. Using results from this survey, I ranked the 2007 list companies by average scores on this question: 'I feel good about the ways we contribute to the community.' For all fifty organizations on the list, positive employee responses to this question ranged between 85 per cent and 90 per cent, and some companies achieved 100 per cent positive ratings. I then looked for common themes in the highest-ranking workplaces on another survey question, which asked employees to describe in their own words what made their company a great place to work at.

Two conclusions jumped out. First, what makes these workplaces great is the people. Employees care and support each other, take part in fun activities, and feel that senior managers or owners genuinely care about them. Words such as *team* and *family* are frequently used. Second, employees view these workplaces as thriving communities in which internal and external relationships are mutually reinforcing. The support, respect, and caring that staff show for each other reach into the community through volunteering, corporate philanthropy, environmental sustainability and ethical actions, and relations with suppliers and partners. The result is a deep sense of pride.

To illustrate, here are representative quotes from employees in several companies in which *all* employees surveyed felt positively about 'the ways we contribute to the community':

- Everyone that works here makes a point of getting to know each other. We participate in events during and outside of company hours.
- The people. Everybody works together as equal members of a team toward common goals, and treats one another with respect. Management has people-oriented values and responds to staff input. We provide a valuable community service.
- I am blessed to have found such an incredibly generous company to work for. They encourage me to be the best that I can be by offering continual personal growth opportunities, fabulous benefits and perks and a tremendously positive, nurturing work environment. In addition, the employees and management are actively involved in giving back to the community regularly.
- I truly get the feeling like I am part of a family here at —— which makes for a fun working environment. I am compensated fairly and am made to feel like my contribution is worth something.
- I work for an amazing company that is very active in the community (over 3000 hours of community service last year). I love that they have onsite fitness classes, a wonderful (inexpensive) cafeteria and a beautiful facility.
- It feels like a happy family here. There is no discrimination towards me with my hearing loss, quite opposite everyone is aware of my hearing loss and accommodates it. Also that we care for the community makes

it special. We also have a monthly international lunch, which we learn about other cultures and food. There are too many positive things to write.

- The emphasis on giving back to the community is astounding. Blows me away every time we do another event. Also, the staff appreciation activities are truly one of a kind. The family BBQ really hit home as something wonderful for us.
- The special events we put on and take care of make a big impact on the community and employees. The events make everyone feel like they are helping and get everyone together to talk and feel more welcome.
- Right from the beginning of my employment with —— I was welcomed as 'one of the family.'
- Everybody in this organization believes in team effort and treats everyone just like a family. We all believe in contributing back to the community.
- We have a unique culture of team and community and our respect toward diversity makes us proud to come to work.
- A genuine concern for its people and community.

Renewing Workforce Capabilities

I am encouraging an integrative approach to organizational sustainability, which taps the synergy between internal people practices and relations with external stakeholders. Thus far, I have focused externally on the social and environmental dimensions of sustainable success. To complement this approach, I now will shift the attention to what you can do internally to recruit, develop, and retain the future workforce. After all, a capable workforce is what drives sustainable success.

There also is demographic pressure to give workforce renewal high priority. Looking at the global economy's meltdown and the sudden threat of mass unemployment, some may conclude that the intense competition for talent that peaked in 2007 is yesterday's concern. I believe they are wrong. Economic cycles do not alter the demographic facts. In North America, Japan, and most of Europe, workforces are aging and there are fewer new workers than will be needed to replace retirees. For example, over half of the workers in Canada are over the age of forty-two. Japan's population is actually shrinking. Across Europe, deaths will outnumber births by 2015. By 2030 people over sixty-five will comprise almost half of Germany's adult population. Even if some older workers postpone retirement in order to make up for savings lost when financial markets tumbled in 2008, the reality is that workforce renewal will seriously challenge many organizations.

If anything, the global recession has provided breathing space to develop longer-term workforce plans. Even firms that were forced by the recession to cut jobs need a long-term strategy to rebuild their workforce capabilities around a repositioned business strategy – just as Trico Homes did. The remainder of this chapter explores different ways that workforce renewal and social responsibility converge, providing ideas for how your organization can build the basis for sustainable success in three areas:

- Workforce diversity strategies dovetail with many organizations' commitment to reflect the changing demographic profile of their customers and communities.
- Meeting the challenge of addressing the needs of three generations of employees offers new opportunities for flexible work arrangements which benefit society.
- Developing long-range workforce plans opens up creative possibilities for aligning workforce capabilities with the future needs of society.

Workforce Diversity Strategies

One socially responsible solution to workforce renewal expands the search for new sources of talent by recruiting a more diverse workforce. Doing so requires a barrier-free work environment that is welcoming and accommodating to individuals from a wider range of backgrounds. The foundations for an inclusive workplace are the organization's people values and a commitment to reflect in its workforce a changing society.

In North America, a workforce diversity strategy enables an employer to better reflect the make-up of society and ensure that all potential sources of talent are being tapped. It's also the socially responsible thing to do. For example, immigrants made up 20 per cent of Canada's workforce in 2006. However, 42 per cent of large employers do not have a strategic plan to foster diversity.[24] The labour shortages prior to the global recession were a big incentive to overcome these barriers. Increasingly, employers in Canada recognized that they would fall short of meeting their recruitment goals unless they created a more welcoming work environment for persons with disabilities, Aboriginal persons, immigrants, and women in male-dominated areas such as construction.

Moving in this direction has the added advantage of forming stronger community ties. I noted in chapter 4 that, for TD Financial, diversity goes beyond a commitment to good corporate citizenship and has become how this North American bank does business. In addition to its Diversity Leadership Council, TD has a workplace accommodation policy that gives job applicants and employees access to an inclusive and barrier-free workplace. The Dedicated Assistive Technology team and accommodation fund support persons with disabilities (1,700 of whom are employed by the bank), providing sign language interpreters, text readers, large screen monitors, and workstation modifications. The bank also adjusts work hours and job scope so that everyone is able to contribute. Diversity managers and coaches work with other managers and supervisors to raise awareness of diversity issues and provide skill development to achieve inclusive workplaces.

Other firms have developed similar approaches, designating managers to lead corporation-wide action plans. Ernst & Young is a leading professional services firm with about 4,000 employees across Canada. The company has a full-time manager of inclusiveness, who is responsible for creating and implementing career development strategies and programs that ensure an inclusive environment. The manager of inclusiveness works closely with the CEO, who chairs the Inclusiveness Steering Committee. Inclusiveness awareness workshops are mandatory for all managers and partners. Recruiters also receive specific training on inclusive hiring practices. Advisory groups monitor and guide gender equity and ethnic diversity practices. To ensure the effectiveness of diversity-related initiatives, Ernst & Young is committed to reviewing diversity data, setting goals, and conducting ongoing focus groups to measure progress.

A diversity strategy also strengthens ties with the community. At a diversity workshop, I recall a Home Depot manager describing how this happened at his store. It used to be, he explained, that hiring persons with disabilities was seen simply as 'the right thing to do.' The few such individuals recruited were given special treatment, with the assumption that they could not do a regular job. So hiring a person with a disability was like a charitable gesture and probably seemed that way. Through closer involvement with community agencies trying to find meaningful employment for persons with disabilities, the store managers and HR team realized that everyone could benefit from a different approach. Rather than trying to fit persons with disabilities into existing job slots, they asked a new question: what can this person do and where in the store do they have the greatest potential to contribute?

This attitude meant rethinking what a job is and altering performance expectations to fit what people can offer. Co-workers' attitudes also had to change so that their idea of a team was more inclusive. The store manager described it as a 'capabilities' approach. One example he provided was the necessity of giving hundreds of in-store plants the required amount of water at regular intervals. This was a task that seemed difficult for high school student part-timers, most of whom had never had to care for plants. The solution came through a community employment agency, which referred to the store an individual with a developmental disability who loved plants, knew exactly how to care for them, and could carefully focus on this one task. She quickly became a valued member of the greenhouse team.

Many other organizations also have incorporated diversity goals into their business philosophy and strategy. At Campbell's Company of Canada, which makes soup and other foods, a strong focus on workforce diversity and inclusion defines its business partnerships. Campbell's believes that creating relationships with minority and women-owned businesses is vital to the company's overall success and makes a contribution to the global economy. The company's mission is to increase their diverse supplier base by providing equal access to those suppliers interested in doing business with Campbell's. The result is a stronger supplier base with a broader representation of vendors that better reflects the markets they serve.

In these examples, diversity was one strand in an integrated people strategy that connected employees and the local community. Some of these companies, notably Campbell's, TD, and Ernst & Young, are recognized on lists such as the 50 Best Workplaces in Canada. This reinforces the vital links up the healthy organization value chain, showing in particular how leadership, culture, and vibrant workplaces contribute to sustainable success.

Inspiring Three Generations of Workers

A question frequently asked by HR professionals is 'how do we manage three generations in the workplace?' The three generations most commonly discussed in North America are baby boomers (born 1946–65), Generation X (born 1966–79), and Generation Y (born 1980–95). I believe you will have a far more effective workforce renewal strategy if you understand the needs of these different generations and, rather than 'managing' them, find ways to inspire them over the long term.

As each generation ages and matures, it loses some of the features that labelled it in the first place. That happened with baby boomers. Commentators in the 1960s and 1970s feared that the 'peace and love' ethics of the baby boomers would unleash havoc inside workplaces, weakening the foundations of capitalism. A more accurate assessment is provided by historian Doug Owram, who concludes that the youth revolution of the 1960s was over by 1975, 'with the front edge of the baby boom approaching the magic age of thirty.'[25] Owram quotes one student radical as observing that he had given up his cause in the 1970s because 'it was time to get a job.'[26]

Similarly, Gen-X's initial image was later recast. During the recession of the early 1990s Gen-X was widely described as alienated, powerless, and cynical in the face of hard times. This 'new' generation apparently had scaled down its expectations and rejected many of the values and institutions of its parents. These themes were dissected in academic studies with titles such as *Generation on Hold* and in novels, such as Douglas Copeland's iconic *Generation X*.[27] Yet by 1999 Gen-X had lost its rudderless slacker image. The internet boom was on and many Gen-Xers had ridden the wave. So there were plenty of examples of thirty-year-old entrepreneurs whose eighty-hour weeks were reaping huge dividends.[28]

Generation Y followed the Gen-Xers into the workforce. A recent PricewaterhouseCoopers report of these young graduates in forty-four countries offers a balanced view of what Gen-Y means for workplaces.[29] The report discovered they wanted similar returns from work as older generations, including steady employment with a few employers; they did not want constant job-hopping. What they do bring into the workplace are generation-specific skills and interests, being IT savvy, social networking, globally oriented, and willing to travel. These attributes can benefit employers. For example, consumer electronics retailer Best Buy asked a consultant to price a new employee internet portal. After a quote for several million came back, a group of young employees assembled an informal team of developers and made the portal for $250,000. Now, facing falling sales and profits, Best Buy is looking for novel ideas from its Gen-Y employees to apply the latest technology to marketing and sales.[30]

But the question remains: are there fundamental differences in work aspirations across the generations? The Rethinking Work survey compared employees age thirty or younger with those over forty-five.[31] Not surprisingly, younger workers more highly value career advancement opportunities and older workers put somewhat more importance on benefits, a sense of pride and accomplishment, and freedom to make decisions. However, a core set of features that defines a vibrant workplace is important to all age groups: a work environment that is healthy, safe, and free from harassment and discrimination; training and other opportunities to develop skills and abilities; friendly and helpful co-workers; challenging and interesting work; good pay; and flexible work arrangements.

Employers who are preoccupied with the needs of young recruits are missing a chance to address the quality of work needs of all their staff. Understanding the full spectrum of workforce needs is critical to organizational renewal. Feedback from employees or prospective recruits could reveal, for example, that quite different needs lie behind the high value placed on training. For young workers or new managers, it may mean expanding their skills repertoire. For experienced workers, it could mean adapting existing skills to new roles such as coaching or mentoring. Similarly, 'good pay' means very different things to a twenty-five-year old and a fifty-five-year old.

So, too, does 'flexibility.' Young workers are the least tied down of any age group. Those who are not saddled with large student loans may want time for travel or further education. Flexibility for them also involves teleworking and spread out work time, rather than the traditional 9-to-5 schedule. Middle-aged workers with families are going to want flexibility to meet children's needs. Older workers want hard-earned and long-deferred time for travel, leisure, and volunteer activities – and for some, grandchildren. According to one survey, workers fifty-five and older would prefer to work Tuesday, Wednesday, and Thursday from 9:00 a.m. to noon and to have over six weeks of annual vacation.[32]

Given that baby boomers far outnumber Gen-Y, employers should be enabling a smooth and possibly delayed departure of the boomer generation. In fact, of all the areas where flexibility in workplace policies and practices are required, this presents the greatest opportunity. Finding innovative ways to maximize the contributions of this huge pool of experienced workers means redesigning retirement.

The coming wave of baby boomer retirements has been on employers' radar screens for well over a decade. Yet surprisingly few have taken the steps needed to prepare for this new demographic reality. Employers' human resource policies and practices, workplace culture, and related work environment factors influence decisions by older workers to stay, retire and not work, or retire and re-engage in the workforce. The aging workforce also poses significant risks to employers in terms of lost knowledge, which again requires strategic responses. As U.S. demographer Ken Dychtwald and his colleagues observe: 'In an ideal world, flexible retirement would allow employees to move in and out of the workplace seamlessly, without ever choosing a moment to retire.'[33] By jettisoning traditional notions of retirement, you also will be opening up flexible options for all workers.

There is another urgent reason to do this. Beyond older worker retention and recruitment, a compelling business case for redesigning work-retirement transitions is reduction of the risk of losing core knowledge when experienced baby boomers retire. Retaining the tacit knowledge of retiring workers in critical positions requires more than succession planning for senior management positions. Vital knowledge can be possessed by any worker, from the front lines up.

What I am talking about preserving is tacit knowledge. This is the 'know-how' or 'how-to' knowledge gained from years of doing the organization's tasks, and it usually is not written down. Even sophisticated knowledge management systems do not fully capture tacit knowledge. Solutions require an integration of a firm's knowledge management and human resource strategies.[34] Long-range workforce planning is part of the solution, helping to identify what kinds of tacit knowledge need to be preserved to meet future business goals. It also opens the door to redefining the roles of experienced workers with vital knowledge, giving them time and support to be coaches and mentors to junior staff. Furthermore, the redesign of project teams to include workers with different experience levels also speeds up knowledge transfer. These kinds of innovations often are welcomed by workers of all ages.

Decisions to stay employed or retire are strongly influenced by job quality – as are younger workers' decisions to join, stay, or quit. Among the workers in the Rethinking Work survey, those who are stressed out or dissatisfied with their jobs planned to retire at least a year earlier than co-workers who had a good quality of work life. Furthermore, the biggest incentive for employees to keep working beyond their planned retirement is not money, but the opportunity to do what they are really good at. Flexible hours and schedules, including part-time work, are big attractions. Many are seeking greater personal rewards, such as making a useful contribution to society and having opportunities for challenging and interesting work. Another criterion is a healthy work environment, especially one that is low stress.

A good number of employers soon could be at a disadvantage in the labour market if they do not respond to workforce aging with appropriate action plans. You can start by asking what flexible retirement (if not already in place) would look like in your organization and, more broadly, how the principle of flexibility could be adapted to careers and work arrangements for all workers. As for social responsibility, just think about the potential to improve the quality of life for employees and their families.

Long-Range Workforce Planning

Whether it is flexible phased retirement, empowering Gen-Y workers to contribute their IT skills, or inclusive workplace practices, each of these initiatives will be more effective when they are part of a comprehensive, long-range, workforce plan. Workforce planning may sound dry and technical. But, in fact, it is a sound method for engaging today's workforce to envision and develop tomorrow's workforce – a process that meets all the requirements of healthy change outlined in chapter 6.

The private sector makes extensive use of long-range business planning. A good example is Royal Dutch Shell's 2050 energy scenarios. 'More energy, less carbon dioxide' sums up the global challenge for energy.[35] In one scenario, called 'Scramble,' little action is taken to encourage more efficient energy use or reduce greenhouse gases. The other scenario, called 'Blueprints,' sees the spread of local actions to address three interrelated challenges: economic development, energy security, and environmental pollution. A price is put on carbon emissions, and new green technologies lead to alternative and more efficient energy sources. CO_2 levels go down as a result. Such future scenarios can be used to test corporate strategies in any sector and expanded to anticipate future workforce requirements.

Most large employers have talent management strategies focusing on high-performers and succession plans for senior management positions. However, few have long-range workforce plans that take a broader and future-oriented perspective on organizational renewal. From what I have observed, long-range workforce planning may be more widely used in the public sector, where the workforce is older and heading for retirement sooner than in the private sector. A good example is Edmonton, a western Canadian city of 1 million people and capital of the energy-rich province of Alberta. The city government's approach to workforce planning combines a straightforward process with vision and imagination.

Positioning an organization for future success requires a clear vision of an ideal future and the capacity to adapt plans and goals as the actual future unfolds. Municipalities are big thinkers in this regard, creating planning frameworks that provide direction for their physical, economic and social development.[36] Edmonton's plan is for ten years, but it uses a thirty-year time horizon. Most major cities have such plans and some, such as Seattle and San Francisco, use 100-year time horizons. Edmonton's new municipal development plan, *The Way We Grow*, uses extensive community input to identify the values and growth scenarios that best fit citizens' changing needs and future aspirations. Interestingly, this ongoing work is expected of a city administration, but when a corporation does it, the CSR label gets applied.

To ensure that it will have the right capabilities to guide the municipal plan, the City of Edmonton also created a long-range workforce plan. In a nutshell, workforce planning is a strategy-focused, evidence-based approach for ensuring that an organization has people with the right capabilities in the positions it needs to achieve long-term success. The workforce planning process started with a ten-year assessment of the external and internal environments. The ten-year community plan calls for dramatic changes in roles and skill sets. For example, there will be less need for building management and maintenance expertise and much more environmental knowledge and skill required. Each department identified the implications of the ten-year community plan for its operations, focusing on workforce and workplace changes that would support future roles and goals. The departments' workforce plans were rolled into the corporate workforce plan.

Edmonton launched its workforce planning process in 2003, and it is now embedded into the business planning cycle. The city's three-year HR strategies are guided by the overall workforce plan. The plan has resulted in increased focus on succession planning, leadership development, and talent management as part of an integrated strategy.[37] Successful workforce planning requires HR to play a greater consulting role, supporting operational departments to develop and implement their own workforce plans. HR staff who had focused on program delivery now had to embrace a far more strategic role, and HR provides more data and analysis regarding current and future workforce needs. In short, it adopted an evidence-based approach to identifying and developing the future competencies needed by departments. Workforce planning has its drawbacks. It works best in larger organizations and it can be expensive and time-consuming. But the potential advantages for organizational renewal are significant. Consistent with a healthy organization perspective, it provides a long-term, holistic, and strategic approach to developing the people capacity needed for future success.

Making Progress

This chapter has tied together organizational renewal in terms of the workforce, the workplace, and relationships with society. A healthy organization evolves organically, so it is in a constant state of renewal. But it does so with an eye on the distant horizon, not just on today's challenges. It also seeks innovative ways to balance the needs and aspirations of customers, shareholders, employees, and community stakeholders.

One of the key points made in the chapter is that new directions in strategic CSR have the potential to reposition businesses in ways that benefit all stakeholders. This approach, in my view, is what a sustainable organization is all about. Another key point is that internal and external renewal strategies need to be merged. The long-range workforce plans, inclusive workplace, and flexible employment practices I have described should be viewed as enablers of business strategies that embrace the ethics of environmental and social responsibility.

Measurement also is a prominent theme in the chapter. Workforce planning, as practised by the City of Edmonton, requires the analysis of workforce demographics and skills. Responding to the needs of an increasingly diverse workforce and tracking progress on inclusiveness require that organizations use employee surveys, as TD does. A focus on generational differences in work values inside your organization requires employee consultations or surveys, so you can understand where there is convergence and divergence within your workforce. Socially responsible companies such as Vancity, TNT, and Nexen use annual reporting systems, set targets, commit to improvement actions, and hold themselves publicly accountable for progress. And many of the organizations profiled in this chapter have undergone rigorous independent vetting in order to earn a place on one or more of the lists that recognize ethical, responsible, and sustainable business and people practices. In short, a purposeful use of metrics can inform decisions and actions required to build sustainable organizations. This is the subject of chapter 8.

8 Measuring Progress

Hilti's power tools are prized by professional builders for their durable quality and are much coveted by serious home do-it-your-selfers. What most of its customers may not know about is the Austrian-based manufacturer's rigorous approach to organizational health. Hilti sees the link between employee and customer satisfaction being forged within healthy environments. According to Hartwig Eugster, plant manager at Hilti, 'we have found that satisfied staff are synonymous with improved customer satisfaction and an upward trend in profitability. By means of the measures implemented in the field of corporate culture and workplace health promotion, we have been able to sustainably increase the level of satisfaction among our employees.'[1] Staff and customer satisfaction are measured with different instruments, but by putting these separate indicators side by side, Hilti is able to connect actions on the people side with business results.

Executives at Genentech, one of the world's leading biotech firms, made a discovery of a different kind a few years ago. Stephen Juelsgaard, an executive at Genentech, explained to a conference in 2007 how the biotech company had experienced 20 per cent annual growth since 2001. Throughout that period, it was on *Fortune* magazine's list of 100 Best Companies to Work For In America. Executives realized that the company's improved ranking on the *Fortune* list tracked its stock price. Essentially, they connected two big performance dots. When employees were asked to write down what makes it a great workplace, three qualities stood out: commitment to science and creating innovative treatments, dedication to patients, and valuing and respecting employees – all drivers of performance. What sparked the executive team to connect these data points was their belief that culture lies at the heart of the company's continued success.

In the public sector, a leader in the use of healthy organization metrics is Britain's National Health Service (NHS). The annual NHS Staff Survey measures what staff identified as key drivers and outcomes of healthy work environments. What is notable is how the survey feeds into a comprehensive framework for ongoing improvements in operational and patient outcomes – what really matters to the public. The 600 NHS organizations must take follow-up actions on survey results in order to meet government targets for twenty-four core performance standards. The reporting and monitoring of survey results are the mandate of the Care Quality Commission, an independent regulatory body. Staff survey results are integrated into a comprehensive performance report card, the Annual Health Check.[2] Adding even greater public accountability, complete survey results for every NHS organization are reported on the Care Quality Commission's website.[3]

Hilti, Genentech, and the NHS illustrate, in different ways, how to piece together relevant data to paint a more complete picture of a healthy organization value chain. These organizations have ventured into the frontier of organizational health, creatively using selective metrics to improve the links between people and performance. HR dashboards, balanced scorecards, health promotion return on investment, and 'triple bottom line' report cards – these topics are the focus of growing numbers of management conferences and featured articles in practitioner publications.

This trend is promising, because it opens up more possibilities for making better decisions that contribute to vibrant workplaces, healthy change, and results that are sustainable. Meaningful HR metrics help an organization to track its progress on people goals by creating accountability for the required actions – at least in theory. If it were that easy, more organizations would have a robust system for measuring the human side of performance. But there are many pitfalls to using metrics. One of the biggest risks is that organizations can drown in their own data. Managers can become immobilized trying to make sense of numbers that are meaningless, inaccurate, or overwhelming in quantity. Metrics can become the tail that wags the dog, displacing the original intent: 'learn how we're doing and where we need to do better.'

In this chapter, I examine the promise and pitfalls of measuring progress along your healthy organization trajectory. Throughout the book, I have drawn on various types of data – surveys, qualitative consultations, corporate information, and published research findings – to build a case for investing in healthy organizations. Having the relevant metrics available contributes to healthy change and a positive culture. Now I will help readers to identify what they can do to improve the use of data relevant to their organizational improvement goals. To this end, the chapter addresses five questions:

1. How can you make better use of evidence to plan, implement and monitor organizational improvements?
2. What measurement tools are available to you and how can you adapt them to your needs?
3. What are successful practices for using surveys as catalysts for healthy change?
4. What must you consider when integrating people metrics into a corporate performance reporting framework?
5. What are the basic guidelines you need to follow in order to measure workplace progress effectively?

Using Evidence for Action

The healthy organization model adds an important new dimension to business performance reporting. At the heart of a healthy organization is the relationship between vibrant work environments, employees' capabilities, and results. Once senior managers grasp this connection between individual well-being and productivity, the next step is to use work environment quality and well-being as performance indicators. This puts employees' experiences right next to customer satisfaction, profits, growth, operating efficiency, and social and environmental impact as key performance measures.

From a risk management perspective, unhealthy and unsafe work environments can impose large costs on an employer. These range from lost productivity and overtime costs due to absenteeism to all the direct and indirect costs of a demoralized workforce and underutilized talent. The costs and risks of an unhealthy work environment for employers should be clear by now. Workplace health research does a good job of quantifying the extent of the problem, using measures such as absenteeism rates and costs, health benefit plan costs, the burden of long-term disability, turnover, and the like. But if these measures are flipped 180 degrees, we have positive indicators of well-being, performance, and sustainability. So, as measures go, retention replaces turnover, days at work replaces absenteeism, injury-free days replaces lost-time injuries, and return to work success rates are used instead of long-term disability rates.

This positive approach to people metrics is most consistent with a healthy organization model. However, we cannot assume this sort of information will have any impact, beyond keeping HR staff busy collecting it.

Practical Challenges of Using Evidence

Jac Fitz-enz, the guru of human resource metrics, makes a convincing case for a focused effort to collect, analyse, understand, and use HR data in organizational decisions: 'Information is the key to performance management and improvement. Without it, we have only opinions with no supporting facts and no directional signals ... Human data show us how the only active asset, people, are doing in their quest to drive the organization towards its goals.'[4] Fitz-enz encourages managers and other change agents to share and use the best available evidence in their decisions and plans. However, this presents practitioners with numerous practical challenges.

Monitoring and evaluation are often the weakest links connecting work environments to healthy outcomes. The information gained through these activities can generate a dynamic learning process that contributes to organizational renewal. Data must spark ideas about how to do things better. This is possible only if monitoring and evaluation data are converted into useable knowledge to inform decisions and actions. Fitz-ens calls it an 'information sharing culture,' with a strong emphasis on knowledge for action. Otherwise, measurement and evaluation turn into meaningless organizational rituals that do nothing but waste resources.

We do not have a handy organizational equivalent of a weigh scale or blood pressure gauge for assessing whether a company is healthy. Thus, organizations have no choice but to come to grips with why they need healthy organization measures, what measures are needed, and how to make the fullest use of them. While it is a good idea to incorporate monitoring and evaluation into any change initiative, putting all the pieces together into a more complete picture of organizational health performance takes time. In U.S. firms widely recognized as leaders in linking health and productivity, data integration happened later in the process of creating a healthier workforce and more productive work environment once actions were under way.[5]

Thinking Ahead

Selecting relevant metrics is more than a technical exercise. You need to think ahead to who will use these data, for what purposes, and what barriers stand in the way of effective use of evidence for decision-making. I invite you to use the following examples I have observed to reflect on the challenges of using data in your organization:

- Using metrics takes time and commitment. A meeting of senior management to address the results of an employee survey had to be rescheduled, because only one person had read the survey report. This shaky start to survey follow-up reinforced employees' cynicism that managers do not care about their views.
- Organizations adopt performance reporting systems without helping the intended users understand them. I have seen managers in organizations with balanced scorecards role their eyes, throw up their hands, and make bad jokes about dashboards as 'dartboards' when asked 'what's it like using a scorecard?'
- Many managers need to feel an emotional connection to employee feedback and numbers do not do that. So, when the sceptical CFO sees dozens of anonymous comments from an employee survey saying 'I love working here,' the positive impact of the firm's people strategy suddenly becomes real.
- Managers want to focus on what they can most influence. In a conference discussion of healthy outcomes, senior managers recognized that there are two levels of health drivers, individual and organizational, and that employers should focus on only the latter.
- Some organizations have consistently measured the wrong things. A strategic goal of a natural resources company was the efficient use of human resources. It struggled to find meaningful indicators of this. Advice from HR to change 'efficient' to 'effective' went unheeded by senior management.

In sum, there are big gaps in management's use of evidence for decision making.[6] These gaps partly stem from the failure of academics to transfer knowledge in understandable ways or to examine what matters most to practitioners.[7] Practitioners, for their part, lack time and motivation to distil the relevant implications from a deluge of academic research. And, when presented with recommendations based on solid internal evidence, managers may ignore them or not require data to

Figure 8.1 Key issues identified in a healthy workplace assessment

Wellness strategy success factors	*Major needs*
1. Commitment from senior management	1. Reduce injury risks and absenteeism
2. Collaboration between management and unions	2. Mental health and stress
3. Participation of employee groups in the design and implementation	3. Health trends in an aging workforce
Strengths to build on	*Barriers to change*
1. Solid foundation of health and safety programs	1. Some employees do not feel valued
2. Lost-time work injury reduction	2. Managers perceive employee dissatisfaction
3. On-site Health Centre	3. Post-strike mood of general distrust
4. Employee and family assistance program	4. Perceived lack of recognition among senior managers that improvements
5. Joint Health and Safety Committee	are required

justify a particular people investment. Still, as more senior managers understand the strategic value of work environments, culture, and human resource practices, we can be sure that better use will be made of people metrics.

The Value of Qualitative Consultations

But let us not get carried away with metrics just yet. Obviously, to make progress and even be thinking about how to measure it, you need a starting point and a clear direction. In fact, some of the most useful information for planning actions is qualitative, obtained through employee consultations. The added advantage of employee consultations is that people come to better understand each other, develop shared goals for their workplace, and have opportunities to take ownership for solutions. Change agents at earlier stages of planning healthy change may find useful lessons in the following examples of how two organizations used consultations in the early stages of developing their healthy organization trajectory.

Senior managers and health and safety professionals at Teck Cominco's Trail Operations had been considering the launch of a workplace wellness strategy. In the wake of a strike by production workers, there was a heightened sense of mutual distrust on both union and management sides. However, rising disability costs, an aging workforce, and an intensely competitive market for skilled trades underscored the urgency of expanding the traditional health and safety focus to a more comprehensive approach to total wellness. Some 80 per cent of workers were in skilled manual jobs and many were nearing the end of long careers with the company. As a first major step, informal discussions were held with key individuals – managers, union representatives, occupational health and safety experts – to define wellness and identify priority needs and opportunities for progress. This was 'phase 1' of the wellness strategy. A 'phase 2' would implement actions around specific improvement goals. The organization approached any major change initiative in this way.

Figure 8.1 provides a summary of what the phase 1 assessment found and shows how simple and direct the messages were. Consultations identified key points in four areas: factors that would ensure success of the wellness strategy; existing strengths the organization could build on; major needs; and the biggest barriers to moving down the wellness path. This information provided a solid foundation from which to launch a joint union-management wellness committee to coordinate, plan, and implement specific initiatives to address the three major needs. The importance of taking stock before moving forward is clearly illustrated and must be done in a way that is consistent with how the organization goes about problem-solving. It also must build a common change agenda around a few consensus needs.

As a new university committed to creating a healthy workplace culture, UBC Okanagan established a Healthy Workplace Advisory Group comprising administrative and service staff, faculty, unions, and the executive. One of the first things the group did was to consult with co-workers to identify what they saw as the elements of a supportive culture at UBCO. Students with training in qualitative research were involved as note-takers for the consultation sessions. This input was then used to define the core values that will guide UBCO to achieve its distinctive mission and vision. An online survey asked respondents to provide written responses to three open-ended questions:

1. What values do you believe are essential to achieve a healthy workplace culture (list up to 3)?
2. What is the best thing about your current workplace?
3. Describe one change that would make your workplace better.

A thematic analysis of the written responses were both validating and revealing; it provided a clear picture of the most important features of a healthy culture. Four value themes emerged, the most widely mentioned one being respect. This was followed by quality of work life, mainly expressed as work/life balance and flexibility in work arrangements. Third-ranked was a supportive community, referring mainly to supportive relationships and a supportive environment. Fourth was communication, which, like respect, was usually stated as a single word. A total of twenty categories were created, in order to capture the diverse language and wide scope of the values provided by survey respondents. In the end, some categories were combined. For example, the value of respect also could include tolerance, openness, diversity, fairness, caring, and compassion. Similarly, the concept of a supportive community included a positive atmosphere, professional development, appreciation and recognition, and services and facilities.

This qualitative consultation and the list of values that emerged helped to energize ongoing conversations about the culture. One clear result was a collectively understood shortlist of healthy workplace culture building blocks. These provided solid ground for ongoing initiatives with wider involvement from employee groups.

Measurement Tools

In this section, I offer suggestions for how you might approach healthy organization measurement. I start with an overview of what needs to be measured, then share some ideas on measurement tools and research design, and end with a brief discussion – and some cautions – about calculating returns on investment in workplace wellness initiatives.

Measures

Healthy organization indicators measure a range of social, psychological, organizational, and physical determinants (drivers); processes (factors or activities that influence how determinants affect outcomes); and outcomes (effects). Figure 8.2 organizes measures by their level of analysis and their position in the causal sequence. Indicators can provide information that enables action at four different levels: individual, job, work unit or team, and the organization as a whole. Individual-level data can be aggregated and reported at the work unit or organizational level to obtain a diagnosis of performance and quality of work life out-

Figure 8.2 Examples of evaluation measures by level of analysis and position in the causal sequence

Level of analysis	⇨ Position in the causal sequence ⇨		
	Determinant	Process	Outcome
Individual	Employee's sense of job autonomy	Timeliness and usefulness of performance feedback	Self-reported health and well-being
Job	Challenging and meaningful tasks	Job scope and design	Job satisfaction
Unit or team	Mutual respect	Policies and practices to support and recognize team effectiveness	Team morale
Organization	Leadership commitment to people development	Annual hours of training per full-time equivalent employee	Career development opportunities

comes such as morale and work/life balance. It is important to clearly distinguish these outcomes from their underlying 'causes.' Factors influencing employee experiences are the vibrant workplace ingredients outlined in chapter 3, in four broad categories: relationships, job, teamwork, and supports.

As also noted in chapter 3, the characteristics of an inspired employee suggest relevant outcome indicators, although the most basic measures here would include employee satisfaction, commitment, pride, and sense of accomplishment. To round out the assessment of performance, at the organizational level it is possible to use employee surveys either to assess performance-relevant outcomes – such as perceived team performance or actual use of skills and initiative – or to rely on other data sources, such as customer satisfaction surveys.

In terms of process, referring back to the healthy organization value chain, we see there is a layer in that model that I called 'effective people practices.' These are the systems, resources, and programs that ensure the determinants will, in fact, have a positive impact on outcomes.

Tools

An important decision in planning an evaluation is whether to create your own measures, use measures from external sources, or use some combination. Existing measures could be extracted from administrative data (e.g., absenteeism, voluntary turnover, and overtime). Building your own evaluation tools could involve developing an employee survey or adding new questions to an existing survey. You could also review existing tools available in published academic research, through licensing arrangements or from consultants. Regardless of whether you borrow or build or buy, it is important to assess the accuracy of the measures and the usefulness of the data they generate for decision-making and action within your organization.

Academic researchers offer various tools for assessing culture, work environments, quality of work life, workplace health and safety, and other relevant topics. Usually, measurement tools published in academic journals are in the public domain and can be used with no cost as long as you credit the source. Advantages of using assessment tools created by academic researchers include the following:

- Documented validity (they measure what they are intended to measure) and reliability (they measure the same thing across different groups and over time).
- Clear definitions of the concepts being measured.
- A solid theoretical foundation, explaining how the concepts measured are interrelated.

However, there are trade-offs. Academic tools can create technical and conceptual overload, giving more than you need to meet your immediate organizational goals.[8] And measures designed to test academic theories may not have practical applications. Still, you might find what you need or get good ideas for adapting measures to suit your purposes.

Qualitative information is a complement or alternative to the quantitative evaluation methods described above. Examples include open-ended questions in surveys, focus groups, other forms of in-person or Web-based employee consultation, and individual interviews. These techniques can be useful at an early stage of planning an intervention, for example, to identify areas of concern or needs. Or they could be a follow-up to a quantitative evaluation to further probe and explain findings or to develop solutions. For some organizations, a qualitative approach is a more personal way to connect with employees and involve them in the change process than conducting a survey.

Design Options

Actually, there is no 'best practice' to conduct evaluations in workplaces. Practically speaking, the best method is the one that fits your context and meets your objectives. Become acquainted with the pros and cons of the evaluation approach you are considering. And, most important, do not go overboard trying to find the perfect methodology. It may be useful to search scholarly e-journals and practitioner publications, online databases (e.g., Medline, ABI-Inform), and Google Scholar for recent publications relevant to your plans. Partnerships with universities can help to tap available expertise on methods. Also useful are informal communities of practice, comprising practitioners who share a similar vision or approach to workplace improvements.[9] If you decide to hire an external consultant to conduct the evaluation, being well informed will ensure you get what the organization most needs in terms of actionable information.

Using rigorous scientific evaluation methods is possible, but often not practical. Here are three examples showing how teams of researchers and practitioners have carried out this type of evaluation. As you read these examples, think about whether these methods would provide value-added to your organization's healthy change process.

Reducing musculoskeletal injuries is a goal of all health care organizations. The Occupational Health and Safety Agency for Healthcare in British Columbia (OHSAH), Canada, evaluated in partnership with employers and unions an integrated injury prevention and return to work process.[10] The goal of the program (called PEARS, which stands for Prevention and Early Active Return to Work Safely) is to reduce the incidence, duration, time loss, and related costs of workplace musculoskeletal injuries through early intervention and the implementation of preventative strategies such as ergonomic assessments and workplace accommodation. Evaluation of pilot sites tracked incidence rates for injuries and the duration of associated time loss.[11] While results showed no reduction in incidence, the program was effective in returning to work more quickly injured nurses and health science professionals. The evaluation calculated savings in time loss and compensation, providing support for expanding the program. It also demonstrated the benefits of union - management cooperation on healthy workplace issues.

Randomized controlled trials (RCT) – considered the 'gold standard' in evaluation research methods – are rarely used to assess organizational change. This is because of the commitment of time, resources, and management required and the disruption of workplace routines. Here is how RCT was used to assess the efficacy of nurse-manager consultation and problem solving meetings for improving staff morale and care quality and reducing absenteeism.[12] Thirteen in-patient units were randomly assigned to treatment and control groups, and the experimental group received training from university experts in a cooperative form of problem solving. Outcomes were measured through a survey of employee morale and absenteeism. Incident reports and patient satisfaction were used to assess the quality of care. The results showed significant improvements in perceptions of the work environment and working relationships in the experimental groups, compared with the control groups.

An entirely different approach to implementing and evaluating workplace change is 'participatory action research' (PAR). PAR combines research with organizational development, with a big emphasis on stakeholder participation. Some organizations, for example, UBC Okanagan, use the approach without labelling it PAR. Employees (and sometimes customers or community stakeholders) are actively involved in defining common problems or they change goals, designing a plan to bring about improvements, then reflecting on the changes and adjusting the plan accordingly. PAR can utilize standard qualitative or quantitative data-gathering and analysis tools to enable learning.[13] The experience and practical knowledge of front-line employees are as important to the process as 'expert' knowledge obtained from scientific research. PAR is an interactive cycle of collective observing, reflecting, and acting. The approach includes a wide spectrum of grass-roots, team, or committee-led change initiatives with a research or evaluation component.[14]

Return on Investment

The U.S. Centers for Disease Control and Prevention (CDC) offers useful guidelines for assessing the financial impact of workplace illness prevention and health promotion programs.[15] This is referred to as 'return-on-investment,' or ROI. The CDC defines the cost effectiveness of an intervention as the ratio of an intervention compared with an alternative as the net costs divided by net health outcomes. Cost-benefit analysis assigns a monetary value to all program outcomes. Realistically, cost-benefit information should be only one of many inputs for decisions about resource allocations in workplaces.

When asking for ROI data, managers need to be aware that providing such information can be an onerous task. Not surprisingly, many organizations shy away from ROI analysis on HR programs because of the volume and quality of data required, lack of in-house research expertise, and the long-term commitment needed to both the program and the evaluation process. Even when 'business case' data are required, there can be a double standard of evidence required by employers for investing in workplace health interventions that are proactive and preventative. Employer-sponsored health plans fund expensive medical treatments that are based on evidence of efficacy, rather than on ROI data. As a team of U.S. workplace health experts observed: 'The health promotion field, however, is continually challenged to prove something medical researchers cannot – that the financial benefits of health promotion exceed its costs.'[16]

What is more, some decision-makers do not need to be convinced of the benefits of healthy workplaces. An organization's core values may be the rationale for setting and meeting people goals. Just think of all the organizations that invest heavily in employee training. Very few systematically evaluate their return on training investment, assuming that training is a necessary human capital investment for both the firm and its employees. The same is true for healthy workplace investments. For example, as the manager of Health and Productivity at Chevron Corporation in California commented about the company's disability management system: 'The return we have achieved has not always been well documented from a financial point of view, but the consensus from our management is that health promotion has added to Chevron's financial success by helping achieve Chevron's goals.'[17]

My intent is not to steer you away from ROI analysis, but rather to offer a word of caution: know what you are wading into. Change agents should be especially sceptical when asked for an ROI-based business case *before* they proceed with a change. It is far more realistic to incorporate an evaluation component into the implementation strategy, using the results as part of the learning and improvement process. This will provide a home-grown business case that will be difficult for senior management to ignore.

Using Surveys for Healthy Change

More organizations are using surveys to evaluate work environments and obtain employee input. Doing a survey is the easy part. A greater challenge is learning from survey results. Look at surveys as one tool for building a better workplace through staff engagement and communication. Surveys are opportunities to involve staff in planning and implementing changes based on survey findings. Surveys also open up communication channels with employees. Effective follow-up requires extensive two-way communication so decision-makers can hear employee reactions to the survey findings and their ideas for improvements.

Survey Guidelines

Expanding on these points, I list below detailed guidelines to help you and other change agents translate results from surveys or other evaluations into action.

1. A senior manager, project team, or committee needs a clear mandate to 'champion' or sponsor the survey from start to finish, especially by involving others in the follow-up process.
2. Recognize that no survey can be definitive. Treat the survey as one mechanism for getting employee feedback. There may be few surprises. Chances are the findings will reinforce what you already know intuitively or from other sources of information.
3. A constructive focus can be achieved by reporting only the percentage of positive responses for evaluative questions on the survey. This also makes results easier to interpret.
4. Follow-up actions are a shared responsibility and should involve employees, unions, supervisors, managers, human resources, occupational health and safety or wellness, corporate communications, and the executive team.

5. Human resources departments must be prepared to assess and readjust current human resources policies and practices in light of survey findings.

6. Consider a sequential approach to reporting, beginning with the executive, followed by managers and supervisors, employees at company forums or team meetings. Consultations give the committee and survey champion opportunities to refine, focus, and validate the priority action areas and key messages.

7. A survey without concerted follow-up action is an expensive and demoralizing waste of resources. To enable follow-up, employees need time to undertake action planning and implementation. The executive must make this a priority.

8. The survey committee should review the results and identify areas of strength and two or three opportunities for improvement. Present these key findings as the committee's view, and ask others for their interpretations.

9. Action planning has to happen within each work unit, so data need to be reported in this way to enable meaningful discussions and action. Give units their results in a form that compares them with those of the rest of the organization. Balance corporate-wide priority action areas with unit-specific actions.

10. Most medium-size and large organizations have 'pockets of excellence' – a few work units in which employees are truly inspired. The survey can help to identify such units, so their 'story' can be shared across the organization.

11. The committee should also examine the data for variations by demographic groups, looking for groups that stand out as being considerably higher or lower than average. Targeted or corporate-wide improvements can be planned based on this group analysis.

12. Coordinating actions at the organization-wide, work unit, and individual levels is an important ongoing role, often taken on by human resources, the survey committee, or the survey champion.

13. If you used open-ended questions, categorize the responses by theme and use the results to amplify and give a human face to the numbers in the survey. All senior managers should read these written responses.

14. Share the complete survey findings with any employees who are interested. This is easily done on an intranet site, but hard copies should be available to employees who do not have computer access.

15. If you are repeating a survey, distil the key trends for communication and follow-up purposes. Where are you making progress, holding your own, or backsliding? Did you achieve or exceed any improvement targets set previously?

Finding a Clear Direction from Survey Data

I have seen many organizations launch a survey only to become immobilized by the results. Several years later, they still lack a clear sense of direction. If this is your experience, consider stepping back and taking another more focused look at the survey findings. One organization I worked with was inundated with people concepts. These sounded similar – positive culture, supportive relationships, workplace community, engaged employees – but were not clearly defined. As a result, it was difficult to find a clear direction for follow-up to a recent employee survey. Working with HR, the executive team took a step back and organized all the concepts it was using into three categories: drivers (i.e., implied 'causes' or enabling conditions); outcomes for employees; and outcomes or goals for the organization. It consolidated the concepts, creating a compact and actionable strategy statement that linked people and performance:

> We aspire to be a high-performing organization, fulfilling our mandate by providing excellent services through teamwork and leadership. The key to excelling at our mission is a highly capable workforce. This requires all employees to be engaged in their work and feel commitment and pride towards the organization. A capable, engaged, committed, and satisfied workforce is only possible if we create and sustain positive work environments and supportive people management practices. Each workplace must strive for positive working relationships guided by core values of fairness, respect, and competence.

Then the HR team revisited the employee survey findings in search of key indicators of employee engagement and its main drivers. The survey contained ten questions that measured aspects of engagement (and led to endless debates about which one was most important). Statistical analysis reduced the ten items to four items that were combined into an Engagement Scale, which simplified reporting by using a single score. The scale score provided a meaningful key performance indicator for tracking and reporting progress on this strategic goal. These scale items are as follows:

- I am proud of the work carried out in my work unit.
- I feel committed to the work that I do in my job.
- My job gives me a feeling of accomplishment.
- Overall, how satisfied are you with your job?

The re-analysis of survey data was pushed further, identifying which of the many potential drivers of engagement had the biggest 'net impact' (i.e., after taking into account other drivers, along with employee demographics) on the new engagement scale score. Again, multiple indicators were combined into four distinct scales measuring people leadership, work unit relationships, training and learning, and job resources. By far, the biggest influence on engagement is people leadership, capturing the quality and consistency of corporate-wide communication, values, and culture. All four of these driver scales contained between three to seven survey questions, each with clear action implications for managers and employees.

Having a model of drivers and outcomes of a healthy organization will help to guide decision-making about which human resource investments, policies, and practices would be most beneficial for the employer and its employees. Most organizations have implicit models that link people and performance. So a useful whiteboard exercise for senior managers as a group is to map this out, guided by a simple question: 'what drives our business results?' This model can then be validated in discussions with middle managers, front-line supervisors, and employees. It should be built from all the major pieces of the HR strategy.

Using Survey Results for Leadership Development

The federal governments in the United States and Canada are among their nations' largest employers. In each country, they also carry out extensive employee surveys in terms of the numbers surveyed and the scale of the follow-up actions. Canada's Public Service Employee Survey (PSES) has been conducted since 1999, most recently in fall 2008. Public service-wide results are published online, in a model display of government transparency.[18] Trends over time show some improvements in the work environment, career development, satisfaction, and commitment. Anyone considering a public service career can use the data to identify the best federal government workplaces. And existing federal public servants can see which department or agency would be a better place for them to work.

The Canada Public Service Agency, the central government HR unit, facilitates survey follow-ups at the department and agency level. It also supports a range of ongoing initiatives to develop an engaged, high-performing workforce and healthy and supportive workplaces across the public service. Faced with a serious demographic crunch due to the large number of retiring baby boomers, many of whom are managers, for the past decade the public service has emphasized leadership development and succession planning.

Worth noting is how indicators on the PSES can be directly linked to the leadership behaviours that are cultivated and rewarded in the public service. Figure 8.3 shows on the left side the percentage of employees responding to the 2005 PSES who were positive or most positive on six basic measures of effective supervision. These include keeping promises, being open to different opinions without reprisal, keeping employees informed, providing recognition, discussing results expected, and providing feedback. When positive and most positive responses are combined, all scores are in the 70 per cent range. But the goal is to increase the 'most positive' part of the bar in the figure. Now, looking at the right side of the figure, you will see ten of the leadership skills and abilities that are the focus of leadership training programs. There is not a direct correspondence between all the survey items on the left and the leadership skills on the right. However, we can assume that any supervisor who had all these skills in abundance likely would be rated 'most positive' by her or his direct reports on the survey. For a large and very complex organization, this basic use of survey indicators to track and inform leadership development shows what is possible and practical.

Integrated Performance Reporting

Most large and mid-sized organizations conduct employee surveys, but relatively few use indicators from these surveys in corporate report cards. Yet there are promising developments in this regard, as some organizations expand their existing balanced scorecard, executive dashboard, or annual reporting to include people and social responsibility metrics. A balanced scorecard guides an organization to measure how well it is implementing its strategy by giving equal emphasis to financial, operational, customer, and employee development goals. An executive dashboard or report card is a similar but simpler reporting method. The triple bottom line – referred to as 'people, profits, and planet' – expands

Figure 8.3 Measuring how supervisors support employees to succeed

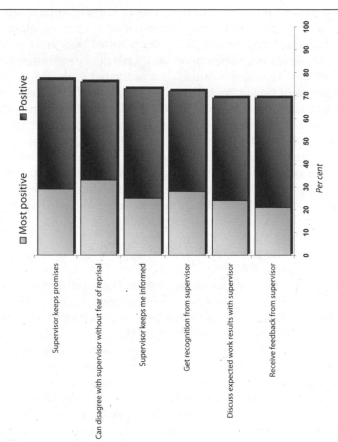

■ Most positive   ■ Positive

Supervisor keeps promises

Can disagree with supervisor without fear of reprisal

Supervisor keeps me informed

Get recognition from supervisor

Discuss expected work results with supervisor

Receive feedback from supervisor

0   10   20   30   40   50   60   70   80   90   100

Per cent

Note: Response categories on all items are 'strongly agree' and 'agree' for most positive and positive, respectively.
Source: Government of Canada, Public Service Employee Survey, 2005
http://www.tbs-sct.gc.ca/pses-saff/2008/index-eng.asp.

Examples of the leadership skills, abilities, and characteristics needed in the federal public service, guided by integrity and respect:

–   Fosters a climate of transparency, trust and respect
–   Builds a safe and healthy work environment
–   Teaches and learns from others
–   Shares information
–   Promotes collaboration
–   Encourages open constructive discussion of diverse views
–   Follows through on commitments
–   Solicits and listens to input
–   Communicates with clarity and commitment
–   Coaches, challenges and provides growth opportunities

Source: Canada Public Service Agency, Key Leadership Competencies, 2006. www.psagency-agencefp.gc.ca

business success criteria to include social and environmental objectives. Compared with traditional financial reports, these approaches are more integrated, holistic, and comprehensive. With the inclusion of the appropriate people, community, and sustainability metrics, these types of integrated performance reporting systems become powerful tools for achieving and sustaining healthy organization goals.

Examples of Effective Performance Reporting

I now want to provide lessons from research and practice in organizations that have included HR metrics in corporate performance reporting systems. Keep in mind, though, that the 'art and science' of organizational performance metrics is evolving, so it is more appropriate to extract lessons from organizations known to have created integrated performance reporting systems that are tied to managers' incentives and rewards. These organizations have taken that extra step to hold decision-makers accountable. Other users of people metrics are not there yet.

Following the basic idea of a balanced scorecard or a triple bottom line, each organization must find its own way to translate its strategy into a compact dashboard of key performance indicators. Metrics become integrated when their interrelationships are known. Metrics become meaningful only when managers, in particular, know exactly what actions make these metrics go up or down. The actual measures in the following examples differ, reflecting the distinctive contexts and goals of these organizations. Here are three examples of different approaches to integrated performance reporting:

- *Ernst & Young.* This global professional services firm developed a system for measuring the impact of work environments on the bottom line as part of its People First strategy. Three pillars refreshed their corporate strategy in the late 1990s: people, quality, and growth. At the global level, each executive must have two people goals. Accountability is achieved using a balanced scorecard approach. The tool they use is People Point, an online rating by any employee for each executive. One item, 'Fosters a positive work environment and helps people grow,' tells what behaviour supports the rating. This system has changed executive behaviour more than any prior performance management system used by the firm. It is now applied to all managers. A Global People Survey with thirty worldwide questions and local supplements also is used. A Business Effectiveness Index, comprising eight survey items, correlates with business performance. Ernst & Young also developed a People Commitment Index, which correlates with performance.

- *ArcelorMittal Dofasco*. Dofasco views its 'innovative, productive and empowered workforce' as critical to being the most profitable steelmaker in North America. It carefully tracks health and wellness, safety, engagement, and productivity at the individual and organizational levels. The following composite indicators are used: job satisfaction; overall health, fitness, and energy levels; productivity and efficiency levels; and absenteeism rates. These metrics are derived from quarterly employee feedback surveys, annual employee satisfaction surveys, focus groups, cost benefit analyses, health audits, program attendance and evaluations, and fitness improvements. Management responsibility for health and wellness has been integrated into Dofasco's existing performance management system and department-level business plans. Dofasco also is committed to the triple bottom line of sustainability (environment, community, profitability) and makes an annual Report to the Community.
- *Vancity Credit Union*. This financial services institution based in the Vancouver area, with 2,000 employees, uses performance indicators to assess how well it is living up to its Statement of Values and Commitments. All high-level performance indicators are publicly reported using a balanced scorecard framework. One of the five commitments is 'We will ensure that Vancity is a great place to work.' This is reported annually with improvement targets, using these metrics: (1) Overall employee satisfaction, measured by a six-item 'engagement index' reported for the organization as a whole, operating divisions, and major employee demographic groups. (2) Percentage of employees agreeing that Vancity's statement of values and commitments provides meaningful direction in their work. (3) Staff turnover. (4) Percentage of employees agreeing the balance between their work and personal commitments is right for them (an 'employee health and safety' measure). Vancity pioneered in Canada the 'social audit' process, which is how it annually assesses its economic, social, and environmental performance and presents the results to the public in accountability reports.

The above examples describe developed systems, so it is useful to look behind the scenes at how organizations go about creating integrated performance reporting. I will use the example of a major logistics and transportation company I worked with. The company spent several years developing and introducing HR metrics into its operationally focused performance report card. Some executives and line managers saw the need to put key people indicators alongside operational metrics, which the company had spent considerable time in perfecting. The challenge was identifying what people outcomes to measure, then how to roll them into a single indicator. As the executive team realized the complexities of measuring and reporting – the company had dozens of key performance indicators 'owned' by different managers and teams – it opted for simplicity.

Basically, HR and operations managers took several runs at trying to create a high-level HR indicator that could be used in quarterly corporate performance reports. The search for a single measure was consistent with how operational performance was measured; for example, a team had recently developed a customer service quality index reported monthly. The goal was to create an HR metric that was a business driver and could be used to calculate the cost of a lost day of work. Working with operations managers who created the service quality indicator, the HR team implemented a workplace health index on a pilot basis. Designed for use at the work unit level, the index includes lost-time injury frequency and severity, short-term disability, turnover, and overtime. Several pilot work units used the index to take action on psychosocial work environment issues related to stress, absenteeism, and turnover. No doubt the index will evolve as work units provide feedback. But for now, the organization has found a way to use HR metrics to create wider responsibility for work environment improvements.

Triangulating Your Existing Data

These examples show what is possible when an organization is diligent and purposeful about using a people-focused measurement and reporting system. But you do not need a sophisticated corporate report card system to put together a bigger picture of performance. Rather, look for easy ways to 'triangulate' existing data – basically, connect the dots (see figure 8.4). Triangulation taps into existing sources of administrative data and combines these data with information from employee and customer surveys. The key to data triangulation is using a standardized reporting category for all data, such as department, functional unit, or worksite. Using a Microsoft Excel spreadsheet, you can present data

Figure 8.4 Triangulating existing data for learning and improvement

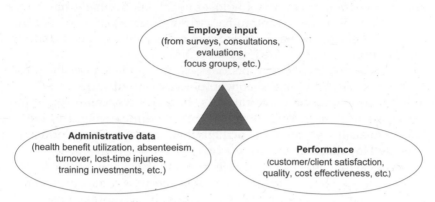

from different sources side by side and look for patterns. When you look at these patterns, ask questions such as 'are units high in employee satisfaction also low in overtime utilization and absenteeism as well as above average in customer satisfaction?'

As you consider your organization's readiness for integrated performance reporting, there are several points to bear in mind. Effective corporate performance measurement systems transform data into information. This makes it critical to understand how the corporate strategy has been translated into dashboard metrics. Furthermore, there needs to be a group within the organization that 'owns' the metrics and dashboard, communicates to the CEO and executive the strategic and operational issues identified in the dashboard, and identifies the supports and resources required by line managers to use the metrics to take action. Metrics must foster learning. For example, dashboards are a powerful tool for internal benchmarking and learning from your own centres of excellence. It is necessary, of course, for the dashboard to be used constructively as a diagnostic tool for learning and improvement. Dashboards also are accountability tools and should be linked to annual performance appraisals and performance-based compensation, as Ernst & Young has done.

Guidelines for Measuring Improvements

To summarize our discussion, below I list guidelines for you to consider when planning, evaluating, and tracking change. I encourage you to adapt these guidelines to fit your healthy change trajectory. They can be usefully applied to a new program, practice, or initiative intended to improve work environments, employee health and wellness, or organizational performance. They can be narrow or broad in focus, aiming to create positive outcomes for individual employees, teams, and the organization.

1. *Be Goal-Focused*. Always keep your objectives front and centre. It helps to create a shared vision of the kind of work environment you are striving to create. If you are having difficulty figuring out how to evaluate a program, perhaps it has too many goals or fuzzy goals. Do not let the tools or methods drive the process. Rather, always keep your eye on the objectives of the changes or interventions and use only evaluation tools that specifically address them.
2. *Model Your Vision*. Every step of the intervention process must contribute to your organization's vision of a high-quality work environment. Evaluation is not simply data collection, but an opportunity for collaborative learning and organizational development. A robust evaluation process will give managers, employees, and teams more control over improvements in their environment. It also contributes to their ongoing learning.
3. *Take a Positive Approach*. Evaluation should help the organization to improve. It should encourage group learning and workplace innovation. Avoid the use of measures for punitive actions. Examples of what to avoid are using absenteeism data to target specific individuals through an absenteeism management program that does not address underlying causes, or inferring that the managers of specific units where survey results show low morale are poor managers. Evaluation data should encourage constructive discussions among stakeholders, beginning with the question: 'how can we better support the employees in this team or work unit?'
4. *Create a Model*. A model maps out your common-sense understanding of how specific changes should improve quality of work life and contribute to other organizational performance goals. Establishing a 'causal relationship' in scientific terms is difficult, but you can still build a convincing case and a model will help to do this.
5. *Integrate*. Look for opportunities to integrate different kinds of measures, creating a composite picture of how the intervention contributes not only to employees but also to organizational goals such as the quality of customer services or products and operational excellence. Connecting the data dots in this way makes your evaluation far more compelling to decision-makers.

6. *Make Metrics Meaningful and Actionable.* Think of the end-user. Collect and analyse only the data you need – and are prepared to act upon. Report your findings in ways that support learning, action planning, and change implementation. Who will use the evaluation information and for what purposes? The knowledge generated by the evaluation must be a catalyst for actions in support of high-quality work environments. To this end, consider translating some of the indicators into costs, such as calculating overtime costs, costs of lost-time injuries, and the cost of replacing an employee who voluntarily leaves.

7. *Mine Existing Data.* Most organizations have data that can be useful for evaluations on outcomes such as absenteeism, time-loss injuries, incidence and length of disability, and voluntary turnover. Try to analyse and report these data in ways that assess the impact of an intervention. Look for ways to link surveys of employees, and customers or clients – which is most easily done by using a uniform reporting unit, such as worksite, functional unit, or employee group.

Healthy Organization Measures Are Good Public Policy

Good measurement tools and reporting frameworks for progress on organizational health goals also can be developed at the sector, regional, or national levels. If a group of employers sees mutual gains by raising the floor for workplace health promotion or the overall quality of the work environment, they can collaborate to create shared approaches.

A leading example of this approach to create healthier organizations is found in the United Kingdom, where the Health and Safety Executive (the national body responsible for occupational health and safety) developed evidence-based good management practices to reduce the risks of work stress.[19] Industry was a partner in the development and dissemination of the standards and related assessment tools. The business case was clear-cut: 36 per cent of sickness absenteeism due to work-related illness or workplace injuries in the United Kingdom is caused by stress, depression, and anxiety. As a result, between 30 per cent and 40 per cent of the direct costs of sickness absenteeism can be attributed to these causes. The Confederation of British Industry estimates that the average direct and indirect (including reduced customer satisfaction, lower productivity, and higher staff turnover) costs of work stress to be approximately $3,000 per worker per year.[20]

The Health and Safety Executive's (HSE) preventative approach aims to promote healthier outcomes for employees and organizations by establishing 'management standards.' Its six evidence-based standards for reducing work stress address work demands, employee control over their work, support, relationships at work, role clarity, organizational change, and culture. Consistent with the healthy change model I laid out in chapter 6, the HSE advocates a bottom-up approach to changes required to reduce stress risks. Standards define the future state the organization should strive to achieve; risk assessment identifies the hazards that need to be reduced.

The standards are not legally enforceable but are principles designed to help employers to meet their legal obligation to provide employees with a hazard-free workplace. This is a continual improvement process. Baseline measures are established and progress is tracked using an employee survey tool that asks a series of questions derived from each of the standards. The standard is set for 85 per cent for each indicator (e.g., 85 per cent of employees saying they are able to deal with the demands of their jobs). Standards are considered an effective, practical way to reduce work stress.

The HSE approach resembles the United Kingdom's successful human resource management standard, the Investors in People program. However, experience with the Investors in People standard shows the limits of a voluntary model. One study of its impact suggests that some organizations that attain a standard for people practices may already have these in place. Furthermore, as a result of following the standards, these already high-performing organizations may have ended up linking training to business needs rather than employees' developmental needs, as they had done previously.[21]

The overall sustainability of organizations will surely become the focus of corporate and government leaders in the coming decade. If anything, the global economic crisis may speed up this process, having focused collective attention on organizational survival. We can expect rising health care costs to prompt employers to find solutions by promoting healthier work environments. A promising step in this direction is the proposed Healthy Workforce Act, before the U.S. Congress in 2009, which would give tax incentives to businesses that introduce comprehensive workplace wellness programs.[22] As one of the components of the Obama administration's health care reform plan, the goals are to improve the health of the workforce and reduce health care costs.

As I have argued, workplace wellness programs are ideal launching pads for more far-reaching strategies to create healthy organizations. Continued labour and skill shortages in some occupations and sectors will put a premium on finding better ways to unleash workers' productive potential. So will the steady stream of new information technologies. Strains on the environment and communities will only heighten the pressures on organizations to 'do good' and 'give back.' If we can measure a company's carbon footprint, calculate the value of its human capital, and feed a wide range of performance data into corporate balanced scorecards, surely we can construct meaningful metrics for tracking the overall health of an organization and its people.

My recommendation to governments is to collaborate with employer groups, employee organizations (e.g., professional associations and unions) and university researchers to create a Healthy Organization Index. Just as measures of Gross Domestic Product for the economy have evolved and expanded to include environment and society, it is entirely possible to create a composite of existing employee, workplace, and organizational measures that any organization can use to self-assess progress. This is already happening in Europe in the area of job quality, using the European Survey of Working Conditions conducted biannually in all member states of the European Union. In Canada, it would be feasible to include a select set of workplace and organizational indicators in the Canadian Community Health Survey. This Statistics Canada survey already has good measures of work-related stress and employees' overall health. However, unlike the organizational changes discussed throughout the book, this public policy initiative requires something different to get off the ground: political will.

9 Designing a Healthy Organization Strategy

This final chapter provides an action-oriented summary of key insights and practical suggestions provided throughout the book. My intent is to offer readers a guide for planning and implementing a healthy organization change strategy in their workplace.

To reiterate one of my opening points, I am aware that organizations are at different places on a healthy organization trajectory. And for each of you, that trajectory looks somewhat different, reflecting the distinctive circumstances of your organization. Some of you will already have a healthy organization strategy mapped out, so you will be thinking in more tactical terms about implementation. Others will be looking for ideas than can help to launch a strategy. So I'm not offering a prescriptive guide. Rather, I present issues and pose questions for your reflection, discussion, and, most important, action. I firmly believe that you have to find your own way forward; coming up with answers to the questions I raise below can be a catalyst – in keeping with the organic nature of change in a healthy organization. It is also a good way to collaboratively design a change strategy.

I encourage the flexible application of the suggestions below, as well as the tools and resources presented in earlier chapters. Please use them in any way that is helpful, adapting entire sections, using figures or checklists as organizational development tools, or pulling together pieces from different sections to meet your particular needs. As you and your co-workers tailor these suggestions to fit your organization's immediate needs and challenges, you will find there is considerable room for creativity. As I have shown through examples, regardless of your formal position, as a change agent you have the scope to exercise positive influences within your own sphere of the organization.

What follows are invitations to ongoing discussions that lead to ac-tion. In fact, I like to think of this chapter as a general guide for extended conversations that you could have with your co-workers or employees. Another way to use the suggestions I offer is personal reflection on the current health of your organization and the possible roles you could play in moving it to the next level.

I have taken this approach here because of the positive experienc-es I have had with numerous organizations, watching what happens when employees and managers are collectively challenged to envision a healthy path forward for their organization. When designing these workshops, I try to learn as much as I can about the organization, its goals, and the challenges faced by change agents. So the starting points and direction of the strategy design process would look different, re-flecting these particular realities. In fact, the people in the organization co-design the workshop with me. For example, if you have just refreshed your corporate values, there is a natural stepping stone to framing a vi-brant workplace vision (or healthy workplace, if you prefer). Or, if you have before you results from a recent employee survey, then a helpful starting point is the discussion of survey follow-up. For organizations that have robust social responsibility frameworks, the timing and op-portunity may be right to forge closer links with HR. And so on.

Additional resources to help you to design your own healthy or-ganization strategy are available on the book's website, www.creating-healthyorganizations.ca. I invite you to visit the site, make use of these resources, offer suggestions for further resources, and join an online discussion about what you and your co-workers are doing to move down a healthy organization trajectory.

1. *Use the Healthy Organization Model as a diagnostic and planning tool.*
   - How can you leverage existing workplace health and wellness ini-tiatives to incorporate healthy organization thinking and goals?
   - Using the Healthy Organization Model as an assessment tool, what pieces of it are already operative in your workplace? What are the strengths? Use these strengths as a foundation to build on.
   - Are there teams, units, or departments in your organization that have their own version of a Healthy Organization Model?
   - To expand the case for investing in a healthier work environment, how could you make the connections (using the Healthy Organi-zation Model) to employee engagement, workplace learning, and collaboration?

- How closely does the Healthy Organization Model resemble the strategy model used in your organization to link people with results?
- What language and thinking is used in your workplace to describe how people and performance are connected? Try modifying the Healthy Organization Value Chain to fit your context, looking for new insights about your organization's links in the value chain.
- How can your organization's social responsibility commitments and practices (including philanthropy, community partnerships, support for employee volunteering, and environmental practices) be integrated with people practices? Look for new synergies through this sort of integration. Also look for ways to ensure the consistency of corporate values and ethical commitments made to stakeholders.

2. *Use the idea of a vibrant workplace to get at the 'drivers' of health and performance.*
- What is the evidence-based 'business case' in your organization for investing in employee and workplace health promotion programs? If there is no business case, is that because your organization has strong people values, making these investments the right thing to do? Or is it because no one has taken the time to calculate the costs associated with employee health and wellness? Regardless, you need to be able to explain convincingly to senior managers and co-workers the strategic impact of a vibrant work environment.
- Does the concept of a vibrant workplace help to address current or future challenges your organization faces? If the word 'vibrant' does not fit your context, what would you replace it with, being careful not to loose the holistic focus on workplace ingredients of a healthy organization? You need to find language that is comfortable for co-workers to use and, at the same time, is sufficiently compelling that they will be mobilized to take further action.
- Use figures 2.1 and 2.2 as assessment tools – or at a minimum, a stimulus for discussion – to understand where your workplace is on the health promotion / healthy organization continuum. What specific dimensions of your workplace health promotion initiatives are on the healthy organization side of the continuum? What actions are needed to expand other aspects of workplace health promotion to an organizational perspective?

- What is the need in your organization for the following types of health promotion programs: healthy lifestyle programs, helping employees with chronic health conditions, and comprehensive programs targeting high-risk employees? If the answer to the question is not available, how realistic is it to assess these needs? If you did obtain this information and acted on it, how would that advance you towards healthier organization goals?
- What would be the value to your organization of having a full discussion of the causes and consequences of absenteeism and presenteeism? Do you currently have indicators that suggest either undermines organizational performance and employee quality of life?
- Using insights from the discussion about job stress and work/life balance, how psychologically healthy is your workplace? Would addressing the root causes of stress and work/life imbalance be a good next step to improving overall health and performance?

3. *How can you move beyond engagement to create a truly inspired workforce?*
   - What is your own personal vision of a vibrant (or your own term, as suggested above) workplace? Think about how these conditions would inspire you in your work.
   - Identify an appropriate time and venue for your work group, or management team, to develop a shared vision of a vibrant workplace. If managers were to develop a vision of the ideal 'fully engaged' employee, how would the elements of that vision 'map' onto an employee vision of a healthy or vibrant workplace? The point here is to find ways to help others, particularly managers, connect workplace features with performance-related outcomes, most notably employee engagement.
   - After you have had the discussions just described, write a unifying vision for your organization that clearly describes the six to eight key elements of a vibrant workplace that will inspire employees. This is the 'big picture' of the kind of workplace your organization has the potential to achieve. What would enable actions to strengthen, or create, these workplace elements?
   - Would employees in your workplace view the elements of a vibrant workplace as the major contributors to their overall well-being while at work? If not, what is missing?
   - If employees in your organization were asked to describe one improvement in their workplace that would have the greatest

positive impact on their well-being, what do you think the top three improvements would be? If it is realistic to do so, add this question to an employee survey or conduct consultations or focus groups. The results could generate ground-up initiatives to improve the workplace.

- How might your organization benefit from identifying the biggest gaps between what employees highly value in a job and their current experiences in this regard? What is the most effective way to gather this information and ensure that it will be acted upon?

4. *Talk about your culture and become aware of its power.*
- Create an overall picture of your organization's culture. Is it strong or weak? Is there a widely understood set of core values? What are the main unwritten assumptions or beliefs that underlie workplace behaviours? Do specific groups have their own sub-cultures? The point of this exercise, which can be done by a team or committee, is to identify the aspects of the culture that are the most and the least healthy.
- Do senior managers in your organization talk about culture (or elements of the culture) as providing a competitive advantage? If they do, how can this discussion be expanded so that everyone gains a clearer understanding of how culture contributes to performance (as outlined in figure 4.1)? If managers do not view culture this way, what action can you take to help them to see these links?
- How does culture influence day-to-day working relationships among co-workers, between managers and employees, and with customers and other external stakeholders? How would you rate the level of trust in all these relationships? As a way to build a healthier organization, what concrete steps could be taken to build trust?
- If in the recent past your organization has tried to change the culture, reflect on this experience through a healthy organization lens. What are the key lessons that can help you and others to create a healthier culture?
- Values or guiding principles are powerful catalysts for moving down the healthy organization path. For your organization, would revisiting the values or creating more behaviourally focused guiding principles be a good next step towards a healthier organization? If not, when would be the right time to do so, how

would you position such an initiative, and who would champion it?

5. *Make healthy leadership something everyone does.*
   - How is the term 'leadership' used in your organization today? Is its use exclusive, inclusive, or in-between? What opportunities exist right now to take a more inclusive approach to leadership? Consider the implications of moving in this direction for employee and supervisor training and leadership development programs.
   - To what extent do the leadership competencies promoted in your organization (either through formal leadership development programs or implicitly through promotions, succession planning, or talent management) foster healthy values, behaviours, and relationships? Consider the best ways to go about making these connections between leadership and culture visible and stronger.
   - Actions to create healthier organizations can be led from many places and positions. In your workplace, who has taken this kind of leadership? What support have these change agents had? Extract the key lessons from these experiences that can inform more grass-roots change in future.
   - Specifically, what does your executive team need to do in order to empower and mobilize others to take healthy workplace actions? Realistically, is there anything you can do to help the executive team become champions and enablers of healthy workplace change, so that improvement goals become more of a shared responsibility?
   - Take another look at the six elements of inclusive leadership. Think of ways you and your co-workers could use the six elements as an organizational development tool. Options include using it as a basis for assessment and discussion at workshops, management or team retreats, at workplace wellness committee meetings, or HR department meetings. If your organization invests in leadership development, this opens up possibilities for discussing the benefits of inclusive leadership.
   - Try approaching the concept of healthy leadership from another angle: supervisors' people skills and behaviours. Look at current supervisor selection criteria, training, and performance incentives. How can these systems be revised to include concrete skills and

behaviours that cultivate healthy and productive working relationships?

6. *Design any change to be a healthy experience.*
   - Reflect on your organization's healthy change trajectory. Is it on a pathway that will raise health and performance standards and outcomes? If your answer is 'no,' collaborate with co-workers to map out an ideal healthy change trajectory for your organization.
   - Do executives, people professionals, and line managers in your organization understand the importance of making change a healthy process? If not, how can you or your team raise awareness about this issue?
   - Groups can be powerful engines of change. Which groups (e.g., teams, committees, and informal networks) are best positioned, and have the capabilities, to positively influence change, moving it along a healthy trajectory?
   - After reviewing the five principles for guiding healthy change, write down a list of 'guiding principles for healthy change' that would resonate with your colleagues. These principles would apply to any change, resulting in more successful implementation.
   - Take a recent healthy workplace, wellness, safety, or HR initiative and assess it using these criteria: How effectively were changes in structures, processes and culture aligned? Did everyone involved and affected understand how this change contributed to the business strategy? How well did the organization learn from this change experience, and have these lessons contributed to more innovative practices?
   - Try using the Change Readiness Assessment tool (figure 6.1) to identify sources of resistance, inertia, readiness, and momentum for any planned healthy organization change.

7. *Adopt an integrated approach to renewing your stakeholder relationships and workforce capabilities.*
   - Examine your CSR approach through the healthy organization lens. Assess three things: How firmly connected is CSR to the organization's culture, especially its values? Have the potential synergies between CSR and the organization's approach to HR been tapped? What are the best opportunities for taking a 'strategic' approach to CSR, building social and environmental goals into products or services?

- What would sustainable success look like for your organization? Identify current practices that are not sustainable over the next five to ten years. Then identify the practices and other organizational features, including culture, that already contribute to sustainable success.
- What capabilities has your organization developed for renewing the workforce? Do you have processes, systems, expertise, and other resources that effectively meet employee recruitment, retention, and development goals? Look for ways to more closely link workforce renewal with workplace improvements that move in the direction of a healthier organization.
- How inclusive is your workplace? What steps could be taken to implement some of the healthy organization changes above (e.g., especially focusing on culture, values, and relationships) with the specific goal of making a more welcoming environment?
- Identify an effective and easy way to document the needs of different age groups in your workforce. This might be accomplished by re-analysing existing survey data, adding new questions to your next employee survey, running an online pulse survey, or conducting focus groups. Look for both similarities and differences, focusing on ingredients of vibrant and inspiring workplaces.
- Is your organization taking appropriate steps to retain older workers with critical competencies and to transfer their essential knowledge to junior colleagues before they depart? How can the concept of 'flexibility' be adapted to HR policies and practices to meet the needs of all age groups, particularly older workers?
- Long-range workforce planning is a significant commitment and often becomes an umbrella for all people-related plans, programs, and practices. Consider the pros and cons of developing a long-range workforce plan in your organization. If there are significant advantages, how would you go about getting such a plan on the senior management agenda for consideration?

8. Develop and make full use of meaningful metrics.
- Consider how effectively managers in your organization make use of internal and external evidence when planning change. Does the culture support evidence-informed decision making? If it does, then your challenge will be to elevate HR metrics to the same level of quality and relevance as other business performance data.

- Identify your specific short-, medium-, and long-term healthy organization goals. For each goal, develop a meaningful indicator that will help to track progress (or select from among existing people metrics). The key criterion for the selection of any indicator is its ability to generate learning and further action.
- There are many examples throughout the book of how organizations use internal data, usually from administrative databases or employee surveys, to document needs, find strengths to build on, identify gaps that need closing, and plan improvements. These examples provide reference points for reviewing how your organization uses its existing employee data to achieve healthy organization goals. Based on this review, what are the best opportunities to better mine these data?
- When you look at your current HR and other people metrics, including safety, how integrated are they in your corporate performance reporting system? If you have a balanced scorecard or performance report card, what relatively easy modifications could be made to incorporate one or two new people metrics?
- Healthy cultures are built around values, relationships, and behaviours. How can existing people metrics be used to create accountability among managers at different levels for living the values, cultivating healthy and productive relationships, and personally demonstrating healthy behaviours? What would be the implications for your organization's performance management system? How can this model of accountability be extended to all employees?
- Employee surveys are useful tools for obtaining employees' assessments of the 'drivers' of organizational health. All the ingredients of a vibrant workplace can be measured in well-designed surveys. Assess your existing employee survey to determine how well it measures the drivers of organizational health. Do the relevant questions in the survey provide actionable results? If your survey lacks such questions, consider making the appropriate modifications. And if you do not conduct an employee survey, now is a good time to start.

Moving an organization further along a healthy trajectory, plotting its future course, and keeping it moving in that direction – this is hard work. That is why I have emphasized the importance of inclusive leadership, healthy change as a shared responsibility, and the need for managers and employees to co-create vibrant workplaces. As your next step, why not take the ideas from this book that resonated most with you back to your co-workers, start a discussion, and collectively explore the possibilities.

Notes

Introduction

1 De Smet, A., Loch, M. and Schaninger, B. (2007). Healthy organizations. *Executive Excellence*, 1 September.
2 Beer, M., and Eisenstat, R. (2000). The silent killers of strategy implementation and learning. *Sloan Management Review*, 41 (4), 29–40.
3 Karasek, R., and Theorell, T. (1990). *Healthy Work: Stress, Productivity, and the Reconstruction of Working Life*. New York: Basic Books.
4 Ibid., 2.
5 Dutton, J.E., and Glynn, M.A. (2007). Positive organizational scholarship. In *Handbook of Organizational Behavior*, edited by Cooper, C., and Barling, J. Thousand Oaks, CA: Sage.

1. The Healthy Organization

1 Malzon, R.A., and Lindsay, G.B. (1992). *Health Promotion at the Worksite: A Brief Survey of Large Organizations in Europe*. Copenhagen: World Health Organization, Regional Office for Europe. European Occupational Health Series No. 4, 9.
2 Lim, S.Y., and Murphy, L.R. (1999). The relationship of organizational factors to employee health and overall effectiveness. *American Journal of Industrial Medicine* Supplement, May, 64.
3 European Network for Workplace Health Promotion (2003). *Healthy Employees in Healthy Organisations*. Essen, Germany, 6 (www.enwhp.org).
4 Becker, B.E., Huselid, M.A., and Ulrich, D. (2001). *The HR Scorecard. Linking People, Strategy, and Performance*. Boston: Harvard Business School Press. Pfeffer, J. (1998). *The Human Equation: Building Profits by Putting People First*.

Boston: Harvard Business School Press. Huselid, M.A. (1995). The impact of human resource management practices on turnover, productivity, and corporate financial performance. *Academy of Management Journal*, 38, 635–72.

5 Rucci, A.J., Kirn, S.P., and Quinn, R.T. (1998). The employee-customer-profit chain at Sears. *Harvard Business Review*, January, 82–97.

6 Quoted in Macey, W.H., and Schneider, B. (2008). The meaning of employee engagement. *Industrial and Organizational Psychology*, 1, 7.

7 Prost, M. (2007). Failure to inspire. *Human Resource Executive On-line*. 1 November. http://www.hreonline.com/HRE/story.sp?storyId= 43275541

8 *Economist*. (2007). Something new under the sun: Special report on innovation. 13 October, 4.

9 Garvin, D.A. (1999). *Learning in Action*. Boston: Harvard Business School Press, 42.

10 Gephart, M.A., Marsick, V.J., Van Buren, M.E., and Spiro, M.S. (1996). Learning organizations come alive. *Training and Development*, December, 35–45.

11 Senge, P.M. (1990). *The Fifth Discipline. The Art and Practice of the Learning Organization*. New York: Currency Doubleday.

12 Marosszeky, M. (2005). Best practice in the construction supply chain. *ASQ World Conference on Quality and Improvement Proceedings*, 217–28.

13 Adler, P.S., and Heckscher, C. (2006). Towards collaborative community. In *The Firm as a Collaborative Community*, edited by Heckscher, C., and Adler, P.S. Oxford: Oxford University Press.

14 Phua, F. and Rowlinson, S. (2004). How important is cooperation to construction project success? A grounded empirical quantification. *Engineering, Construction and Architectural Management*, 11 (1), 45.

15 Berry, L.L. (2004). Leadership lessons from Mayo Clinic. *Organizational Dynamics*, 33, 228–42.

16 Stubblefield, A. (2006). The Baptist Health Care Journey to Excellence: Creating a culture that WOWs! Presentation at the Great Place to Work Institute Conference. Boston, 7 April.

17 Stubblefield, A. (2005). *The Baptist Health Care Journey to Excellence*. Hoboken, NJ: John Wiley, 95.

18 Russell Investment Group data courtesy of Great Place to Work Institute.

19 Fulmer, S., Gerhart, B., and Scott, K.S. (2003). Are the 100 Best better? An empirical investigation of the relationship between being a 'great place to work' and firm performance. *Personnel Psychology*, 56, 965–93.

20 Edmans, A. (2007). Does the stock market fully value intangibles? Employee satisfaction and equity prices. Unpublished paper. Wharton School, University of Pennsylvania. http://ssrn.com/abstract=985735.

21 Harter, J.K., Hayes, T.L., and Schmidt, F.L. (2002). Business-unit-level relationship between employee satisfaction, employee engagement, and business outcomes: a meta-analysis. *Journal of Applied Psychology, 87*, 268–79.

22 Wagner, R., and Harter, J.K. (2006). *12: The Elements of Great Managing*. New York: Gallup Press.

23 Sirota, D., Mischkind, L.A., and Meltzer, M.I. (2005). *The Enthusiastic Employee: How Companies Profit by Giving Workers What They Want*, Upper Saddle River, NJ: Wharton School Publishing.

24 On high performance workplaces, see Pfeffer, J. (1998). *The Human Equation: Building Profits by Putting People First*, Boston: Harvard Business School Press; Appelbaum, E., Bailey, T., Berg, P., and Kalleberg, A.L. (2000). *Manufacturing Advantage: Why High-Performance Work Systems Pay Off*. Ithaca, NY: Cornell University Press.

25 Pfeffer, *The Human Equation*, 90.

26 From the International Finance Corporation, which is part of the World Bank. http://www.ifc.org/ifcext/economics.nsf/content/csr-intropage.

27 Verma, A., and Gomez, R. (2008). Does employee relations occur in a vacuum? Recent evidence on corporate social responsibility and employee relations in Canada. Paper presented at the Second International Workshop on Work and Intervention Practices. Laval University, Quebec City, 27–29 August.

2. Beyond Workplace Health Promotion

1 For information see: http://www.hpb.gov.sg/hpb/default.asp?pg_id=2115.

2 Buffett & Company Worksite Wellness Inc. (2009). *National Wellness Survey Report* 2009. Whitby, Ontario: Buffett and Company Worksite Wellness Inc.

3 For the evidence see Engbers, L.H., van Poppel, M.N., Chin, A.P., and van Mechelen, W. (2005). Worksite health promotion programs with environmental changes: A systematic review. *American Journal of Preventive Medicine, 29*, 61–70; Pelletier, K.R. (2001). A review and analysis of the clinical- and cost-effectiveness studies of comprehensive health promotion and disease management programs at the worksite: 1998–2000 update. *American Journal of Health Promotion, 16*, 107–16; Ozminkowski, R.J., Goetzel, R.Z., Santoro, J., Saenz, B., Eley, C., and Gorsky, B. (2004). Estimating risk reduction required to break even in a health promotion program. *American Journal of Health Promotion, 18*, 316–25; Shain, M., and Kramer, D.M. (2004). Health promotion in the workplace: Framing the concept; reviewing the evidence. *Occupational and Environmental Medicine, 61*, 643–8; Belkic, K., Schnall, P., Landsbergis, P., and Baker, D. (2000). The workplace

and cardiovascular health: Conclusions and thoughts for a future agenda. *Occupational Medicine: State of the Art Reviews*, 15, 307–21; Pelletier, K.R. (2005). A review and analysis of the clinical and cost-effectiveness studies of comprehensive health promotion and disease management programs at the worksite: Update VI 2000–2004. *Journal of Occupational and Environmental Medicine*, 47, 1051–8.

4 Max, W. (2001). The financial impact of smoking on health-related costs: A review of the literature. *American Journal of Health Promotion*, 15, 321–31.

5 Kuyumcu, N. (2008). Helping employees butt out generates big savings. *Benefits Canada*, 22 April. www.benefitscanada.com.

6 World Health Organization. Obesity and overweight Web page. http://www.who.int/dietphysicalactivity/publications/facts/obesity/en/

7 Canadian Institute for Health Information (2006). *Improving the Health of Canadians: Promoting Healthy Weights*. Ottawa: CIHI. http://secure.cihi.ca/cihiweb/products/healthyweights06_e.pdf .

8 DiNubile, N.A., and Sherman, C. (1999). Exercise and the bottom line: promoting physical and fiscal fitness in the workplace: A commentary. *Physician and Sportsmedicine*, 27 (2), 37-43.

9 Briner, R.B. (1997). Improving stress assessment: Toward an evidence-based approach to organizational stress interventions. *Journal of Psychosomatic Research*. 43:61–71. Barling, J., Kelloway, E.K., and Frone, M.R., eds. (2005). *Handbook of Work Stress*. Thousand Oaks, CA: Sage.

10 Burton, W.N., Conti, D.J., Chen, C.Y., Schultz, A.B., and Edington, D.W. (2001). The impact of allergies and allergy treatment on worker productivity. *Journal of Occupational and Environmental Medicine*, 43, 1–16.

11 Riedel, J.E., Baase, C., Hymel, P., Lynch, W., McCabe, M., Mercer, W.R., and Peterson, K. (2001). The effect of disease prevention and health promotion on workplace productivity: A literature review. *American Journal of Health Promotion*, 15, 167–90.

12 Bertera, R.L. (1990). The effects of workplace health promotion on absenteeism and employment costs in a large industrial population. *American Journal of Public Health*, 80, 1101–5.

13 Goetzel, R.Z., Anderson, D.R., Whitmer, R.W., Ozminkowski, R.J., Dunn, R.L., and Wasserman, J. (1998). The relationship between modifiable health risks and healthcare expenditures: An analysis of the multi-employer HERO health risk and cost database. *Journal of Occupational and Environmental Medicine*, 40, 843–5; Powell, D.R. (1999). Characteristics of successful wellness programs.' *Employee Benefits Journal*, 24(3), 15–21; Leonard, B. (2001). Healthcare costs increase interest in wellness programs. *HRMagazine*, 46 (9), 35–6; Goetzel, R.Z., Juday, T.R., and Ozminkowski, R.J. (2005).

Estimating the return-on-investment from changes in employee health risks on the Dow Chemical Company's healthcare costs. *Journal of Occupational and Environmental Medicine*, 47, 759–68; Brown, D. (2001). Wellness programs bring health bottom line. *Canadian HR Reporter*, 17 December.

14 White, J. (2008). Companies signal an active approach to employee health. *Benefits Canada*, 4 April. http://www.benefitscanada.com/benefit/health/article.jsp?content=20080404_150857_2232.

15 Marshall, A. (2004). Challenges and opportunities for promoting physical activity in the workplace. *Journal of Science and Medicine in Sport*, 7 (1).

16 See for the United States: Hutchins, J. (2001). Optimas 2001 – Partnership: Labor and management build a prescription for health. *Workforce*, 80 (3), 50. In Canada, Chrysler and the Canadian Auto Workers Union have successfully introduced the Tune Up Your Heart program and other wellness initiatives. www.workingtowardwellness.ca.

17 O'Donnell, M.P. (2000). Health and productivity management: The concept, impact, and opportunity. Commentary to Goetzel and Ozminkowski. *American Journal of Health Promotion*, 14, 215.

18 Murphy, R., and Cooper, C.L. (2000). *Healthy and Productive Work: An International Perspective*. London: Taylor and Francis.

19 Sainfort, F., Karsh, B.T., Booske, B.C., and Smith, M.J. (2001). Applying quality improvement principles to achieve healthy work organizations. *Journal of Quality Improvement*, 27, 469–83.

20 See the QWQHC website. http://www.qwqhc.ca/indicators-healthy-workplaces.aspx.

21 Canadian Institute for Health Information. (2006). *Improving the Health of Canadians: Promoting Healthy Weights*. Ottawa: CIHI. http://secure.cihi.ca/cihiweb/products/healthyweights06_e.pdf. Also see http://www.husky.ca/.

22 Edington, D.W. (2001). Emerging research: A view from one research center. *American Journal of Health Promotion*, 15, 341–9.

23 Health and Safety Executive, United Kingdom. (2006). HSE press release E009:06 – 31 January. http://www.hse.gov.uk/press/2006/e06009.htm.

24 Recovre Corp Health. (2009). *Well Aware Absence Management*. http://www.recovre.com.au/LinkClick.aspx?link=brochures_pdf%2FWell+Aware+DL_Web+view.pdfandtabid=270andmid=972.

25 Ruiz, G. (2006). Tallying the true cost of absenteeism. *Workforce Management*, 19 April. http://www.workforce.com/section/00/article/24/33/85.html

26 Statistics Canada (2007). *Work Absence Rates, 2006*. Ottawa: Statistics Canada, Catalogue No. 71-211-XIE.

27 U.S. Department of Veterans Affairs, Office of Inspector General. (2004).

Evaluation of Nurse Staffing in Veterans Health Administration Facilities. Report No. 03-00079-183, 7.

28 Davey, M.M., et al. (2009). Predictors of nurse absenteeism in hospitals: A systematic review. *Journal of Nursing Management*, 17, 312–30. Lovell, B.L., Lee, R.T., and Frank, E. (2009). May I long experience the joy of healing: Professional and personal well-being among physicians from a Canadian province. *BMC Family Practice*, 10, 18.

29 Edington, Emerging research, 346.

30 Hemp, P. (2004). Presenteeism: At work – but out of it. *Harvard Business Review*, October, 49–58.

31 Schultz, A., and Edington, D. (2007). Employee health and presenteeism: A systematic review. *Journal of Occupational Rehabilitation*, 17, 547–79. For an overview of return-to-work best practices, see Institute for Work and Health. (2007). *Seven 'Principles' for Successful Return to Work*. Toronto: Institute for Work and Health.

32 Goetzel, R.Z., Long, S.R., Ozminkowski, R.J., Hawkins, K., Wang, S., and Lynch, W. (2004). Health, absence, disability, and presenteeism cost estimates of certain physical and mental health conditions affecting US employers. *Journal of Occupational and Environmental Medicine*, 46, 398–412.

33 *Canadian HR Reporter*, 21 April 2008. www.hrreporter.com

34 Karasek, R., and Theorell, T. (1990). *Healthy Work: Stress, Productivity, and the Reconstruction of Working Life*; Siegrist, J. (1996). Adverse health effects of high-effort/low-reward conditions. *Journal of Occupational Health Psychology*, 1, 27–41; Maslach, C., Schaufeli, W.B., and Leiter, M.P. (2001). Job burnout. *Annual Review of Psychology*, 52, 397–422.

35 Rethinking Work was conducted by Ekos Research Associates Inc. and The Graham Lowe Group Inc. In the fall of 2004 a worker survey was conducted using a random sample of 2002 individuals who were either employed, self-employed, or unemployed (but who had held a job at some point in the past twelve months). The sample is considered to be representative of the Canadian workforce and has a margin of error of up to +/−2.2 per cent, nineteen times out of twenty.

36 See Eby, L.T., Casper, W.J., Lockwood, A., et al. (2005). Work and family research in IO/OB: Content analysis and review of the literature (1980–2002). *Journal of Vocational Behavior*, 66, 124–97.

3. How Vibrant Workplaces Inspire Employees

1 Ford, R.C., Wilderom, C.P.M., and Caparella, J. (2008). Strategically crafting a customer-focused culture: An inductive case study. *Journal of Strategy and Management*, 1, 143–67.

2 Ibid., 157.
3 Allen, J., Hamilton, B., and Reichheld, F.F. (2005). Tuning in to the voice of your customer. *Harvard Management Update,*10 (10). http://hbswk.hbs.edu/archive/5075.html.
4 See http://www.health.qld.gov.au/qhafe/htm/mr090425.asp.
5 See http://www.authentichappiness.sas.upenn.edu/seligman.aspx. Seligman, M.E.P., Steen, T.A., Park, N., and Peterson, C. (2005). Positive psychology progress: Empirical validation of interventions. *American Psychologist*, 60, 410–21.
6 Helliwell, J.F., and Huang, H. (2005). How's the job? Well-being and social capital in the workplace. National Bureau of Economic Research (NBER), Working Paper No. W11759.
7 Sharp, I. (2009). *Four Seasons. The Story of a Business Philosophy*. Toronto: Viking Canada.
8 Aaserud, K., Cornell, C., McElgunn, J., Shiffman, K., and Wright, R. (2007). The golden rules of growth. *Profit*, May, 72.
9 Ipsos MORI. (2008). *What Matters to Staff in the NHS*. Research study conducted for Department of Health, England.
10 Lowe, G.S., and Schellenberg, G. (2001). *What's a Good Job? The Importance of Employment Relationships*. Ottawa: Canadian Policy Research Networks. www.cprn.org.
11 This section draws on Lowe, G.S., Schellenberg, G., and Shannon, H.S. (2003). Correlates of employees' perceptions of a healthy work environment. *American Journal of Health Promotion*, 17, 390–9.
12 I also have called this a 'job quality deficit' score. See Lowe, G. (2007). *21st Century Job Quality: Achieving What Canadians Want*. Research Report W-37. Ottawa: Canadian Policy Research Networks. www.cprn.org
13 There are other ways to do this. You can add together the positive responses (the fourth and fifth categories) on both response scales and make the gap calculation that way, or you can use average scores on the response scale.
14 Gaps are calculated using the most positive response category (response category 5 on the five-category 'agree' and 'importance' scales used to answer the questions).

4. Positive Cultures

1 Johnson, J., Dakens, L., Edwards, P., and Morse, N. (2008). *SwitchPoints: Culture Change on the Fast Track to Business Success*, Hoboken, NJ: John Wiley.
2 Liker, J.K. (2004). *The Toyota Way: 14 Principles From the World's Greatest Manufacturer*. New York: McGraw-Hill.

3 Heskett, J.L., Sasser, W.E., and Wheeler, J. (2008). *The Ownership Quotient: Putting the Service Profit Chain to Work for Unbeatable Competitive Advantage*. Boston: Harvard Business Press.

4 For an overview of the Walkerton tragedy, see Wikipedia. http:// en.wikipedia.org/wiki/Walkerton_Tragedy#cite_note-Walkerton-part-1-1. This quote is from that website.

5 DeCloet, D. (2007). Sweat luxury. *Report on Business Magazine*, April, 42.

6 Dofasco news release, 17 September 2002. http://www.dofasco.ca/bins/ content_page.asp?cid=2347-2349-2534.

7 Sutton, R.I. (2007). *The No Asshole Rule: Building a Civilized Workplace and Surviving One That Isn't*. New York: Business Plus.

8 http://caib.nasa.gov/news/report/pdf/vol1/full/caib_report_volume1. pdf.

9 Solomon, R.C., and Flores, F. (2001). *Building Trust in Business, Politics, Relationships and Life*. New York: Oxford University Press, 5.

10 Colquitt, J.A., Scott, B.A., and LePine, J.A. (2007). Trust, trustworthiness, and trust propensity: A meta-analytic test of their unique relationships with risk taking and job performance. *Journal of Applied Psychology*, 92, 909–27.

11 Quoted in Pitts, G. (2007). Community-ship v. the decision maker. *Globe and Mail Report on Business*, 30 October, B2.

12 Kanter, R.M. (2008). Transforming giants: What kind of company makes it its business to make the world a better place? *Harvard Business Review*, January, 43–52.

13 Collins, J.C., and Porras, J.I. (1994). *Built to Last: Successful Habits of Visionary Companies*. New York: HarperCollins.

14 www.vancouver2010.com. Also see Brethour, P. (2007). Shaped by the crucible of culture. *Globe and Mail Report on Business*, 28 May, B3.

5. Inclusive Leadership

1 Mintzberg, H. (2004). Enough leadership. *Harvard Business Review*, November, 22.

2 Dinham, S., Aubusson, P., and Brady, L. (2008). Distributed leadership as a factor in and outcome of teacher action learning. *International Electronic Journal For Leadership in Learning*, 12 (4). http://www.ucalgary.ca/~iejll/ volume12/dinham.htm.

3 Baker, G.R., MacIntosh-Murray, A., Porcellato, C., Dionne, L., Stelmacovich, K., and Born, K. (2008). Trillium Health Centre. In *High Performing Healthcare Systems: Delivering Quality by Design*, edited by Baker, G.R. et al. Toronto: Longwoods.

4 Kouzes, J.M., and Posner, B.Z. (2007). *The Leadership Challenge*. 4th ed. San Francisco: John Wiley.

5 Ibid., 338. Emphasis in original.

6 Covey, S.M.R. (2006). *The Speed of Trust. The One Thing That Changes Everything*. New York: Free Press, 40.

7 Fullan, M. (2001). *Leading in a Culture of Change*. San Francisco: Jossey-Bass.

8 Wheatley, M.J. (2005). *Finding Our Way: Leadership for an Uncertain Time*. San Francisco: Berrett-Koehler.

9 Ibid., 88–9.

10 Goleman, D. (2006). *Emotional Intelligence*. New York: Bantam, 149.

11 Rethinking Work. 2004 worker survey and 2005 employer survey.

6. Healthy Change

1 Lowe, G. (2004). *Healthy Workplace Strategies: Creating Change and Achieving Results*. Ottawa: Health Canada. www.grahamlowe.ca.

2 Beckhard, R. (1997). The healthy organization: A profile. In *The Organization of the Future*, edited by Hesselbein, F., Goldsmith, M., and Beckhard, R. San Francisco: Jossey-Bass.

3 Hackman, R.J., and Edmondson, A.C. (2008). Groups as agents of change. In *Handbook of Organization Development*, edited by Cummings, T.G. Thousand Oaks, CA: Sage.

4 Pfeffer, J., and Sutton, R.I. (2000). *The Knowing-Doing Gap. How Smart Companies Turn Knowledge into Action*. Boston: Harvard Business School Press.

5 The relevant reports and documentation can be accessed at http://www.ubc.ca/; http://web.ubc.ca/okanagan/welcome.html.

6 Becker, B.E., Huselid, M.A., and Ulrich, D. (2001). *The HR Scorecard. Linking People, Strategy, and Performance*. Boston: Harvard Business School Press, 9.

7 Axelrod, R.H. (2000). *Terms of Engagement: Changing the Way We Change Organizations*. San Francisco: Berrett-Koehler.

8 Tushman, M., and O'Reilly III, C.A. (1997). *Winning Through Innovation: A Practical Guide to Leading Organizational Change and Renewal*. Boston: Harvard Business School Press, 200.

9 Kotter, J.P. (1996). *Leading Change*. Boston: Harvard Business School Press.

10 Beer, M. (2003). Building organizational fitness. In *Organization 21C: Someday All Organizations Will Lead This Way*, edited by Chowdhury, S. Upper Saddle River, NJ: Financial Times Prentice Hall, 311–28.

11 Barber, F., and Strack, R. (2005). The surprising economics of a 'people business.' *Harvard Business Review*, June, 84.

7. Sustainable Success

1　See Nexen, *Balance: 2008 Sustainability Report*. www.nexeninc.com/about_us/corporate_profile.

2　Nexen's Community Investment Policy: www.nexeninc.com/files/Policies/CommunityInvPolicy.pdf.

3　Franklin, D. (2008). Just good business. A special report on corporate social responsibility. *Economist*, 19 January, 4.

4　Levenson, E. (2008). Citizen Nike. *Fortune*. 24 November, 165–6.

5　Johne, M. (2007). Show us the green, workers say. *Globe and Mail*, 10 October, C1.

6　Reingold, J., and Tkacyzk, C. (2008). Ten new gurus you should know about. *Fortune*, 24 November, 153.

7　Ulrich, D., and Smallwood, N. (2004). Capitalizing on capabilities. *Harvard Business Review*, June, 119.

8　Lister, T. (2008). What keeps HR executives up at night? *Canadian HR Reporter*, 7 April, 17.

9　Blackwell, R. (2008). The double-edged sword of corporate altruism. *Globe and Mail Report on Business*, 10 November, B5.

10　https://www.vancity.com/MyBusiness/AboutUs/.

11　Johne, Show us the green, workers say.

12　Franklin, Just good business.

13　http://www.imaginecanada.ca/en/node/49.

14　http://www.fivewinds.com/uploadedfiles_shared/CSRCaseStudy-HomeDepot.pdf.

15　Franklin, Just good business, 6.

16　Maitland, A. (2004). Corporate care in the global community. *Financial Times*, 8 January, 12.

17　TNT. *Sure We Can. Corporate Responsibility Report 2008*. http://group.tnt.com/Images/tnt-corporate-responsibility-report-2008_tcm177-427051.pdf.

18　TNT recognised for consistent contributions to community. (2009).*Traffic World*, 16 January.

19　Porter, M.E., and Kramer, M.R. (2006). Strategy and society: The link between competitive advantage and corporate social responsibility. *Harvard Business Review*, December, 88.

20　Ibid., 86.

21　www.ge.com.

22　A lean, clean electric machine. (2005). *Economist*, 10 December, 77–9.

23　Boston Consulting Group. (2008). *Making a Difference: BCG's Partnerships and Projects for Social Impact*. http://www.bcg.com/impact_expertise/publications/files/Making_a_Difference_Dec_2008.pdf.

24 Conference Board of Canada. (2007). *Report on Diversity.*
25 Owram, D. (1997). *Born at the Right Time: A History of the Baby Boom Genera-tion.* Toronto: University of Toronto Press, 281.
26 Ibid., 306.
27 Côté, J.E., and Allahar, A.L. (1994). *Generation on Hold: Coming of Age in the Late Twentieth Century,* Toronto: Stoddart; Coupland, D. (1993). *Generation X: Tales for an Accelerated Culture.* New York: St. Martin's Press.
28 Miller, M. (1999). Gen-X working its 'lazy' label off. *Edmonton Journal,* 17 October, E10 (reprinted from the *Los Angeles Times*).
29 Cited in Generation Y goes to work. (2009). *Economist,* 3 January, 47–8.
30 Ibid.
31 Lowe, *21st Century Job Quality.*
32 *The Competition for Canadian Talent.* (2008). RBC Survey conducted by Ipsos Reid. http://www.rbc.com/newsroom/20080415survey.html.
33 Dychtwald, K., Erickson, T., and Morison, B. (2004). It's time to retire re-tirement. *Harvard Business Review,* March, 55.
34 DeLong, D.W. (2004). *Lost Knowledge: Confronting the Threat of an Aging Workforce.* New York: Oxford University Press. On the importance of tacit knowledge for firms, see Dixon, N.M. (2000). *Common Knowledge: How Companies Thrive by Sharing What They Know.* Boston: Harvard Business School Press.
35 http://www.shell.com/home/content/aboutshell/our_strategy/shell_global_scenarios/shell_energy_scenarios_2050/shell_energy_scenarios_02042008.html.
36 http://www.edmonton.ca/city_government/city_organization/plan-edmonton.aspx.
37 City of Edmonton, Office of the City Auditor. (2008). *Human Resources Branch Audit.*

8. Measuring Progress

1 European Network for Workplace Health Promotion. (2003). *Healthy Em-ployees in Healthy Organisations.* Essen, Germany, 10. www.enwhp.org.
2 http://www.cqc.org.uk/_db/_documents/0708_annual_health_check_overview_document.pdf.
3 http://www.cqc.org.uk/usingcareservices/healthcare/nhsstaffsurveys/2008nhsstaffsurvey.cfm.
4 Fitz-enz, J. (2000). *The ROI of Human Capital: Measuring the Economic Value of Employee Performance.* New York: AMACOM (American Management Association), 22.
5 Riedel, J.E., Baase, C., Hymel, P., Lynch, W., McCabe, M., Mercer, W.R., and

Peterson, K. (2001). The effect of disease prevention and health promotion on workplace productivity: A literature review. *American Journal of Health Promotion*, 15(3), 167–90.

6 Pfeffer, J., and Sutton, R.I. (2000). *The Knowing–Doing Gap. How Smart Companies Turn Knowledge into Action*. Boston: Harvard Business School Press.

7 Editors' Forum on the Research–Practice Gap in Human Resource Management. (2007). *Academy of Management Journal*, 50(5).

8 For job and organizational assessment tools, see Field, D.L. (2002). *Taking the Measure of Work: A Guide to Validated Scales for Organizational Research and Diagnosis*. Thousand Oaks, CA: Sage.

9 For resources on communities of practice, see www.co-i-l.com/coil/knowledge- garden/cop/index.shtml.

10 OHSAH website: www.ohsah.bc.ca.

11 Davis, P.M., Badii, M., and A. Yassi. (2004). Preventing disability from occupational musculoskeletal injuries in an urban, acute and tertiary care hospital: Results from a prevention and early active return-to-work safely program. *Journal of Occupational and Environmental Medicine*, 46, 1253–62.

12 Weir, R., Stewart, L., Browne, G., Roberts, J., Gafni, A., Easton, S., and Seymour, L. (1997). The efficacy and effectiveness of process consultation in improving staff morale and absenteeism. *Medical Care*, 35, 334-53.

13 Hughes, I., and Seymour-Rolls, K. (2000). Participatory action research: Getting the job done. Action Research E-Reports, 4. www.fhs.usyd.edu.au/arow/arer/004.htm; Reason, P., and Bradbury, H., eds. (2001). *Handbook of Action Research: Participative Inquiry and Practice*. London: Sage.

14 A useful guide to participatory ('high involvement') organizational change is Axelrod, R.H., Axelrod, E.M., Beedon, J., and Jacobs, R.W. (2004). *You Don't Have to Do It Alone: How to Involve Others to Get Things Done*. San Francisco: Berrett-Koehler.

15 Harris, J.R., Holman, P.B., and Carande-Kulis, V.G.. (2001). Financial impact of health promotion: We need to know much more, but we know enough to act. *American Journal of Health Promotion*, 15, 378–82.

16 Anderson, D.R., Serxner, S.A., and Gold, D.B. (2001). Conceptual framework, critical questions, and practical challenges in conducting research on the financial impact of worksite health promotion. *American Journal of Health Promotion*,15, 281–8.

17 Whitehead, D.A. (2001). A corporate perspective on health promotion: Reflections and advice from Chevron. *American Journal of Health Promotion*, 15, 367–9.

18 PSES results for 2005 are available at http://www.psagency-agencefp.gc.ca/arc/survey-sondage/2005/index_e.asp. The 2008 PSES results will

be released online in 2009. http://www.psagency-agencefp.gc.ca/svdg/pses-eng.asp

19 Mackay, C.J., Cousins, R., Kelly, P.J., Lee, S., and McCaig, R.H. (2004). 'Management Standards' and work-related stress in the UK: Policy background and science. *Work and Stress*, 18, 91–112.

20 Henderson Global Investors. (2005). *Less Stress, More Value. Henderson's 2005 Survey of Leading UK Employers*. www.henderson.com.

21 Grugulis, I., and Bevitt, S. (2002). The impact of investors in people: A case study of a hospital trust. *Human Resource Management*, 12, 44–60.

22 See http://www.uswwa.org/portal/uswwa/legislation/default. Pear, R. (2009). Congress plans incentives for employers that offer wellness programs. *New York Times*, 10 May.

Index